THE VANCE

The Beginning & The End

By Vance Johnson
with Reggie Rivers

KENDALL/HUNT PUBLISHING COMPANY
4050 Westmark Drive   Dubuque, Iowa 52002

This book is dedicated to my wonderful wife, Holly. I could never have made it without her loving support.

To order additional copies of *The Vance: The Beginning and the End,* call Kendall/Hunt Publishing at 1-800-228-0810. Please have the ISBN listed below handy when you call.

Designed by Scott Steffen of Steffen Design & Advertising
3773 Cherry Creek North Drive, Suite 100, Denver, CO 80203

Contents

Foreword

I was an abusive person.
I hit my wives. I hit my girlfriends.
I yelled at people. I intimidated people.
I had a serious problem.

I apologize to everyone I have hurt over the years. I have no excuses for being emotionally and physically abusive.

It has taken three years of professional counseling, but now I understand that it's not right to hit people. It's not right to push people. It's not right to shake people. It's not right to restrain people. It's not right to threaten people.

It's not right to slap your wife and see the fear and the anger inside of her. It's not right to make her afraid that you are going to kill her.

I feel so sorry for battered women, because so many men think the way I used to think. So many men think they have a *right* to be abusive.

But no one has the right to hurt another person.

I don't expect anyone to forgive me for being an abusive person. The things I did were flat-out wrong, and there's nothing I can say that will make my past behavior acceptable.

I just want to tell everyone that I am working hard to change my life. I don't want to be an abusive person anymore. I'm getting professional help, and I want to help other men learn the lessons that I have learned.

I think the reason God put me into the NFL was so that I could be an example for other people. During my career, I descended to an all-time low as a human being.

I was dirt. I was trash. I was the filth of the earth. I didn't like myself. I didn't have any respect for myself, and it showed in the way that I lived my life.

Now I want people to see that I'm in recovery, and I'm becoming a good person.

I want other men to be able to look at my life and know that if I can change, then they can change, too. They can become good people. They can become good husbands and good fathers.

Anyone can change if he really wants to.

During the past three years, I've been blessed to have people in my life who cared about me and who were willing to stand by me and help me turn my life around.

Now I want to return the favor by helping someone else.

If only one person reads this book and seeks help because of it, then it will be worth it for me.

We have to stop domestic abuse one person at a time.

Spousal abuse has been a hot topic in the media ever since the O.J. Simpson situation began, but it was a reality in the lives of many people long before then.

I don't know if O.J. Simpson is guilty of murder, but I do know that he is at least guilty of being an abusive person.

Simpson needs help, too.

His story of abuse shares a lot of parallels with mine.

Fortunately, my tale has a happy ending. I hope his will, too.

This is a book about abuse and about excess and about chaos. It is the story of my life and my rapid descent into the hell that I used to think was a cool place to be.

As you read this book you will notice that there is very little talk about the big catches I made on the football field or big touchdowns I scored.

I didn't want this to be a typical sports book. In this book, I want to show people the other side of the picture. I want to tell the story of how I let fame and fortune go to my head and how I lost control.

If you're looking for a lot of stories about life inside the Denver Broncos huddle, this book may not be for you.

If you're interested in learning what happened in the tumultuous mind of a maniac…

Turn the page.

1

The Awakening

For most of my NFL career, there were two people inside of me. One was Vance Edward Johnson. He was a nice, shy, insecure guy who loved children and who wanted to live a good life. The other person was "The Vance." He was an extroverted, flamboyant, crazed, publicity monger. He loved to party, drive fast cars, spend loads of money, pick up women and ignore responsibilities.

I'd like to be able to say that I, Vance Edward Johnson, fought the arrival of "The Vance," but I didn't. I'm honestly not sure I ever saw "The Vance" walk into the door of my life. And by the time I realized that he had arrived, he was already sitting in the living room of my mind drinking a beer and talking about living the good life.

He seemed like a cool guy, so I got him another beer and decided to go along for the ride.

Lately, I've been looking back on my career trying to figure out exactly what sparked the birth of that chaotic entity inside of me, but it's tough to pinpoint.

There are probably thousands of little factors that contributed to his birth, but only a psychologist with two or three years of free time on his hands could decipher them all.

Since 1991, I've received a lot of counseling to help me overcome my domestic violence problem. And through that counseling, I have begun to understand who I really am, and why I do some of the things that I do. I have learned to take responsibility for my actions past, present and future. I think I'm learning to be a stand-up guy, but it's not easy. I did a lot of dumb things, and some of them I would just as soon not bring back up to the surface. But I truly believe that for my emotional well-being, and for me to truly change my life, I have to face up to all of the things that I've done in my life. That's one of the reasons I'm writing this book.

Throughout this chapter, I will talk about some of the factors that helped create The Vance, but I'm not offering excuses for my actions. I'm just laying out all of the things that contributed to my problems.

For starters, I obviously had tremendous potential to be a wild, crazy and abusive person. If I didn't have that ability, then a lot of the chaotic events of my life would never have happened. So whether it's because of the way I was raised, or because of a chemical imbalance in my brain, or simply because of immaturity on my part, the potential was there. And when I hit the scene in Denver, that side of me began to flourish.

The second major factor in The Vance's development, was that I became an NFL football player. That alone is often enough to drive a person's ego through the roof and into the stratosphere. When you become a professional athlete, you get immediate fame, a fist full of power and a truck-load of money. For most players — even the ones who are able to hide it from the media — that's a recipe for Instant Ego A la Mode.

That's just a fact of life. Take virtually any 22-year-old off the street and make him the best in the world at his job — in fact, make him so good that people fill stadiums throughout the country to watch him perform. Give him about $500,000 cash with the promise of more in the near future. Get a group of about 50,000 people who can be counted on to walk up to him on the streets and say things like, "Can I please have your autograph?" or "Can I shake your hand? I just want to touch you." And put the guy's face on television, his voice on the radio and his name in the newspaper every chance you get.

If you do all of these things, I guarantee you that kid will change. It doesn't matter what kind of personality he has or how well he was raised. He will begin to develop an ego whether he wants to or not. So much of what we all do every day is based on what other people think of us. Why do people buy Mercedes and BMWs and Porsches? Why do people buy million-dollar houses? Why do people buy custom-tailored suits? Why do people go to expensive restaurants?

It's all ego. When you earn a lot of money, you want to impress people with it, so they will think that you are important. So you buy things that will let everyone know that you make lots of money. As you cruise down the fast lane in your sleek, black, fat-ass Mercedes, part of you is silently thinking that you are better than the person who is puttering down the slow-lane in a rusting, aqua-colored, 1972 Datsun 210.

When any combination of money, fame and power get together, people change.

Having these three things is sort of like having 300 pounds on your shoulders. You can hold up the weight for a certain amount of time, but eventually the load is going to cause changes in your body. Your knees may buckle. Your back may start to bow. Your ankles may give out. Or your shoulders may become bruised. But, the bottom line is that if you hold the weight long enough, the laws of physics will force some changes in you. The human body was simply not designed to hold up that much weight for any length of time.

All of the pressures of fame, fortune and power are the same way. It is such a heavy load that it forces people to change in order to continue carrying it. That change usually comes in the form of increased ego, because a big ego has a much greater carrying capacity for fame, fortune and power, than a small one.

Of course, not every person experiences the massive ego growth that I experienced, but like I said, I had some personality characteristics that made me more susceptible to this type of change. And as those characteristics started to get positive reinforcement, they began to dominate my personality. In fact, I quickly progressed to the point that I did whatever I could to get more attention. Media attention became a drug for me. I couldn't get enough of it. I sought it at every opportunity. Whether it was a new hairdo, a set of earrings, a fancy car or a beautiful girl, I was always doing whatever it took to get attention.

In some ways, I think The Vance was like a little campfire that was burning quietly inside of me for most of my life. As long as I kept it crackling quietly inside a ring of stones, I was fine. But when I entered the NFL, it was like stacking dry straw all the way around that fire and dumping kerosene on the blaze. The flames were jumping higher and higher, and that straw was catching on fire, and the truth was that I thought it was cool. I didn't try to fight it. I just watched like a little kid with a smile on my face as everything around me started to catch on fire.

By the time I realized I was in danger, a forest fire (The Vance) was raging and there was nothing I could do to stop it (him).

But I did try at times.

The media always gave me a hard time when I was The Vance because I was so inconsistent. One day I would complain that I was tired of all the attention I was getting and that I just wanted to go back to being a regular person. The next day, I would do something wild or crazy to get more attention.

This type of flip-flopping was confusing to me, mystifying to the media and not believable to the general public. I was just so many different people all rolled up into one. One part of me wanted to go have sex all the time with whomever I chose. That part of me wanted to have a good time, party, drive fast and live hard. Another part of me wanted to have a wife and a child and a house with a white picket fence and a happy home. Another part of me wanted to be just a shy person who didn't know anyone. I wanted to just sit in my house and read my Bible.

I wanted to be all these people, and I would actually become all these people at different times. Which character I became depended on what night of the week it was and what had happened during the day.

But I think the most powerful of all my drives was the desire to be in love. And that is the one that has caused me the most heartache and pain during the past decade.

But no matter which part of my personality was dominant on a given day, the drive to be famous was always there.

Before the 1987 Super Bowl, I told a reporter that, "I want to be famous so bad it hurts. I want to be famous as hell, and I'll do anything legally possible to get famous."

Less than a year later, I took back those words. After having a court appearance for a traffic ticket blown completely out of proportion by the media. After having the media latch onto and circulate a few of the crazy things that were happening in my life. After dealing with the flop of the Three Amigos at the 1987 Super Bowl.

After all that, I said, "I'm tired of being in the public eye. I can't go anywhere without people mobbing me. Being a celebrity sucks, and I wish I could just go back to my old life."

Days later, I was out doing crazy things again to try to get attention.

Nobody could figure out what the hell was wrong with me. Everyone decided my complaints about fame were bullshit, because I was trying so hard to try to get attention.

But I really did want to change. I just didn't know how.

The Vance seemed indestructible to me. He was that raging forest fire gobbling up everything in my life, and I was standing there ready to fight him, but all I had was a small bucket of water.

In the same way that a real fire needs air and fuel to survive, The Vance just kept gobbling up the two things he needed: Money and Attention. As long as he got those, and not necessarily in that order, he was going to be fine.

Finally, I realized that the only way I could get back into control was to call the fire department, or in my case, professional counselors. With their help, I was finally able to start putting that fire out, one section at a time.

• • • • •

Before seeking help, I was just a spoiled brat running around the city buying up everything I could get my hands on. I enjoyed the feeling of invincibility that came from being a pro football player. I embarked on a career of abusing myself and other people.

It was hard for me to keep my head screwed on straight and my feet on the ground, when all of this ego-increasing stuff hit me. After a while, I started to believe all of the great things that people were saying about me. I started to believe that I was better than other people. And once I started believing that, I was in big trouble, because then I started to think of myself as a god. And when that happened, there was nothing that I wouldn't do, because I didn't think there was anything that I shouldn't be allowed to do.

It reminds me of that board game, I think it's called Scruples, where you sit around asking people questions like, "Would you ever rob a bank, if you knew you wouldn't get caught?" or "Would you ever have an affair if there was no way anyone would find out?" or "Would you kill one of your enemies if there was no way anyone would ever know it was you?"

The entire point of that game is to find out what people will do if they think they won't get caught. I think the common denominator in most of the rules in our society is that people are afraid to get caught. What keeps someone from robbing a bank? Part of it may be their strong moral belief that they should not steal, but I think the real motivator is fear of prison.

I was playing the real-life version of Scruples. Don't look for this brand at your local toy store because you won't find it. I had no fear of punishment, so I did a lot of bad things simply because I could.

Let's say President Clinton managed to get away from the Secret Service guys for five minutes and was out cruising around in a Ferrari doing 120 mph. If a cop pulled him over, do you think he would get a ticket? Hell no! He's the President of the United States. The cop would say, "sorry sir," and let his ass go.

When you reach a certain status in society, either through money or power or fame, people are in awe of you, and they begin to give you freedom to do whatever you want to do. You begin to believe that rules do not apply to you. And when you believe that, you're in trouble.

Plus, I fell prey to another fallacy of logic. I thought everything was fixable. I believed there was no mistake that I could make that I couldn't fix.

If I spent all of my money, I didn't care because I knew I'd make plenty more money. If I treated some woman like shit, I didn't care because I knew I'd have plenty of other women. If I got a speeding ticket, I didn't care because I could just pay the fine and forget about it.

That was my attitude. I didn't believe anything would affect me in the long run. I thought I could do whatever in the hell I wanted to do and no one would dare say shit to me.

The Vance was crazy. He was a piece of fiction that I and a bunch of other people in the country bought into. I made him up, and people started to believe in him. They looked forward to seeing what The Vance would do next. Hell, I looked forward to what The Vance would do next. He was sensational. He was irresponsible. He was wild. He was popular. He drove fast. He partied hard. He spent money like it was going out of style, and he bedded women like it was his birthright.

I can't lie. I had a lot of fun being The Vance, but it got tough, because he quickly became a lot bigger than me. He was smothering me. It was like I had created Superman or Batman or some other cartoon character and after a while, everyone recognized that character. Everyone talked the character as if he had a life of his own. But no one remembered the creator.

Everyone knew The Vance, but no one really knew me — Vance Edward Johnson. I don't think I even knew who I was. It took a lot of professional counseling for me to realize that I had created a monster and that my life was chaos.

I knew that I had to kill The Vance before he killed me.

But I had a hard time sending him away. People expected The Vance to be crazy and unpredictable and entertaining, and I felt pressure to be all those things. The pressure that I felt to do the "wrong" thing probably isn't all that different from the pressure that a lot of people feel to do the "right" thing.

A guy who has a family to take care of may resist buying a convertible Corvette simply because it's not in his family's best interest. If he was a single guy he'd do it in a second, but because he has responsibilities to other people and is expected to act maturely, he resists the temptation. I was the same way with The Vance except, I always felt like I was being tugged toward the negative choices. I felt a tremendous pressure to act a certain way, and I often felt powerless against it.

I couldn't kill The Vance because he made me popular. Ever since I was a little boy I had been shy and quiet and no one really seemed to like me. I didn't think I was a good person, but I had finally found a way to make people like me. I could walk into any club or any restaurant and people would say, "There's Vance Johnson!" and they would go crazy. I thought that if I killed The Vance, no one would like me anymore. I thought people would lose interest in me, and I would go back to being a quiet, unpopular kid again.

So instead of getting rid of The Vance, I kept feeding him. I got crazier and crazier hairdos. I drove faster and more expensive cars. I spent more money. I slept with more women. Of course, I'd be lying if I said I wasn't having a hell of a lot of fun doing all this. But I was exhausted, too. Keeping that crazy, chaotic pace was a full-time job, and to this day, I still don't know how I survived. I treated a lot of people wrongly, and I pissed off a lot of people. By rights, I should be dead right now.

I used to read about people who became addicted to drugs, and I could never understand their addictions. I found it hard to believe that people would spend all of their money on a drug. That they would sell all of their possessions and even their bodies for a drug. I couldn't understand it until about 1990 or 1991. Then I realized that I was addicted to The Vance. I was addicted to the free-spending lifestyle, the fast cars, the women, the crazy haircuts, and, most of all, I was addicted to the attention.

The only way I could cure myself of this addiction was through professional help.

This book is titled *The Vance: The Beginning and The End* because The Vance had to die before I could return to a normal life.

2

Early Years

In my life, as with most people, a lot of my thinking was funneled in a certain direction by events that happened when I was a child.

But before I get into the story of my childhood, I want to make it clear that I don't blame my parents, my family, my friends, or anyone else for the mistakes that I made during my NFL career. I can't blame anyone for all of the extramarital affairs that I had, for all of the children I had, for all of the money I spent, for all of the abuse I initiated or for anything else that has happened during the last decade. I was an adult when all of those things happened, and as an adult, I have to take responsibility for my actions.

I was an adult when I launched "The Vance" persona. I was an adult when I was having affairs with hundreds of women, changing my hairstyle as often as my clothes and being abusive to my ex-wives. I was an adult who was in complete control of his own decision-making process, and therefore, I am wholly responsible for all of my actions.

I've seen famous people like Oprah Winfrey and Roseanne Barr bash their parents and blame their problems on the way that they were raised. I don't want to do that. I love my parents, and I know they did the best job that they could with me.

When I became an adult, I had free choice. Although the way you are raised may put you on a certain path, there comes a time in all of our lives when we decide whether we are going to stay on that path or not. The path you are on may lead straight to hell, but there are always side paths that you can get on that can lead you back to a normal life. Unfortunately, I started out on a path to hell, and I never ventured off that beaten track. I was content to stay on that course and live a chaotic life. It wasn't until I began to take responsibility for myself, and decided to take those first tentative steps off the track that I was able to start working back toward a normal life.

But I am going to talk about my childhood and my family life. I'm not telling this story in an effort to assign blame. I'm just trying to explain my background, so that you can better understand who I was before I got into the NFL, and why I might have done some of the things that I did.

· · · · ·

I was born at Mercer Hospital in Trenton, N.J., on March 13, 1963. My mother, Jean, said that her labor with me was really tough. She said I started my descent into the world, but halfway out of the womb, I must have changed my mind. I had a tenacious grip on something in there, and I flat refused to come out. My mom was screaming and yelling and pushing. The nurses were screaming for her to push. But for a long time nothing was working. Finally, I popped out at 6:30 a.m. and added my tiny voice to the volume in the room.

My mom said that years later she had a chance to meet up with the nurse who helped deliver me and the woman still had scars on her arms from when my mom clamped her fingernails on the lady during the delivery.

They took me home from the hospital, and I became another young black kid destined for trouble in Trenton — my father's home town.

We lived with my grandmother on Pasace Street, which was in a fairly tough part of Trenton. Grandma's house was a narrow three-story affair, like all the other houses in the area. There was no front yard, just steps leading up to the door. All the houses were jammed tight together, so there were no side yards either.

My grandmother's house was pretty big, so there was plenty of room with just my parents and me living there with her.

Despite the decent house and a nice mother-in-law, my mom was just out of place in Trenton.

My mom — who is half Cherokee Indian and half black — was born in Oklahoma. When she was an infant, her parents moved to Arizona and were part of a small group of people who founded the town of Marana — just outside of Tucson. Her family wasn't rich, but they got by. As a child, Jean picked cotton for a few pennies a day.

So Jean lived in southern Arizona and my father, Gene, lived in Trenton, N.J. There was a whole lot of country between them, and no apparent opportunities for the two of them to ever meet.

But that all changed when 20-year-old Gene joined the Army.

His first assignment was at Fort Huachuca (pronounced WAchooka) near Tucson. Everyone called it Fort Hoochie Koochie because of all the lovin' that was going on out there.

Jean was 15 years old when my father came to Arizona, and she was dating an Arizona State University football player. One night, she and her boyfriend went to a dance that was being held on the army base. Because of her age, my mom wasn't allowed to go inside. So her boyfriend left her sitting in the car while he went inside for a few minutes.

Gene, was just arriving at the dance with some friends when he saw a pretty girl sitting in a car all by herself. He went over to talk to her and they hit it off right away. Jean's boyfriend was gone for nearly and hour, and she and Gene talked the entire time.

Before Gene left that night he got my mom's phone number.

A few days later, he visited her in Marana. And a few months after that he went to see her at her high school one day, and asked her to marry him. She said, "Yes."

My mother was 16 and my father 21 when they tied the knot.

About four months after their wedding, my mom discovered that she was pregnant with me. A couple months after that, my dad's three-year stint in the Army was over and he moved back to Trenton with his pregnant bride.

But my mom hated Trenton.

Being part American-Indian, Jean was really fair-skinned, and she had really straight, pretty, black hair with a reddish tint in it. She was very pretty and nice, but that's not how the people of Trenton — especially women — treated her. They were very mean to her, always calling her names and making fun of her pale skin. They said they couldn't tell what race she was, so they called her a Mexican, a Cuban, an Indian, a half-breed and anything else that they could think of to tease her. And they constantly made fun of her hair.

My mom was miserable in Trenton.

But my dad loved the city, because it was his home. It was the place he grew up, and the only place he really knew. All of his family and friends lived there, and he didn't want to leave.

My parents fought all the time about where they were going to live.

Finally, my mom decided that she'd had enough of Trenton, and she was moving regardless whether my father wanted to or not. Years later, she told me that I was about three months old when she packed a couple of bags, scooped me up and jumped on a train back to Arizona. We moved into her parent's home in Marana, and everything was cool for a while.

Then my father caught a train out to Marana and said to my mother, "You're not taking my boy away from me. This is my son." So he packed everything up and loaded my mother and me back onto a train to Trenton. While we were in New Jersey the second time, my mother got pregnant with my sister, Tammy. She's about a year younger than me.

Shortly after Tammy's birth, my mom packed us up again and jumped aboard a train to Arizona with her two kids. Again, my father caught a train out and dragged us all back to New Jersey.

We continued to travel back and forth for the next six or seven years, and I always had fun on the trips. It took three or four days to cross the country on a train and as a little kid, I always had a blast. I thought it was cool to be rolling on a choo-choo, looking out the window, and sleeping on the train. At the time, I don't think I realized that my parents may have been on the verge of divorce during all of that. I just thought they didn't agree on where they wanted to live. And their indecision was creating some fun train rides for me. So even today, I don't remember that situation as being traumatic for me.

But living in New Jersey was definitely traumatic.

Everything around us in Trenton was negative. We were surrounded by poverty, low education, theft, gangs and violence.

As early as I can remember, I knew that a lot of the people around us in New Jersey were involved in some type of crime. Some of them sold drugs, most of the young people were in gangs and a lot of them had been to jail at one time or another.

While we were living in New Jersey, I remember one kid who lived down the street went to prison for attempted murder. He and some of his gang members approached a potato chip delivery van that was parked on the side of the road. When they got there, the driver was filling out a form or something. They demanded money from him. After the driver said he didn't have any money, this kid grabbed the guy, dragged him out of the van and started stabbing him with a knife. While the guy was bleeding on the ground, they snatched his wallet and searched the van. I think they got less than $10 from the man.

The driver lived, but he was in bad shape for a while.

The police caught the kid who did the stabbing later that day, and he was eventually sentenced to serve time in prison. Of course, none of that was really a big deal to everyone in that area. Things like that happened in New Jersey all the time. People expected crime. Men always expected to spend some time in prison in the near future. All of that was just part of the background chaos that was present every day.

It was another — and probably the main — reason my mother didn't want to live there.

As I grew up, I started spending more and more time with other kids in the area. In some ways they scared me to death, because I knew some of them beat people up on a fairly regular basis. I was afraid to hang around with them, but at the same time I was drawn to them. Part of me wanted to be like them. I admired their courage and their toughness, and I envied the confidence they had when they walked down the street.

I was always a real scaredy-cat, and I was always looking over my shoulder when I was in Trenton. But my friends walked the streets like they owned them, and I guess in a way they actually did own those streets.

Despite my fear, one thing I did have confidence in was my ability to outrun people. I was a fast running little kid. I may have been slow coming out of the womb, but that was the last time I was ever slow in my life. When I started crawling, I bet I crawled faster than other kids. When I started walking, I bet I walked faster than other kids, because when I started running, I know that I ran a hell of a lot faster than other kids.

I could flat smoke anyone who wanted to get on the line and race against me.

At age 2, I could outrun most other kids my age. After about age 4, I could usually outrun kids who were two or three years older than me. By the time I was 7, I could outrun kids who were 11 or 12 years old. There was just something in my genes — maybe it had something to do with the fact that my parents names are Gene and Jean — that made my legs fly.

Some of my cousins recognized this talent in me very early in life, and they began to use it to their advantage. They would take me to a park near our house and would make 25-cent bets with anyone who wanted to race me. I was 7 or 8 years old at the time, and they would line me up against guys who much older than me.

I would always win.

One day at the park we made about $9 or $10 doing races like that. You don't have to be a math whiz to figure that I raced a hell of a lot of times to make that much money.

But after a while, I started to get tired. On the last race of the day, I got beat by a kid who was about four years older than me. He asked for his money, but my cousins wouldn't give it to him. There were five of us, and there were five of them, but they were all older and bigger than us. We figured they could kick our asses, but we were standing our ground. We were in the park yelling and screaming over a 25-cent debt. Actually, I said "we" but that's a lie. They were yelling. I was just standing there scared out of my mind and prepared to run at a moment's notice.

The yelling continued, and then someone got pushed. That was our cue to bolt. My cousins and I took off running. We were flying down the street with all of these other kids in close pursuit. I had outrun just about everyone in the park that day, and even though I was tired, I knew that my pursuers wouldn't catch me. I was like a gazelle — my main defensive weapon was my speed. I kept pumping my arms and legs and led everyone as we raced down the street.

I turned down an alley, and jumped over a fence into the backyard of the house that belonged to one of my aunts. My cousins followed me over the fence, and by the time they got over, I was banging on the back door yelling for my aunt.

The boys who were chasing us hopped the fence next and they were closing in on us when my aunt opened the door. She yelled at them to stop and for us all to break up the fighting, but those other kids didn't listen. They just kept coming toward us and eventually fists began to fly. It was like a Bruce Lee movie. Everywhere you looked two guys were engaged in hand-to-hand combat.

But my aunt broke that shit up pretty quick. She came out swinging a broom like it was a kung-fu stick. She wasn't swishing that broom around and patting kids on the butt. She was trying to decapitate people. She hit those other boys in the shoulders, the backs and the stomachs. They were all ducking around and yelling for her to ease up. But she just kept advancing and swinging her weapon. After a couple of minutes they all ran out through the gate cussing and yelling that they'd get back at us later.

We were all laughing and celebrating. We were proud of our aunt for kicking their asses.

We hung out in her backyard for another 15 minutes or so then we walked to the corner store to spend the money we had won that day. We kept looking over our shoulders, but we never saw those other guys again that day.

That was a fairly common day for life in Trenton, and I was learning to survive there. I was still terrified most of the time, but with the help of my cousins, I was learning to hold my own. Unfortunately, I was also learning a standard for relationships that would follow me into my adult life and would eventually force me to seek professional counseling. I was learning to be abusive.

Everywhere I looked, men abused women.

There was absolutely no respect given to women in Trenton, N.J. All of the women were really battered and abused emotionally and physically. It was just a way of life and no one ever did anything about it. And the women seemed to accept it as normal. They never called the police about their husbands or boyfriends. I can remember hearing women screaming as they got hit or slapped or knocked down. If you stood on the porch for 15 minutes you were guaranteed to see some guy beating the shit out of his woman out in front of everyone.

One time I was sitting on the porch and saw a woman get knocked out by her boyfriend right in the middle of the street. They were arguing about something and he threw a round-house punch to her head. She keeled over like she was dead. Her boyfriend looked down at her, and then walked away and left her lying there in the middle of the street.

Abuse was just part of life. And everything happened in front of everyone else. There didn't seem to be any real privacy in New Jersey. If the family down the street got into a loud all-night brawl, then everyone on the street knew about it. I can remember constantly seeing and hearing people around me fighting virtually 24 hours a day.

One incident that sticks out in my mind happened when I was standing on my grandmother's front porch in Trenton. A woman down the street was out cleaning her front stoop with a mop and bucket. Her husband came home, parked the car on the street and started yelling at her because she hadn't yet prepared dinner. She started yelling at him, and the two of them stood out there arguing for a few minutes. Then the man exploded. He pushed the woman backward, and reached down to grab her mopping pail. He turned it over, dumping all of the water and the pail onto the woman's head. I was standing on the porch sort of in shock watching this woman with the bucket on her head.

Then the man punched the bucket really hard and dented it.

The woman fell to the ground and pushed the pail off her head. She was crying really loud, and she had a busted lip that was bleeding really bad. One of our neighbors had apparently heard the commotion and called the cops. But when the police arrived the lady apparently decided not to press charges, because the cops were only there for a couple of minutes before they left.

I was really young at the time, and that scene really scared me.

But that was just a part of our life at the time. In fact, that very night, one of my female relatives got into a fight with her husband and cut him with a knife. He had big wounds across his throat, chest and head. He stumbled to our front door, and my parents ended up taking him to the hospital and staying there with him for most of the night.

When I was a kid, I didn't want to become a violent person. I always told myself that I would never be that way. I thought it was wrong for men to hit women, and I vowed that when I got married, I would never raise my hand to strike my wife.

• • • • •

There was also a lot of womanizing going on in Trenton when I was a kid. It didn't seem to matter if men were married or had serious girlfriends. They'd still go out and try to pick up women every chance they got. In fact, it didn't take me long to figure out that the number of women you bedded was a source of pride. It was something that you should discuss with your friends if you wanted to impress them.

I always heard men bragging about girls they had met. They bragged about the women they had slept with. They bragged about cheating on their wives.

If a man's wife caught him in bed with another woman, it was just something else for him to brag about. Although the men would be pissed off if they ever found out their wives were cheating, they thought it was perfectly normal for men to be unfaithful.

One day a bunch of people in our neighborhood were having a block party. Everyone was cooking up food, drinking beer and playing games. One of the men there was married but his wife and son weren't there. Meanwhile, he was flirting with one of the other girls who was there. He patted her butt, tickled her, rubbed her shoulders and kissed her. Eventually she was sitting on his lap kissing him and laughing. Everyone knew this guy was married, but no one said anything about it. It was like it was okay because his wife wasn't there.

Then his wife showed up. And she was pissed.

She came storming up to him with her son in tow. His wife grabbed the woman by the hair and pulled her off his lap. The woman hit the ground with a grunt, and the wife just kept pulling her hair. The little boy — who was probably about 9 years old — was yelling at the woman, too. His hands were balled up into fists and he was swinging away. He punched the woman in the stomach and chest and even landed a couple on her face.

A bunch of people rushed over to break up the fight, and it took them a couple of minutes to get the mother and child off the woman. Even after they pulled her back, the wife was still yelling and screaming. She was furious.

Her husband seemed really embarrassed. But he didn't seem embarrassed about cheating on his wife. He was more put out by the fact that his wife had created such a scene in front of so many people. He started yelling at his wife asking her what the fuck she thought she was doing. He told her that she had ruined the party for everyone with her craziness. He told her that she needed to take her ass home instead of being out here causing trouble. His wife was yelling back at him. She said this was all his fault, not hers. At one point, she started to charge toward him like she was going to hit him.

He launched a right hand and slapped her hard across the face.

Not only had he been messing around with another woman in front of everyone, but now he had slapped his wife in front of everyone. He had totally disrespected her, and we all knew it. He didn't care. His wife broke down and started crying, and then she grabbed her son and walked quickly away.

After she left, the man started muttering about how the bitch was crazy. He got himself another beer and went to sit down with some of the other men. I heard him talking about his wife and how she was always fucking up. He obviously blamed her for the scene that had happened a few minutes earlier.

Even though I was a little kid, I knew that he was wrong and his wife was right.

Of course, when I became an adult, I had a different perspective of things like that. During my first two marriages, I discovered that I had a real talent for turning things around and pinning the blame on my wife. I often stayed out all night, had an affair with another woman and then came home in the morning drunk as a skunk. My wife would confront me with tears and screams, and I would quickly turn the entire thing around and try to make her think it was her fault.

And I was often abusive. But at the time, I didn't even think that I was an abusive man. I didn't go to the extent of trying to break anyone's arm or putting anyone in the hospital. Those things seemed like abuse to me, and I didn't do that. I was just emotionally abusive and every once in a while I pushed or slapped my wife. I felt like, "I'm not making them bleed. I'm not putting bruises on them and punching them on the face and putting them in the hospital. I just slap the shit out of her when she pisses me off. Or I push her. Or if she hits me, I'll fucking punch her back." That's where I was with it. I didn't feel like I was being abusive, because of all the bad things I had seen in the past.

But years later when I started getting counseling, I learned that abuse occurs if I stand in a woman's way and restrain her. I can't stand in someone's way and tell them that they can't go here or can't go there. I can't grab someone by the arms and hold them in one spot and scream at them and tell them to fucking listen to me. That's abuse. After that, I might lose control or may do something even worse. I might slap her. I might push her. I might punch her. All those things are wrong.

Oops! I've gone off talking about myself as an adult when I should be talking about myself as a child.

• • • • •

Besides hating Trenton for herself, my mom also hated it for the effect that it might have on my sister and me. She didn't want us to grow up and join gangs or go to prison or get killed. She wanted us to have good education, safe neighborhoods, and hope for the future.

So after years of going back and forth from Trenton to Marana, my mother finally made a stand. She took us to Arizona on the train and then called my father and said, "You're not taking my kids, and I'm not going back to New Jersey. So you can either move out here, or you can say goodbye to all of us."

My dad had to think about that for a while. Even now, I recognize it was a hard decision for him. Although he wanted what was best for his wife and kids, New Jersey was his home. He had lived there nearly all his life. His entire family lived there.

Living in New Jersey had forced my mother to leave behind everything she knew. Living in Arizona would force my father to divorce himself from his past. They were both in a tough situation.

But I know my dad loved my mom, and I know he loved us. He wanted what was best for all of us. So he agreed to move to Arizona.

The family settle in Tucson where my father landed a job working as an electrical foreman for Mountain Bell, and my mother worked as a checker at an A.J. Bayless supermarket.

Everything was looking good for us.

• • • • •

I had always loved Tucson during our previous visits, and I loved it when we moved there for good. I think the thing I appreciated most was that it was safe. I wasn't afraid to go outside of my house. I wasn't afraid to walk to school by myself. I wasn't afraid to be outside after dark. I wasn't afraid to go into the bathrooms at school. And I wasn't afraid stay in the playground after school.

Of course, there were some bullies in school, but there were no gangs to deal with, and there were no drug dealers — that I knew of — in school.

Plus, I had some immediate opportunities to play sports in Tucson. I don't think organized sports for kids really existed in New Jersey. I guess the schools in Trenton didn't have the money and the residents didn't have the resources to start any sports leagues for kids. But in Tucson, I was able to start playing sports right away, and that became a huge part of my life.

Although I was blessed with a lot of natural abilities, I still had to develop great work ethic in order to take advantage of my talents. I credit my father for instilling those traits in me. My dad was always a very strict disciplinarian, and he set very high expectations for Tammy and I as far as doing our chores, working hard in school and trying our best in sports.

On weekends when I was young, my father would never let me watch television until all the chores were done. We had gravel in our front yard, and my job was to have all the gravel raked into perfect lines. Every Saturday I picked out all the weeds and raked the gravel into lines for my dad's inspection. In the back yard, I picked up the dog shit, fed the dog and watered the plants. There were a few other chores I had to do, but the bottom line was that I couldn't watch TV or leave the house to play until all of my work was done.

At the time, I was pissed off at my dad for making me do all of this, but today, I can see that he was trying to teach me to have good work ethic and to be responsible.

My Saturday chores also sparked a trend that would follow me for the rest of my life. I became a very early riser. During my youth, I would get up at 5 a.m. on weekends so I could get my chores done early and then watch TV or go play with my friends.

That habit is still with me. Even today, I get up at 5:30 or 6 a.m. every morning — even though I usually don't have to be at work until 9 a.m.

• • • • •

Since my entry into the sports world, my father always told me that he expected a lot out of me. He knew I had great talent, and he wanted me to be a champion. He wanted me to always strive to get better, and he wasn't satisfied with anything less than my best effort.

When I got into organized track in junior high school, my father would always tell the coaches to put me into an older age group. He knew I could outrun all the kids my age, so he wanted me to run against kids who would challenge me more, and who would make me faster. I was 12 or 13 at the time, but I'd be lined up against 14- and 15-year-olds. I won most of my races.

In fact, I was winning so handily during one race that I slowed down at the end and looked over my shoulder to see where my competitors were. I think I had seen a world-class sprinter do that one time, and I thought it looked pretty cool. So I did it.

My father was pissed off at me for not running all the way through the line. After the race, he told me that I shouldn't be out there showboating. I should be working hard and trying to get the best time I can get regardless of what the other runners are doing.

I learned my lesson then, and I don't recall ever doing that type of showing off again, until I got into the NFL.

But it wasn't the last time that I shut down my engine in a race.

As I said before, I was always able to outrun all of the other little kids. But as I got older, everyone around me seemed to get faster and faster. I could still win most of the time, but I sometimes I had to work really hard to win.

When I was in eight grade, I met a kid named Joe who intimidated the hell out of me.

Joe was about my age, and he was faster than me. We were running a 100-yard dash. When the starter's pistol fired and we shot out of our blocks, Joe was already in front of me. That shocked me. No matter what might happen at any other point in a race, no one had ever beaten me out of the blocks. The start was the strongest part of my race. In fact, I'm almost certain that by that point in my team sports career, I had never been beaten in the 100-yard dash during an organized track meet. But during this particular race, I could see Joe slightly ahead of me as we came out of the blocks.

I started pumping faster trying to catch up and pass him, but he kept the lead. He was running as fast as I was and maintaining the one-step advantage he had captured at the start. I couldn't believe it. No one was supposed to beat me. Not even older kids could beat me. Suddenly, I felt like a loser. I knew Joe was going to beat me to the finish line, and I was embarrassed. I was humiliated by the reality that I was going to be a second place runner.

I was used to being the fastest kid in the place. I was used to winning all of my races. I would generally be disappointed in myself if the second place kid finished anywhere close to me. I wanted to win by 15 or 20 yards even in a race as short as the 100 yards.

So when I got into the race with Joe, I didn't know how to handle being behind. I didn't know how to handle not being the fastest person. I didn't know how to handle the reality that I'm not always going to finish first. Instead of dealing with it, I quit.

I stopped running about 60 yards into the race. I didn't just slow down and allow myself to be beaten. I came to a complete stop on the track. All the other runners passed me. I stood there and watched them for a second, then I walked into the infield where I had left my sweats.

Everyone was surprised by what I had done. My dad was really disappointed in me, and he was really embarrassed. So was I. I felt like a failure, and I wasn't sure what to do. I looked over at my dad, and he just shook his head and walked away. He went home and left me at the track meet. When everything was over, I slowly walked about 2 miles back to our house.

But I had a few more events to run that day, and Joe beat me two more times. He took me in the 220-yard dash and the 440-yard dash. I don't think I ever lost an organized race before then, but that day I had two second place finishes and an incomplete. It was not a sterling day in my athletic career.

But I think I did learn an important lesson that day. I learned that sometimes I'm going to work as hard as I can and things aren't going to work out for me. That's life. I just have to be willing to stick to it and I can't quit no matter what happens.

I never stopped running in a race again.

And despite my father leaving me at that particular track meet, he was always there to support me when I was young. Every track meet and every football game, my father was in the stands cheering for me.

He would sometimes get pissed off at me for not working hard enough or for coming in second place, but he was there for me, and that meant a lot to me.

• • • • •

My parents also really supported my other major talent in life — art.

Ever since I was a little kid I had always loved to draw, and I had a lot of ability with a pencil and a piece of paper. As I progressed through elementary school, I gained more and more confidence in my talent, because I was always far and away the best artist in my class.

If I recall correctly, the very first time my father recognized my interest and talent for art came when I was being punished for something at age 8 or 9. Sometimes, when I got in trouble, my father would make me sit behind the television and do my homework. I could still hear the TV, but I wasn't allowed to watch it. On this particular occasion, I was behind the TV doodling instead of doing my work. After about 15 minutes back there, my father asked to see my homework. I walked over to him and showed him my paper and it was covered with pictures. He was mad at me for not doing my homework, but I could tell he was also proud of me for the skill that was evident on the page.

He became one of the biggest fans of my art, and really encouraged me to pursue that field.

Over the years, my parents enrolled me in different art schools, and the teachers would always say, "He shouldn't be in this school. He should be in a better school, because he has a lot of ability."

I think I really began to develop my art, because I was a shy, quiet little kid who had a hard time communicating with people. Art became a way for me to express myself. I felt that I could put any emotion I was feeling onto a piece of paper.

• • • • •

Although we left New Jersey a long way behind us when we moved to Arizona, there were still elements of that environment present in our home.

I think there is a saying that goes something like this: You can take a lion out of the jungle, but you can't take the jungle out of a lion.

That's how life was for us. My father was a born-and-raised Trenton, N.J. native, and he had been surrounded by chaos his entire life. My sister and I had been exposed to it at a very early age, so we understood and even expected a lot of craziness. My mom was not from Trenton but — like the women who lived in New Jersey — she quietly tolerated a lot of abuse.

So even though we escaped from the tough world of Trenton, parts of that world stowed away with us on the trip to Tucson. There were still problems in our house. There were still arguments and the occasional abuse.

Every once in a while my father was abusive to my mother. I was definitely a mama's boy, and I wanted to protect my mother. I always thought that she was perfect. In my mind, she never did anything wrong. She was a good mother to my sister and me and a good husband to my father. So whenever she and my father got into a fight, I always blamed him. So when I was a teenager, I hated my father because I thought he was a mean person. Now that I'm older, I realize that my father's problem wasn't that he was mean — it was that he drank.

He drank quite a bit back then, and — like a lot of men — every once in a while when he was intoxicated, he would be abusive. But every once in a while was too much for me. I used to get really pissed off at my father, and I wanted to stop him.

When I was a sophomore in high school my father — who had been drinking — got into an argument with my mother and he slapped her across the mouth. She was bleeding really bad, and I said, "enough of this shit." I ran toward my father and I told him to let go of my mother or I was going to fucking kill him.

I think my outburst startled him. He stuck his foot out and kicked me in the chest. I fell back against a wall trying to catch my breath. The blow knocked my breath away, and I was just sitting on the floor against the wall feeling disoriented. I was crying. That was the first and last time that my father ever hit me.

When I caught my breath, I walked up to my father and said, "I'm going to kill you when I turn 18." I felt that by then I would be big enough and strong enough to take on my dad.

Then I went to my room, which is the place that I spent most of my young life. I always came home from practice for whatever sport was in season and went into my room to lay on the bed and dream about becoming a professional athlete. It was the only thing on my mind.

• • • • •

Although I constantly dreamed about having a high-profile profession, I was always an extremely shy kid. Throughout high school, I was a loner. I avoided friendships, and in a lot of ways I was kind of a nerd. I was the best football player. I was the best track guy. I was the best artist. But that was all. I wasn't the most popular. No one hung out with me. My peers may not have thought of me as a nerd, because I was good at so many things. I think a lot of them thought I was stuck up, because I kept to myself. But I didn't feel superior to anyone. I was just a quiet guy who was a little bit afraid of people.

I was so shy that during my senior year, when I was voted Athlete of the Year and Artist of the Year at my high school, I was too embarrassed to accept the awards. During the all-school assembly in which they handed out the trophies, I hid outside the gym while my sister went up to the stage in front of the entire student body and picked up the awards on my behalf. I could hear everyone clapping for me inside, and that made me feel good, but I still didn't have the courage to go up in front of that crowd.

Years later when The Vance was running full steam, I never would have passed up an opportunity to jump up in front of a crowd and maybe grab the mike and say a few words. But back then, I was terrified to be up in front of a group of my peers.

Despite this shyness, I always dreamed of growing up and being rich and famous and having nice cars and nice clothes and everything else that went with being a celebrity.

I would go home after school and cut out pictures of guys in GQ Magazine and Sports Illustrated who were wearing really nice suits and work-out gear. I cut out pictures of guys who were really muscular and who had flat, muscular stomachs, because that's how I planned to look. I had the pictures plastered all over my room, because I just knew that I was going to be a high-profile athlete, and I wanted to look like the male models in the magazines.

The other decorations in my room included some of the artwork I had created and the many trophies and medals and blue ribbons that I had won during various athletic competitions. My father would allow me to keep only the first place medals and ribbons that I won. I had to throw away all of the second and third place awards, because they weren't worth anything.

Besides constantly telling me to keep my room clean — which I think most parents do — and telling me to get rid of second place prizes, my father rarely had anything to say about my room. I was free to decorate it however I wanted.

But one night my father came home drunk. I was sitting in my room day dreaming as usual. It was about 9 p.m. when my father walked in and said, "Your room is a mess."

I could tell that he had been drinking a lot, and I hated it when he got like that. I looked around me. My bed was made. Everything was put away neatly, but there were two shirts and a pair of shorts on the floor.

He started screaming at me that I need to keep my fucking room clean. Although he was yelling at me about the clothes on the floor, I could tell he was really mad at me about other things, and it didn't take long for the real concerns to surface. He didn't understand why I was so uncommunicative.

"Why do you spend all your time in this damned room instead of coming out and being with the family? Why don't you talk to anyone in this house?"

I just stood there and didn't say anything.

He wanted to know why I didn't try to make friends. Why I never made or received phone calls? Why I never talked to girls? Why I never tried to be social with anyone?

Looking back now, I think my father was really concerned about me. He really wanted to know if I had a problem, and what he might be able to do to help me. But I didn't get that interpretation at the time. He was drunk, and I was scared, and my silence only pissed him off more.

Then he looked up and saw all the pictures of the men on my walls and just exploded.

"Why the fuck you got all these pictures of men on the wall?" he said. "Why Vance? You're a fucking faggot aren't you? You're a fucking faggot. You have pictures of men all over your walls. No wonder I never see you with any girlfriends. You must like fucking men!"

There was a young guy who lived in our neighborhood in New Jersey — I'll call him Roberto — who was a self-proclaimed homosexual. That night my dad screamed at me, "You're just like Roberto!" He started ripping the pictures off the wall, and throwing my trophies on the ground. He knocked the desk over. He kicked things. He flipped the bed up. He broke more than half my trophies. I was really hurting inside. I wasn't gay. I didn't have any girlfriends, because I was shy. I had pictures of men on my wall, because they were my role models. I wanted to explain myself to him, but I didn't know how. I felt completely inadequate.

When my dad ran out of steam he looked at me sadly and walked out of my room. I sat on the floor and cried for a long time, then I slowly started to clean up the damage in my room. I threw away all of the pictures of men.

• • • • •

Not long after that incident, I started dating a girl — I call her Joanie. I think I was 17, and she was 16 years old. She was my first relationship, and I fell deeply in love with her. I was crazy about her. I planned to spend forever with her. Now, I realize it was just puppy love, but at the time it felt very real to me.

Joanie was the girl I would marry.

But while we were dating, she was going through some serious emotional stress. Her mother and father both died of cancer within a couple of years of each other, and, naturally, Joanie was having a tough time dealing with that.

Sometimes, she would have drastic mood swings, and it would completely throw me off balance. I was playing the role of a boyfriend for the first time in my life, and it was a mistake because I don't think Joanie was emotionally capable of any type of commitment at that time.

I didn't realize that then. I gave her my heart, and I desperately wanted her to fall in love with me.

I was still a virgin when I started dating her. I had never even kissed a girl before. So I never even tried to have sex with Joanie. Part of the reason for my reluctance to lose my virginity was that a coach had once told me that sex would ruin me as an athlete. My understanding of sex was that if I had it, I would become addicted to it and would want to have it all the time. I would lose my competitive edge. I'd lose my desire to go to football or track practice. Eventually I would lose all my skills. I still dreamed of becoming a professional football player, so the last thing

I wanted to do was risk that by having sex. So I didn't.

Another huge factor was that I was scared to have sex with Joanie or anyone else, because I had never done it before. I was afraid of being embarrassed if she found out I was a virgin, so I just avoided the issue.

To give you an idea of how emotional and how in love I was with Joanie, I'll tell you about a track meet during my senior year in high school. The meet was at my school, and my parents were in the stands. Joanie was supposed to be there watching me, but she hadn't arrived yet. I kept looking for her face in the stands.

I was by far the fastest man on our track team and everyone was counting on me. We really needed to win that meet, and I was one of the biggest factors in whether we would score enough points to win or not.

That day I was competing in the long jump, the 100-meter dash, the 200-meter dash the 400-meter relay and the 1600-meter relay — in that order.

I ran down the long-jump runway and leaped into the pit for my first attempt in that event. Then, since I had a long time to wait until my second jump, I began jogging around the track. I looked up into the stands, and I could see my parents sitting up there, but Joanie still had not arrived.

Then I happened to glance through a gate leading out of the stadium, and I could see Joanie in the park right across the street. She was there with three guys from my school. I stopped jogging and just stood there and stared. From where I was standing it looked like she was all over those guys. She appeared to be hugging one of them, and the other guys kept touching her body.

My feelings were really hurt, and I was really pissed off. Tears were forming in my eyes as I stood there watching my girlfriend hanging all over some other guys.

I was so upset that I couldn't compete. I heard my name announced to be on deck for my second attempt on the long jump, but I didn't want to go.

Instead, I just walked into the locker room, changed clothes really fast and got into my car and drove away from the track meet. I didn't care that I had a lot of competing to do that day. I didn't care that my teammates and my coach were counting on me. I was emotionally devastated by what I had seen, and I had to get away.

After I drove around for a while, I cruised over to the park where I had seen Joanie, but she wasn't there.

When I finally got home, my parents were there, and they were really disappointed in me. My coach was really pissed off at me, and he kicked me off the track team. A couple of days later I had to go apologize to my coach and my teammates and ask them to let me back on the track team.

Now as I look back on my life — especially my dating life — I can see that I was always very emotional and unpredictable when it came to women. When my feelings got hurt there was no telling what I was going to do. And beginning with Joanie, I developed a fear of women. I didn't think they were trustworthy, so I tended to put up a mental wall between my true self and all of the women that I met during my adult life. Now, I understand that my feelings were built on a shaky foundation.

Joanie was a teenager who had just lost both parents, and I was waiting for her to love me. I waited and waited, and the longer I waited the more hurt I felt. The reality was that she probably wasn't capable of loving me at the time. She was probably closing off her feelings so that she wouldn't get hurt again.

But I didn't realize that. All I saw was that I had given my heart to a girl, and she had hurt me. I wasn't going to let that happen again.

Until I got counseling and got into a relationship with my wife, Holly, I was never able to be truly intimate with a woman.

In fact, after Joanie, I could never even kiss a woman on the mouth.

Before my relationship with her, I had never french kissed anyone. I didn't even know what that term meant. But she quickly taught me that french kissing is simply kissing someone with your mouth open instead of with pursed lips. I tried it with her, but I hated it.

When she wanted to french kiss, she would pool a big glob of spit on her tongue and would want me to swallow her saliva. Sometimes she would stick out her tongue and let spit drip off the end of it before we started kissing. It really grossed me out. It made me feel sick to my stomach. It's weird when I look back on it, but I had an unbelievably strong negative reaction to that. She was the first girl I ever kissed, and since my very first kissing experience was so bad, it really affected me.

I never wanted to kiss anyone with my mouth open again. In fact, I never wanted to kiss anyone on the mouth again.

I guess it would be like someone nearly drowning the very first time they ever got into a swimming pool. That person might develop a lifetime fear of water.

That's what happened to me. My wife Holly is only the second person that I have ever kissed on the mouth.

During the chaotic years of "The Vance" I was having sex with hundreds of women and the issue of kissing came up hundreds of time. Kissing is what people traditionally do first when they are having sex. But not me. If I was talking to a girl I was planning to have sex with, I would tell her that I never kiss. I'd tell her that I have a problem with kissing that stems back to my childhood, so I just don't do it.

Most of the time just telling a woman that would keep her from trying to kiss me later. I think kissing is a very intimate act, and I didn't want to be intimate with most of the women I was with. I just wanted to fuck them and they just wanted to fuck me. So the lack of kissing was no big deal.

On the rare occasions when a woman did try to kiss me on the mouth, I would just turn my head away. She would say, "Oh yeah. I forgot you said you didn't kiss."

If I could have learned to turn my dick away instead of my head, I probably would have had a lot fewer problems over the years.

But once again, I'm jumping ahead of the story.

Despite all of the negative things that happened with Joanie during the three or four months that we dated, I carried a torch for her for many years. She was my first love, and I maintained my love for her from when I was 17 until I was drafted into the NFL at age 22. In fact, during my very first newspaper interview during training camp that year, I talked about Joanie and how much I loved her and how I could have been her husband and spent the rest of my life with her. But at the end of the interview, I said, "Goodbye Joanie. I don't love you anymore."

Even though I was putting her out of my life at that time, her influence has stayed with me for many years. My relationship with her molded the way that I treated women as far as intimacy was concerned. Until Holly, I never really allowed myself to be both physically and emotionally intimate with a woman. Sure, I had sex with a lot of women, but I didn't "make love" to them.

Looking back at this during my counseling sessions, I began to understand that I didn't think I could make love to anyone. In my mind, I was still waiting for Joanie to love me. She was my first love, and in my mind, until I made love with her, I was incapable of making love to anyone else. Of course, that was all a lie, but it was something that I believed for a long time.

Over the years, I think I fell in love with a lot of women emotionally, but the moment we had sex, that emotional tie was severed. I just couldn't be intimate with a woman both physically and emotionally. For some people, sex becomes the culmination of an emotional relationship. When they feel especially close to a person, they have sex with them to create an even deeper emotional bond.

I was the exact opposite. If I felt close to someone, having sex was the quickest way to destroy that bond. Having sex, put me so physically close to a woman that I felt threatened, and I would put up a wall to protect my feelings. I'd become a hard, uncaring person. During my NFL career, my longest-term relationships always developed with women who refused to have sex with me.

• • • • •

When I was 18, my father was yelling at my mother in the kitchen. I had the reached the point that I wasn't willing to put up with any more abuse of my mother. I ran into the room and said, "It's time." I stood there looking at my father.

"What the fuck are you talking about?" he said.

"It's time for me to kick your ass," I said. "I want you to bring your fucking ass outside." My adrenaline was pumping really hard. I kicked open the screen door and marched out into the front yard which was all gravel. I was screaming for him to bring his ass outside because I was going to kill him.

My father finally came outside, and said, "You ain't gonna do shit." I could tell that he was drunk.

I grabbed him and flipped him onto the ground. He was laying there on his back and I sat on top of him and grabbed him by the throat. I told him that I was going kill him.

"Well, just kill me then," he said quietly. "My son doesn't love me anymore. Just kill me." He was lying there crying, and I felt like shit.

"If you ever touch my mother again, I'm going to kill you, because I'm tired of this shit," I said. That was the first time that I really stood up to him, but I felt terrible afterward.

I felt like I was becoming the person that I always said I wouldn't become.

• • • • •

At the end of my senior year in high school, I had a lot of opportunities to choose from. I could have gone to the Colorado Institute of Art on scholarship. Or I could choose from 12 different colleges on football and art scholarships. I selected the University of Arizona because I wanted to be close to my mother.

I wanted to be an architect, but I wasn't very good at math. So I decided that I would study commercial art.

I did a lot of art work back then. I worked really hard at it. I got really good grades. But it started to slow down as college continued, because there were so many new things happening in my life. I still loved art, but college is a crazy time, and it was difficult to find time to draw.

My father used to say to me, "Boy, you've got a better shot of going to the moon than becoming an NFL player, so you'd better concentrate on your art work."

But I missed a lot of time in a bunch of my art classes. Even though I really enjoyed art, I didn't go to class, because I didn't think I needed to. In an art class, a big portion of your grade is determined by the production of one major project, and I always knew that I could quickly produce a painting. So I'd skip class and skip class, and then at the end of the semester, I would whip up a painting to turn in, and I'd get a good grade. But as I went along, more and more teachers began to make "attendance" part of the grading process. So it didn't matter how good an artist you were, if you didn't go to class all the time you weren't going to get a good grade.

At one point during my college career, I was in danger of getting kicked out of the school of art, because I had missed so many classes and my grades were really suffering because of it.

The dean of the school called me in and said that he was thinking about kicking me out of school. Art was really important to me, so I changed my attitude a bit and started attending classes. I didn't want to get kicked out.

Besides, despite missing classes, I was generally pretty excited about my art classes. Artists are strange people. They're not all there. They're in outer space. If you sit down with some of them, they couldn't carry a conversation with you. But if you give them a piece of paper or a stage or a canvas, they can produce something that explains Einstein's theory of relativity. It's just the way artists express themselves. Many of them can express themselves better through other mediums than they can through conversation.

That's always how I was, too. Sometimes it was hard for me to express my feelings or my concerns or my desires in real life. But if I got out a piece of paper and a pen, I could pour all of my feelings onto that paper. As I got older, I began to do the same type of expression on the football field. I was able to express myself through the way I played. I invented things as a football player just like I did with my art.

I always did a lot of art as a way to make myself feel better. It was kind of a therapy for me. When I first got into the NFL, I noticed an artist named Patrick Nagel whose pictures of women really appealed to me.

So that's something I decided to do.

But my sketches of women really meant a lot to me, because I had so much fear of women. I began to draw pictures as a way to have women in my life who couldn't hurt me. At one point during my NFL career, I was drawing four or five pictures of women every night. I had a bunch of pictures hanging on my walls. I'd walk into my house and look at those pictures and know that those women would never be mean to me. They'd never hurt me. They'd never turn their backs on me.

Sometimes I'd even talk to them. I'd say good night to them.

I trusted them.

3

Fame & Fortune

During my four-year tenure at the University of Arizona, I was a very accomplished athlete. I started at tailback for the Wildcats Football Team all four years, and I was the fastest man on our track team, too.

In track, I won the NCAA championship in the long jump when I leaped 26-feet-11-and-3/4 inches. That was the longest jump of my life, and my teammates told me that I took off nearly a foot behind the front of the board. If their estimates are correct, then that leap was definitely the greatest thing I had ever done in the long jump pit. I went nearly 28 feet. When I realized how far I had jumped, I was excited because I thought I had broken the barrier at 27 feet. I thought that I might start jumping over 27 feet all the time. But I never did jump that far again.

Our 400-meter relay team — on which I was the lead-off guy — crossed the line in first place at 39.24 seconds during the 1981 PAC-10 meet.

In the 100 meter dash, I wasn't always the fastest guy in each meet, but with a speed of 10.25 seconds, I was always in the top three. I also ran the 200 meter and 400 meter dashes occasionally. Our 4 x 200-meter relay team was awesome. In fact, there was a three-month period in which our team had the world's fastest time in that event. We set the record in 1983 with a time of 1:20.8 — I can't remember exactly, so I might be off by a second or two.

Besides playing in the NFL, one of my long-time dreams was of competing on the American team in the Olympics. That dream nearly came true during the 1984 Olympic Trials.

Down at the Los Angeles Coliseum hundreds of athletes competed for several days each trying to earn one of the few coveted spots on the Olympic team. I was one of the best long jumpers in the country, and that was the event in which I had the best shot of making the Olympic Team.

We had been jumping all day long to qualify for the team. There were a couple hundred jumpers competing for only three spots on the team, so the competition was fierce. Each guy got 6 attempts, and there were some leapers in the group. I wasn't intimidated, though, because I had done this type of thing all my life. I was always faster than everyone. I could always outperform everyone athletically.

So I was very excited, but not surprised, to find that after a full day of jumping I was in the top three. My leap of 26-feet-9.25 inches was ranked third, and I knew the top three guys would make the Olympic Team. I felt really confident. I was almost there. Only two or three more men had attempts left, and none of them had even come close to my distance on their previous jumps. There was one guy — named Jason Grimes — that I was worried about, because I had seen him long jump before, and I knew he had the potential to beat me. But so far that day, he had not been jumping well.

It turned out that Grimes was the very last jumper of the day. He was down to his last attempt. I was sitting in third place, on my way to the Olympics — which were being held in Los Angeles that year. All I needed from Grimes was a jump like his first attempts, or a scratch. Either would be fine, as long as he got it over with.

He, like everyone else, desperately wanted to make the Olympic Team. And unlike most of the other competitors, he actually had the ability to be among the top three. Going into the Olympic Trials, he was one of the three favorites. Everyone had predicted that he, Larry Meyers and Carl Lewis would represent the United States in the long jump. All day long Grimes had had a large contingent of fans cheering for him from the stands.

It was like a Hollywood movie.

Grimes was standing on the runway, rocking back and forth, his eyes glazed over looking down at the sand pit. He was probably thinking that he was about to make his last jump. If he didn't make it he'd be going home. He had to beat me to get on the Olympic Team. The air was electric with the excitement of the moment. Everyone in the stands started clapping in sequence. Every other second a collective CLAP ripped through the air. There seemed to be no other sound. I was sitting on the ground with a bunch of other jumpers, and I looked at Grimes' face. I could see that he was fired up. He knew this was his last chance, and I could tell he was prepared. He was pumped up.

Something inside of me said, "Oh my God, he's going to do it." Another part of me was saying, "Please God, stop him from doing it."

He rocked backward one final time, and started running down the asphalt. I'm sure he was sprinting pretty fast, but the entire thing seemed to happen in slow motion to me. I could see his arms pumping, his legs churning, his cheeks filling up as he shot air out of his lungs. He got to the end of the runway, planted his foot firmly on the takeoff board, pinwheeled his legs and arms a couple of times before he extended his feet out in front of him. He was a long way from the launch point when he hit the sand, and the crowd roared its approval.

I was praying for a red flag from the official which would have indicate that the jumper had stepped over the line. But there was no red flag. The tape measure came out. The officials marked off the distance. Then the announcement came that he had jumped 26-feet-9.5 inches. He had beaten me by a quarter of an inch on the last jump of the day in the Olympic Trials.

I felt sick. It killed me to be so close to this monumental goal only to lose it at the very last moment.

I was really disappointed, but I found a little bit of solace in the fact that I was an alternate for the team. If one of the first three guys was unable to compete for any reason, then I would still have an opportunity to go to the Olympics.

I walked over to the stands where my parents were watching everything. I said, "Well, at least I'm an alternate. Maybe one of those guys will get sick or something. Maybe one of them is on steroids and he'll get busted." I was grasping at anything, because I had my heart set on going to the Olympics.

Fortunately for them, and unfortunately for me, none of the first three guys developed any problems before the Olympics, so I did not compete. I didn't even go to the Olympics — although I could have as an alternate — because I wanted to concentrate on football.

But the Olympics Trials were just one of the exciting things that were happening in my life at that time. The NFL draft was rapidly approaching — and so was the emergence of The Vance persona.

In 1984, during my senior year at the University of Arizona, The Vance was nothing more than a "spark in his father's eye." I had always been a very shy person throughout high school and college, but during that year, I discovered a way for me to be more popular. Throughout the 1984-85 NFL season, guys like Jim McMahon and William "The Refrigerator" Perry of the Chicago Bears were getting a lot of attention. They were completely crazy and flamboyant and fun. People loved them. And as a result of their outgoing personalities they were doing national commercials for sunglasses and refrigerators. You could hardly watch TV without seeing their faces.

I envied those guys. I wanted to be like them. I wanted to be famous. I wanted to do commercials. I wanted people to look at me with envy and say, "Damn, he leads a fun and exciting life."

I wanted people to like me.

I knew I could do what those guys were doing. I could do commercials. I could be a personality. I could be flamboyant. I could be crazy.

This type of thinking was just a seed in my mind at that point, but on draft day in 1985, all of the hoopla really began to kick in, and it was like watering a seed inside of me. In most people this seed, called the ego, ranges in size from a small house plant to an oak tree. My tree was an overachiever. It would eventually earn a leading role in Jack and the Bean Stalk.

On draft day, I was a projected first-rounder, so all of the press in Tucson were at my house. One part of me was really excited to have all of the media there. I was dying for the phone to ring so that I could officially proclaim myself a professional football player. And the media could be counted on to broadcast my good fortune all over the state. They could make me famous. They could help me get commercials.

But at the same time, the shy side of me didn't really want the media to be there. I was nervous because I thought I might not get picked until the fourth or fifth round, and if that happened I would feel like an idiot. I would be embarrassed and humiliated. And I certainly wouldn't want to have the press standing there staring me in the face as round after round ticked by without a phone call.

But when the draft started my mood improved because a couple of teams expressed interest in me. The Dallas Cowboys called during the middle of the first round just to see if I would be interested in playing for them. I said, "Yes, of course."

Later in the round the L.A. Raiders called to tell me they were going to take me with their next pick, and I was really excited.

"Hey, I'm going to be an L.A. Raider," I told everyone. "I'm moving to Los Angeles!" They were all very excited for me.

I was really relieved by that phone call, because for months everyone in the media had been saying, "Vance Johnson is certain to go in the first round." They had been talking about it and talking about it. So on draft day, every time a team made a selection — and it wasn't me — I got more worried. There were only about four or five picks left in the first round when the Raiders called me. I was happy to learn that I would definitely be a first-rounder, and I wouldn't have to deal with the embarrassment of not living up to all of the hype that the press had created.

So as I sat watching the screen, the television news cameras were rolling, the newspaper photographers were poised, everyone was waiting to record my reaction when Commissioner Pete Rozelle said my name.

Then the commissioner stepped up the podium and said, "The Los Angeles Raiders select...wide receiver...Jesse Hester."

I was still smiling for a couple of seconds after hearing this, because when I heard the words "wide receiver" I stopped listening. I knew it was going to me. They had just called and told me they were going to pick me.

When I realized that they had selected someone else, I was shocked. I couldn't believe it. How could a team call and say they were going to draft you and then turn around not five minutes later and take someone else? I was really hurt and embarrassed. All of the media in Tucson were at my house. Even the media seemed kind of embarrassed for me, which made me feel even worse. You know you're in trouble when reporters start feeling sorry for you.

So I sat there feeling stupid as the rest of the first round rolled past. Fortunately, I didn't have to wait too long into the second round before I was selected. Denver made a trade with Houston that moved the Broncos up four or five positions. When a coach from the Broncos called to say that they were going to take me with their next pick, I just sat on the phone saying, "yeah, sure, whatever." I wasn't going to believe anything until I heard my name on TV. I wasn't going to get my hopes up, because I didn't want to get my feelings hurt again.

When the commissioner went to the podium and said, "the Denver Broncos select…wide receiver…Vance Johnson," I was elated.

Everyone in the house went wild. My family was laughing and yelling and the press was cheering. I felt really proud. And I was really happy to be going to Denver. The Broncos already had seven former Arizona Wildcats on the roster, so I figured I would fit right in. (The seven other players were: Al Hill, wide receiver; Chris Brewer, running back; Mike Freeman, offensive guard; Marsharne Graves, offensive tackle; Randy Robbins, cornerback; Steve Broadway, linebacker, and Ricky Hunley, linebacker.)

Draft day was one of the most exciting days of my life.

I later heard rumors that the Houston Oilers — who specialized in short, fast receivers, as opposed to the normal tall, slower guys — were planning to draft me with the third pick of the second round. But the Broncos, who held the eighth pick of the second round, called the Oilers and negotiated a swap of picks. I don't know what all the details of the trade were, but my understanding is that the Broncos told the Oilers that they were planning to select a different player. After the trade was completed, the Broncos picked me, and the Oilers were pissed off.

But I was really excited to be a Bronco. I was looking forward to catching passes from John Elway. Later that day, I ran out to the Jeans West store to pick up a cool jeans outfit to wear to Denver.

The next day, I flew to Denver, and I told some of the passengers on the plane that I was Vance Johnson, and that I was glad I was going to be playing for the Broncos. Everyone seemed really excited to meet me, and the flight attendants even moved me up to first class and gave me a bottle of champagne. I felt like a king.

That was really the first item on a long list of special treatments that I got simply because I was a Bronco. At the time I didn't think much about it, but looking back on it, it's clear to me that draft day was when The Vance first emerged.

On that wonderful April day in 1985, a beautiful mistress named the National Football League went to bed with Vance Johnson from the University of Arizona, and they conceived a child. A couple of months later, after a very short pregnancy, a kicking and screaming infant, named The Vance, was born.

He would become a holy terror.

It was a crazy situation. One day I was a 22-year-old college student living on $150 a month. I didn't have a job and I was barely getting by in school with my grades. The next thing I knew, I was a professional football player. I was flying first-class to a new city. I got to Denver and my name was on the front page of the newspaper. Everyone in the city was excited to have me on the team, and even John Elway said he was looking forward to throwing to me. It was mind-boggling.

During the Broncos three-day mini-camp immediately following the draft, all of the new players were tested for strength and agility and speed. Of course, I beat all comers when they started timing the 40-yard dashes. We were running on a slow field with high grass, but I still crossed the line after only 4.36 seconds. I can still hear the whistles, wows and grunts from the coaches as they looked at their watches.

I could run like the wind, and I could see by the faces of the coaches that they couldn't wait to get me into a football uniform.

This was exactly the sort of thing that The Vance thrived on. I loved being the center of attention. I loved getting special treatment. I loved impressing people. And I was determined to do everything that I could to get even more attention.

Before training camp started my rookie year, I decided to get a perm and dye my hair red, so people would be able to recognize me easier. But something went wrong with the dye and my hair came out sort of an orange-ish color. That was okay with me though, that would just make me stand out even more.

When I returned to Tucson after rookie camp, my agent — who I will call Kevin — picked me up and said, "Vance, now that you're in the NFL, you can have anything you want."

During my college tenure, I constantly stopped at the Porsche dealership on Broadway in Tucson. I'd pull up during the evenings after the place had closed, and I'd just look in the window and dream about having one of those cars.

So when Kevin told me I could have anything I wanted, my response was immediate.

"I want a Porsche," I said.

So he drove me to the dealership on Broadway and said, "Pick one out."

I was in heaven. I couldn't believe that I was going to be an NFL player. I was finally going to have so many of the things that I had dreamed about all my life. I was going to have a nice car and cool clothes and lots of women and lots and lots of money.

Porsche models are differentiated by numbers, and as I walked through that showroom I saw 911s and 924s and 928s and 944s. My first love was a Porsche 911, but that day I was experiencing a rare, fleeting, marginally responsible mood. I decided to get a Porsche 944 — one of the less expensive Porsches — and I would later upgrade to a 911 after I was established in the NFL.

I selected an maroon Porsche 944, and I was in heaven. My agent, Kevin went into the back room with the manager of the dealership, and when he came out a few minutes later he handed me the keys and said the car was mine. I didn't have to sign any forms. I didn't pay any money. I didn't do anything except grab the keys and drive home.

One of my lifelong dreams was to own a Porsche and suddenly I had one. I was on my way to Denver, and I didn't have a penny in my pocket, but I had a Porsche. I didn't even have money for gas, but I had a Porsche. And I sure didn't have any money to make car and insurance payments. But I had a Porsche.

I drove the hell out of that car.

I was still living in Tucson for about a month after the draft, and I was cruising around town and around campus in my Porsche. I thought I was the shit. I was hanging out with people who weren't my friends before, but who suddenly decided that they wanted to be my friends.

I started lying and telling people stories about how hard John Elway throws a football. My visit to Denver had only lasted a couple of days, and I hadn't even seen John yet, but I was already telling war stories.

After the draft, but before I signed my contract, my agent loaned me $5,000 to tide me over. About a month and a half later he loaned me an additional $4,500. I used this money to buy myself some new clothes. Some of it was flash money that I would pull out of my pockets in a big wad to impress people. I started taking my parents out to nice restaurants for dinner everyday.

It was crazy, too. When me and my parents went out to eat, we could have jumped into one of their cars, but I wanted to drive the Porsche. So we would all squeeze into that little sports car to go out for a nice dinner. My dad would wedge himself into the back seat, and we would be off and running.

After a couple of months of testing my spending wings, I was ready to move to Denver to start living the really fast life.

Not long after I got to Denver, I was pulled over by a Denver cop who clocked me doing about 90 mph in a 55 mph zone. When he walked up to my car, I had already hidden my driver's license, because I thought I'd have more time to talk him out of the ticket if my license wasn't immediately handy. I was fumbling through my wallet pretending that I couldn't find any identification.

"Dang officer, this is all I have," I said, handing him one of my football cards.

"Oh, you're Vance Johnson," the police officer said smiling.

We sat there talking about the team for a few minutes and then he let me go with no ticket. "Just slow down a little bit," he said as he walked back to his car.

I couldn't believe it. I had gotten out of a ticket just because I was a Bronco. At the time, I thought this was way past cool, but it was one of the many incidents that contributed to the growth of The Vance. With every passing day, I was becoming more and more spoiled as a Broncos' player. I didn't think I had to take responsibility for my actions, and everywhere I went people were confirming that for me. I got away with everything.

After I signed my contract, I got a check for $450,000. Did you hear me? I said I'm 22 years old, I've got a Porsche and a check for $450,000!!! It's an amazing feeling to have that much money. It's like winning the lottery. I wasn't thinking about saving that money. Why the hell would I save it? I'd been poor all my life. I'd struggled. I'd worked hard. And now that my labor had finally paid off, was I going to continue to live in poverty in order to save the money? Hell no! I was going to spend that money as fast as I could. I wanted cars and clothes and furniture and a house and more cars. I wanted it all. And I was going to have it.

That was my attitude. I didn't worry about the money, because I had so much God-given ability that I knew I would play in the NFL for a long time and make more money. But even though I was eager to spend the money, it was hard at first because everywhere I went, everything was free.

I would go to restaurants and get seated immediately no matter how long the waiting list was. Later the managers would always come to my table to thank me for coming in and to tell me that my meal was free. I would go to the mall, and they would give me 40 or 50 percent discounts on the clothes. I'd go to the movie theater and walk right in without buying a ticket. I'd just waltz right past the usher, pretend I didn't even see him. No one ever said a thing to me.

It was like this everywhere I went, and I loved it. I began to thrive on it. I loved the attention. I loved the special treatment. I loved the way that women threw themselves at me when I went to clubs. I loved the way people's eyes bulged out when I pulled out a big wad of cash. I loved the way people looked at my Porsche with envy. I loved all of it.

I became so well-known in Denver, that I started calling myself the Black John Elway, because I had never heard of a black guy with the Broncos who was that popular.

My desire for all of this attention was further fueled by my insecurity and my competitive nature. Although I've always strived to be the best at everything in life, I've always had this deep-seated fear that people didn't like me. So that insecurity and competitive fire became The Vance's chief characteristics. When I saw some of my teammates driving flashy cars and dating beautiful women, I felt inadequate. I felt that I had to do better than them, so I was always trying to outdo them. I always had to have the prettiest woman in the club, or to be dating a more beautiful woman than any other player on the team. I always had to have the nicest car. I always had to be the most popular player.

Eventually, I had thousands of women chasing after me. I knew I had more women than most of my teammates could even imagine, and that made me feel good. It gave me a sense of accomplishment, like I had done something really great. I was buying a new sports car every couple of months, and I loved it when the other players would say, "Damn VJ!! That's a sweet-ass Porsche you've got." Everywhere I went people recognized me because of the crazy clothes I wore and the wild haircuts I sported.

I thought people respected me because I had so much money and so many women and so many cars, and because I was just so damned crazy. I thought all these things were signs of power and success.

But no one respected me.

I was running around partying all of the time hanging out with very low class people. Those people became the mirror of the world that I was looking at, and I quickly lost perspective of what was important to me and what wasn't. You see, the mirror I was using was warped. It was like one of those circus mirrors that are concave or convex that make you look taller or fatter or shorter. If you stared into that mirror long enough, and you never consulted a regular mirror, you would start to believe that that's what you really look like.

Imagine that you are a fit person, who worked out hard to maintain your healthy body, and deep down your motivation is that you are terrified of ever getting fat. Say you consult a mirror every morning to check how your body looks, and let's say that mirror is the type that makes you look tall and skinny. Although you fear becoming fat, it would be a very easy thing for you to unknowingly do, because everyday your mirror lies to you and tells you that you are skinny.

Now there was nothing accidental about the changes in me. I wanted to change. I wanted to be famous and to be known as a wild and crazy guy all over the world. So I walked into this hall of mirrors and everything I looked at gave me a false picture of the world. I was doing a lot of things that ranked as cool in the crowd that I was in, but in the real world, a lot of what I did was just stupid. I was this evil person who was out there just destroying himself. At first I didn't know I was killing myself. Later, I didn't even care.

Even though I eventually realized what kind of people I was running with and the type of life I was leading, I denied it. I wasn't a low-class person like those other people. I was The Vance. You know, Vance Johnson, the guy who was catching all of those passes for the Broncos. The young star of the Denver Broncos. I felt like I was different from them. I felt like I was better than them.

It took me a long time to figure that the only person I was fooling with all of that stuff was myself.

4

The Vance in His Prime

When I was in my prime "Vancing" years, people generally thought of me as a fast-moving, irresponsible, philandering sex maniac, who slept with a different woman every night and got the hell out of her house in the morning before the kid was born.

To those people I say, "Congratulations! You were right." To claim your prize, please send a self-addressed stamped envelope to my attention at the San Diego Chargers headquarters. Your prize will be one self-addressed stamped envelope.

During my heyday, I bedded a lot of women, and I was extremely irresponsible, and I rarely thought about the consequences of my actions.

But one thing about me that will probably surprise a lot of you who have followed my stormy life and career is this: I was a virgin until age 20.

I think a lot of people always thought of The Vance as a hell-raisin' son-of-a-bitch, who came out of the womb driving a turbo Porsche, wearing a pair of shades and sporting a funky hair cut. They probably figured I lost my virginity at the tender age of 2 and set out deflowering my fellow, female preschoolers, while all the other kids were taking naps.

But that image is a long way from the truth. Until my early 20s I was very shy.

I had a few opportunities to lose my virginity before my 20th birthday, but I was too insecure to ever go all the way with a girl. Of course, whenever the subject of sex came up among my peers in high school or college, I would lie about my experience.

Like a lot of kids, I thought everyone was having sex except for me, so I was embarrassed about my virginity.

There were a few girls who wanted to have sex with me during my first couple of years at the University of Arizona, but I thought they were all non-virgins, so I didn't want to mess with them. It wasn't that I had to have a girl who was "pure" and "untainted." I was afraid to have sex with an experienced girl, because she might have been able to tell that I was a virgin, and laugh at me. Or, worse, she might tell everyone at the school that I was a virgin. I didn't think I could handle that kind of embarrassment, so I kept my dick to myself.

Then when I was 19, I was dating a girl named Ana. She was really pretty, and nice and I really loved her a lot. She was also a virgin, which gave me some confidence. I figured that if I had sex with her and I did something wrong, she wouldn't realize it because she was as inexperienced as I was.

So we talked about having sex, and finally on March 12, 1983 — the night before my 20th birthday — we decided that it was time.

We went to a convenience store, and she sat in the truck while I went inside to get condoms. I had never purchased condoms before, so I was really embarrassed that night. Whenever I watch movies that show a teenager acting nervous while buying condoms, I always think about myself. That's exactly how I was. I thought the clerk was smirking at me. I thought the transaction would be recorded on the store's security camera and the employees would be watching the tape and laughing at me later. I was afraid that someone would walk in and see the small box of three Trojan condoms sitting on the counter. I thought the whole world knew that I was about to get laid. I was sweating when I handed over the money, but I tried to act cool as I walked out of the store.

We drove to a park right next to my old high school in Tucson, and got ready to have sex right there in the cab of my father's Ford F-150 pickup truck.

I pulled a condom out of the box and started to unroll it. I had never worn a condom before, so I wasn't exactly sure how it worked. There was no way in hell I was going to embarrass myself by turning on the dome light and reading the directions, so I just tried to put it on the way that seemed right. I had the condom rolled pretty much to the bottom when the tip ripped open. Damn!

I pulled out another condom and started to put it on. Shit!! I ripped that sucker too.

I just didn't know how to put the damned things on. I was pulling them real tight all the way to the bottom. In later years, I would brag that my dick was just too big for a normal-sized condom, but at the time, I wasn't thinking about jokes. I was panicked, scared and embarrassed. But I was trying to play it cool, because I didn't want Ana to realize that I didn't know what the hell I was doing.

So I pulled the third and final condom out of the box. I had it most of the way on, when it too developed a small tear in the tip. I couldn't believe it. I had ruined all three condoms. But it was dark and Ana couldn't tell what was happening, so I didn't say anything.

There were several reasons I pretended that everything was okay. For starters, I didn't have anymore money. Second, even if I did have the cash, there was no way in hell I was going back into that convenience store to buy more condoms. Third, I didn't want to admit that I didn't know how to put on a damned condom. And, fourth, I was so close to finally losing my virginity that it seemed stupid to stop at that point.

So Ana and I had sex that night with a busted condom.

Nine months and three days later my wonderful, beautiful daughter Nicole was born. My first sexual foray had made me a father.

I was batting 1.000.

A few months after that first sexual encounter, I sort of broke things off with Ana and started seeing a girl named Lisa.

I would visit Lisa at her mother's house, and her mom would always leave the front room so that Lisa and I could have some privacy. We would play cards or watch television or just talk, but no matter how long I stayed, her mother never came out to check on us.

So when we had sex for the first time, it was right on the floor in the living room of her mother's house. We weren't really worried about her mother catching us, because we knew she wanted to give us time alone. Besides, our first sex was so damned fast that if her mother had walked out of the bedroom right when Lisa and I started having sex, I would have been finished, dressed and drinking a soda before she reached the front room.

Sex for Lisa and I was always kind of a spur-of-the-moment thing, which meant that we never knew when we were going to have it, and I never had condoms with me when we did it. That was fine with me, because I didn't want to fool around with condoms anymore. My ego couldn't handle the pressure of purchasing them or trying to put them on. Besides I thought the likelihood that another girl would get pregnant from me was pretty low. We were using the rhythm method and it seemed to be pretty effective.

But, as luck would have it, Lisa was pregnant within a month of our first sexual encounter. Nine months later, in May 1985, my second child, Vance Jr., was born. That was just a couple of weeks after I was drafted by the Broncos.

At age 22, after two years, two women and two sexual relationships, I had two children. During the next year, Lisa and Ana would also file two paternity suits against me.

It's no wonder I chose the number Eighty-*Two* when I got into the pros.

After Lisa, I dated a woman named Bettina (pronounced BuTEENa). We had sex together a lot, but we were a lot more careful. We took precautions to make sure that we wouldn't have a child together.

There was virtually no chance that was going to happen with Bettina. Although I was irresponsible, Bettina was a very responsible person who was really into college and who was working hard toward her degree. She cared about her future, and she made sure that we were careful, because she knew she wasn't ready to take care of a child at that point in her life.

Whew! That was a load off my mind. The last thing I needed at age 22, was another child.

Nine months later. . . just joking. HA! HA! Fortunately, Bettina and I managed to avoid getting pregnant.

Right after I was drafted by the Broncos, Ana and Lisa each asked for $1,500 a month in child support, plus back pay. I said, "no way." At that point, I hadn't yet signed a contract with the Broncos. In my entire life, I had never even seen $1,500. That sounded like a shitload of money to me, so I offered them $500 a month instead. They said, "no way." So we all went to court.

It was a weird situation. I knew Ana and Lisa were the ones who had custody of my children, and they had to take responsibility for all of the kids' daily needs. Although I wanted to visit my kids a lot and be a good father for them, I wasn't the one who was physically raising them. So, I felt that Ana and Lisa were completely justified in asking for monthly child support. Besides, I love my kids, and I want them to have everything they need to be happy.

The problem was that I felt the women were trying to take advantage of me just because I was going to be rich after my contract was signed. So I held out.

Ana and Lisa filed paternity suits against me midway through my rookie year, and the Denver newspapers carried the stories. I was really upset about the entire thing, because I knew people would think that I was a jerk who knocked up these girls and then abandoned them. That wasn't true. I never denied that Nicole and Vance, Jr. were my children, and I never shrugged off my responsibility for them. I wanted to pay child support.

In court, the Judge ordered me to pay $750 a month in support to Ana, plus about $20,000 in back pay. To Lisa, I paid $980 a month plus $5,000 or $10,000 in back pay. Plus, I had to pay both of their attorneys' fees which totaled between $10,000 and $15,000.

That's what the judge ordered and that's what I paid. It's important to me that people understand I never tried to escape responsibility for my children. I love them and I want to take care of them in every way. If it were up to me, I would have custody of my kids.

I don't get to see them very often, and I really miss them a lot.

• • • • •

Ana and I first started seeing each other in high school. I have always liked really tall women, and that was part of the reason I was so attracted to Ana. She was about 5-feet-10, and she had a great body because she ran track at my high school. She was Hispanic and had dark skin and long dark hair. She had big, pretty, brown eyes, and she was really soft-spoken and vulnerable. She was a sweet person, and she never really caused any problems for me. Actually, she was basically an angel — until I drove her crazy.

During my senior year in high school, Ana and I were an item, but we weren't in a really serious relationship, even by adolescent standards. We liked each other, and we hung out, but that was about it. We were both shy and quiet, so it was kind of hard for us to be together. We never really talked about the future, and we didn't have sex back then. We used to talk about making love every once in a while, but we never actually tried to perform the act. Ana was a virgin, but she didn't know that I was a virgin, too. So she just thought I was being a gentleman, and I was willing to wait until she was ready. The truth was that I was scared to make a move on her.

Ana was a year younger than me, so when I graduated from high school and enrolled at the University of Arizona on the other side of Tucson, we didn't see each other as much. We'd still go out together every once in a while, but we were in completely different environments. Our relationship was in limbo. At the time, I had mixed feelings about Ana. I really liked her a lot, but I wanted to find a girl on my college campus whom I could date. Unfortunately, I was still really shy, and I didn't really approach or talk to many girls on campus. There were a few girls who were interested in me, but I didn't pursue them. Part of my fear was due to me being a virgin. I figured that all college girls had sexual experience, so I was afraid to mess with any of them.

Ana and I kept seeing each other off and on for nearly two years, and during that time, I was getting more and more eager to lose my virginity. I figured that if I could just get some sexual experience, I'd be able to deal better with college girls. So Ana and I started to talk about having sex.

At the beginning of 1983, we began to date more like a regular couple. We saw each other probably two or three times a week for about three months. We'd drive around town together or rent videos or grab a pizza. We were pretty much together all the time when she wasn't in school, and I wasn't in football or track practice. All of this led up to the night that we lost our virginities together.

After our rendezvous in the pickup truck, Ana and I had sex every chance we got. I was really excited because I wasn't a virgin anymore, and I really wanted to go out and meet some other girls.

Then came the shock.

About a month after the first time we had sex, Ana told me that she was pregnant. She had been worried for a while because her period hadn't come. She finally broke down and went and bought one of those home pregnancy tests.

It was positive.

We were both scared to death. We didn't know what to do. The only thing I knew for certain was that we were going to have the baby, because I don't believe in abortion. I was raised to believe that you should never hurt a child, and abortion is simply inflicting a fatal wound to a child. It's murder, plain and simple, and I won't allow that to happen to my child.

I really developed strong feelings about abortion when I was in high school, because one of my football coaches talked to me about it all the time. He really had a great relationship with a lot of the students, and he was the type of person that guys turned to when they were in trouble. I hate to stereotype anyone, but I think a lot of athletes are very irresponsible, and they (like me) get girls pregnant and then they don't know what to do. When a high school guy gets a girl pregnant, he usually doesn't have a job — which means he has no money. He doesn't want to go to his parents, because he's afraid they'll be really disappointed in him. The girl can't go to anyone, because she's afraid of what they might say. So the guys at my school would typically go to the football coach for help.

My coach talked to me about this a lot. He would try to come up with the money so the pregnant girl could get an abortion. He was really against abortion, but he didn't know what else he could do for all those students. He knew that abortion was a tragedy, but it might be a double tragedy for a child to be born to a 15-year old girl. So he helped the students, but every time he did it, it tore him up a bit. He hated abortion, and through him, I began to develop pretty strong feelings against abortion.

But it got even deeper than that. A girl I was close to during high school had five abortions during a three-year period. She was younger than me, and every time she got pregnant, I — like my football coach — helped her scrape together money for an abortion. I was the one who took her to the hospital, and waited for it to be over. It was always really painful for me, because killing the baby seemed so wrong. There was a life inside of her when she went into the hospital. That life was gone when she came out.

I never told this girl how I felt about abortion, because I loved her and I wanted to support her. Whenever she got pregnant, she didn't really have anyone to turn to. The guys who got her pregnant usually didn't know she was pregnant, because she was afraid to tell them. If she did tell him, there was nothing he could do. He didn't have any money to help support the baby or to pay for an abortion. The girl was afraid to tell her parents or any of her teachers or anyone at church. She was afraid to tell any of her female friends, because she didn't want everyone at school to know that she was pregnant. So, she came to me. I knew she was too young to be having children, so I helped her have abortion after abortion after abortion.

But every time I sat in the hospital waiting for it to be over, it hurt me. I vowed that I would never allow a child of mine to be aborted. I would never kill any of my kids regardless, whether they were 3-year-old toddlers or 3-month-old fetuses. Their lives are just too precious. I don't care if it's my wife who is pregnant or some woman I slept with only one time. I don't want anyone who is carrying my child to ever have an abortion.

So when Ana told me that she was pregnant, I knew that we would have the child, and I was excited about it. I was also terrified by the tremendous responsibility that a child would be. We talked once or twice about getting married, but I wasn't ready to get married, and neither was she. I knew that a child was not the right reason to get married.

Besides — I know this is a terrible thing for me to say, but — I still wanted to meet other girls.

So when Ana was about three months pregnant, I met a girl named Lisa at a nightclub in Tucson. The way I met her was kind of weird. It was the first time I had ever gone to this particular club. I didn't go to clubs very often because I was very shy. I was standing against the wall with one of the guys from my college football team when we saw this beautiful girl walk into the club. It was Lisa. She was wearing a black-and-white dress. It was all black on one side and all white on the other side. And the white side was sort of see-through. Even in the bad lighting of the club, you could "just" see the outline of her thong underwear. She looked incredibly sexy. She was about 5-feet-9 or 5-feet-10. She was half-Puerto Rican and half-white, and she had beautiful strawberry blonde hair. Her body was gorgeous.

Although I really wanted to meet her, there was no way in hell I could approach a girl like that. At that point in my life, I just didn't have the confidence. Fortunately, I didn't need it. She walked past my friend and me once, and she looked right at me. A couple of minutes later, she came back.

"Aren't you Vance Johnson?" she said.

"Yes," I said. "How'd you know my name?"

It turned out that Lisa had run track at a high school in Tucson that was a rival of my old school. She had seen me a lot at track meets and football games. Plus, since I had enrolled at the local college, I was still receiving a lot of publicity in Tucson.

She was in great shape because of her track background. Her body was one of the big reasons that I was initially attracted to her.

We started dating after that. Mostly our dating consisted of me driving over to her house, and the two of us sitting in her mother's living room playing games or watching television. One surprising thing about Lisa was that she was incredibly smart. I'm pretty sure she earned all A's in school. A lot of times when we were hanging out at her house, we'd watch Jeopardy. I have never known anyone in my life who could answer more than five or six questions on any one episode of Jeopardy. But every time we watched Jeopardy, Lisa would answer damned near half the questions before the contestants did. She was amazing.

I guess if we hadn't been watching so much Jeopardy, we might have had sex even sooner than we actually did. We had sex for the first time about a month after we met. And a month after that, Lisa was pregnant. Again, there was no way I was going to let her have an abortion.

So there I was. Twenty-two years old, with one child already born and another one in the oven. You would think that would have a sobering effect on me and cause me to slow down, but it didn't. Instead, I did something that would become the general theme of my life in later years.

I started looking for a new girl to date.

I don't know why I did that. I guess I was afraid to be committed to Ana or Lisa. And even though I was opposed to abortion, I didn't want to deal with the responsibility of a child.

I was still seeing Ana occasionally, and I continued to see Lisa, but my main girlfriend was Bettina. I was hanging out in the commons area on campus one day with one of the guys on my football team. All of a sudden this girl walked by wearing these really short jean-shorts. The bottoms of her butt cheeks were just peeking out, and she looked very sexy. She had on two-inch pumps, and a white tank-top shirt.

My friend and I both sucked in a breath when we saw her, because she was an absolute knockout. She was about 5-feet-8, and she was half-Spanish and half-white. She had short, dark hair, and big brown eyes.

She had just passed us when I ran up to her and said, "Hi."

The initiative in trying to meet her really surprised me, because I normally would never approach a girl to talk to her. But I didn't really think about it at the time. My jumping up to talk to her was just a reaction to her. I just had to say something, so I said, "Hi."

Actually, I didn't just say "Hi". I "yelled" the word.

She started laughing, because I sounded funny, I guess. We stood there and talked for probably 30 seconds. I was really nervous, but she was really nice. I wanted to get to know her better, but I was afraid to ask her out on a date, and I was afraid to ask for her phone number. She started to say goodbye, because she had to go to class, and I blurted out, "Maybe, I'll call you sometime. I mean, um, if you give me your phone number."

She laughed again and said, "sure." She gave me her number, and I was in heaven.

We started dating each other after that, and the more I saw her, the more I realized that she was a sweet person.

Bettina's brother died of AIDS shortly after she and I got together, so she was having a really tough time emotionally. We spent a lot of time together, and we became really close. I think to a certain extent we were clinging to each other because of the things that had happened in our lives. She was struggling to accept her brother's death, and I was trying to deal with the responsibility of suddenly having two children.

So that's the backdrop against which my last semester at Arizona began. Bettina was my steady girlfriend. However, I was still occasionally seeing Lisa, who was pregnant with Vance Jr. — due in early May. And I was still occasionally seeing Ana, who was the mother of Nicole, my first child.

They were The Three Amig*as*.

There were a lot of hurt feelings floating around Tucson during that time — including mine — and all of that tension simmered for a while until it finally erupted into a boiling pot of verbal and physical abuse.

Ana was really pissed off at me, because I had gotten her pregnant, and then I had left her. I think she may have wanted me to marry her, but at the very least, I think she wanted me to hang around and be with her. But I didn't do that. She was stressed with the pressures of taking care of Nicole, plus her parents were really mad at her. They didn't like the fact that a black guy had gotten her pregnant, and I think at one point they were planning to disown her.

While Ana was struggling with all of that, I was in a relationship with Lisa, and she was pregnant with my child. That really hurt Ana and pissed her off even more. She decided to deny my visitation rights with Nicole. Although I wasn't taking daily responsibility for Nicole, I loved her dearly, and I visited her as often as I could. But when Ana cut me off, there was nothing I could do. For months I tried, unsuccessfully, to visit Nicole. Ana lived with her parents out near Old Tucson — where all of the western movies are shot — which is about 20 miles outside of Tucson proper. Their house set off the main road at the end of a dirt driveway that was probably about 100 yards long.

Whenever I drove out to the house to see Nicole, Ana's father would see my car kicking up dust on the driveway. He would walk out onto the porch and tell me to turn the fuck around and get off his property. I'd tell him that I just wanted to see Nicole, but he would say, "You aren't gonna see shit, so you better just get the fuck out of here."

I was young and her father scared me, so when I drove out to their house, I would always leave after a couple of minutes. One day when I visited, he told me that his brother or cousin or someone in his family was a police officer, and if I didn't stay away he would have me arrested for trespassing.

Although I could understand why Ana was upset with me, it still made me furious that I couldn't see my daughter. I didn't know what to do. I had already gone for several months without seeing Nicole. When Ana's dad told me that he was going to have me arrested, that really popped my cork.

I decided to go talk to Ana at the graphic arts office where she worked. I was furious when I confronted her in the parking lot in front of the place. I cussed at her and called her names, and told her that she had no right to keep me from seeing my daughter. I demanded to see Nicole. In the face of my tirade, Ana stood her ground, which tells you a little bit about how pissed she was at me. Like I said earlier, Ana was a really nice, quiet person, and she didn't get crazy, until I drove her to that point. She cussed and yelled names right back at me, and told me I could go fuck myself, because I wasn't going to see Nicole.

We were making quite a scene. People were watching us from store windows, from the sidewalk and from their cars, but at the time neither of us seemed to care.

She screamed that I was never going to see my daughter again, and that just made me absolutely crazy. I lost control. I grabbed her by the shoulders and started shaking her and yelling at her. I shook her like a fucking rag doll. Then I threw her on the ground and told her that I would "fucking kill her" if she didn't let me see my daughter.

That was when I noticed all of the people who were coming out of stores and standing in the parking lot yelling at me to "leave her alone." I looked around in amazement. Don't you all understand what she is doing? Don't you know that she is keeping my daughter from me? She deserved to get pushed around. She is being a bitch, and she needs a little straightening out.

But I could tell that none of these people were on my side. I knew someone had probably called the police, and I was afraid of being arrested. So I ran to my car and drove away quickly.

That incident with Ana was the first time that I was ever violent with a woman, and to tell you the truth, at the time I didn't even think there was anything wrong with what I did. I believed that she really did deserve it. Men around me had been beating the fuck out of women for as long as I could remember, so pushing Ana around didn't seem like a bad thing to me. I thought physical abuse was a normal and inevitable part of any relationship.

After that fight, our relationship became more and more abusive with each passing day. We were still seeing each other off and on, and we got into a lot of physical fights. One time Ana got so mad at me during a verbal argument at the townhouse that my sister and I shared that she shoved me backward, and I tripped over something and fell through the stucco wall right into the fireplace. The fireplace was designed so that the wall that enclosed it protruded about two or three feet from the main wall of the house. When she pushed me, I fell through one of the side walls of the fireplace. I completely knocked a hole through the damned wall. That pissed me off, so I jumped up and slapped the shit out of her.

Ana and I had a lot of fights in those days, and we always fought about the same two things. It was either because I was pissed at her for not letting me see Nicole, or she was pissed at me for having these other girlfriends instead of being with her.

When we fought, I would push her or shake her or slap her with an open hand. Since I never made her bleed, and because I never gave her black eyes or a bloody lip, I didn't think I was really hurting her. I thought I was just teaching her a lesson, and once she learned that lesson, I wouldn't need to hit her anymore. At the time, I thought of it like spanking a child, nothing more.

Actually, back then, based on my definition of abuse, I was not an abusive person. In the movies they always show wives and children getting beat up because the husbands and fathers are drunk or they're mad about work or mad about something else. To me, that was abuse. Since I only hit when I was in an argument, I didn't think that was being abusive. I thought that was just being angry and getting into a fight. That didn't seem wrong to me. When I look back at it, I think that's how Ana saw it , too.

I was becoming increasingly violent. I started to be abusive every time we got into an argument. After a while, Ana would leave my house whenever I got into a rage just to get away from me. Despite all of our fighting, Ana continued to come back because she wanted to be with me.

And despite my abusiveness, I was still trying to be nice to Ana, because I didn't want her to be so unhappy and sad. She did have my child, and I knew she was having a hard time with a lot of things. I cared for her in that sense, but I didn't want to be with her. I didn't know what to do.

Meanwhile, things were pretty shaky between Lisa and me, too. One day Ana came to my townhouse to talk to me about something, and we were sitting together on the couch. Well, Lisa drove up, saw Ana's car parked outside and went totally ballistic. Like Ana, Lisa was pissed because she was carrying my child, but I was still seeing two other girls. She revved her engine and drove her purple Monte Carlo right into the side of the building.

There was a loud crash that scared the shit out of Ana and me. I ran into the bedroom and I could see the imprint of a car sticking into my bedroom. You know the clay masks that are sometimes used in stage acting? The kind in which you can see the outline of the nose and the mouth and the eyes, but you can't see the actual features themselves? That's what my stucco wall looked like. It was like the wall was made out of clay and someone had just pushed the front of the car into it to create that outline. If she had been driving a Rolls Royce or a Jaguar, I would not have been surprised to see the imprint of the hood ornament sticking out of the wall.

I went back to the living room and told Ana to wait inside for me.

When I got outside, Lisa was sitting in her car with her head in her hands crying.

"Are you fucking crazy!" I said. "I can't believe you drove into my house. You are out of your fucking mind."

A bunch of my neighbors had come outside after they heard the crash, so we had quite an audience for the show.

"Why don't you just get the fuck out of here," I yelled to Lisa. I was so pissed off that I could barely stand to look at her. "Just go! Leave! I don't want you here!"

Meanwhile, Ana was standing at the front door telling me to come back inside. Lisa was trying to talk to me and Ana was calling me. I had both of them going at me at the same time, and I didn't know what to do.

Finally, I told Lisa that I was going to call the cops if she didn't get out of there, so she left, and I went back inside with Ana.

I can't remember what ended up happening with the wall. I think I lied to my parents and said that I had accidentally driven my car into the wall.

In later years, when I looked back on the whole situation it made me laugh so hard that I'd start choking. I later told some of the fellas in the Broncos locker room that one time a girl wanted to sleep with me so bad that she drove straight into the bedroom. She did not go to jail. Did not pass go. Did not collect $200. She just drove her car through the wall and into the bedroom.

It was just another funny story in The Vance's life.

After the draft, things just got progressively worse between me and the women in my life. I knew I was on my way to Denver, and I couldn't wait to get there. I was dying to live life fast. I had a fast car, and I wanted a cool home and nice clothes and lots of cash to spend. I was pulling up my roots and replanting them in the Denver nightlife. I was excited and couldn't wait to move on.

But, I'm sure Lisa had an entirely different perspective of the situation. Although we had been broken up for months, she was still seeing me occasionally, and she had just given birth to my son. Now I was moving away, and she was definitely going to have to raise the child by herself.

I didn't really know her parents that well. I was just Lisa's boyfriend, and they never seemed to want to have anything to do with me, but after the draft, all of that changed. I was invited to the house for dinner. I was invited to go do other things with her family. I had a chance to do a lot of things with them, and it felt good to be treated like that. But at the same time it felt weird, because I thought it all revolved around my being drafted into the NFL.

Her parents sat me down one day and told me that they expected me to marry their daughter and raise my child and be a respectable young man.

I sat on their couch very wide-eyed and eager, and basically told them whatever they wanted to hear. "Yes sir. Of course, we're going to get married," I said.

But I knew I was lying. Lisa and I had been broken up for a while, and I knew a child was not the right reason for two people to get married. I was irresponsible for getting Lisa pregnant, but I wasn't going to compound the problem by marrying someone I didn't love.

But I told Lisa that I was going ahead to Denver to find a place to live and get situated and then I'd fly her up and everything would be great.

But when I got to Denver, I never called her again.

Now I wish that I had handled that entire situation better. Lisa has a lot of bitterness toward me and she has really made it impossible for me to have a relationship with my son. When I left Tucson after the draft, I had every intention of helping Lisa and Ana with the children financially. Although I didn't want to marry either of the women, I still loved my children, and I wanted to be a father for them.

But my departure to Denver pissed off the women so much, that it really severed any hope of my developing a close relationship with my kids.

I see my daughter Nicole fairly regularly, but I haven't seen my son Vance, Jr. since his first birthday party in May 1986.

I miss him.

5

Take This Show To Denver

When I moved to Denver in 1985, a couple of months before my first training camp, my father came with me to help me get settled. I had never really gone anywhere by myself before, so it was a relief to have my father with me as I moved to my new home.

Although my relationship with my father had been bad when I was growing up, it got a little better while I was in college. But it wasn't until we drove up to Denver that our relationship really improved dramatically. My dad and I loaded up the car for the trip from Tucson to Denver, and we started driving. During that trip was when I got to know my dad. Although I had been alive for 22 years, I didn't really know or understand my father.

Enroute to Denver, my father told me how proud he was of me, and how sure he was that I would do well in Denver. During that 12-hour trip, I found out that my dad had emotions. I realized that he was a human being and that he struggled with things at times. I realized that he cared about me. I began to understand that he had never meant to hurt my feelings when I was growing up. He was just trying to raise me in the best way he knew how.

I was sitting in the passenger seat — my dad drove all but about three hours of the trip — thinking about my father. I decided that I loved him, and I wanted to try to have a good relationship with him before one of us passed away.

Today, my father and I have a wonderful relationship, and I'm glad that he has always been there to support me no matter what was happening in my life.

•••••

Even after my experiences with the Three Amigas in Tucson, I was still very shy around strangers — especially women. Bettina was still officially my girlfriend, but I didn't know how long that would last. I was hoping to get a new girlfriend in Denver. But I didn't have any social confidence in clubs or bars. I could never bring myself to walk up to a strange woman and buy her a drink or ask her to dance. I was too insecure at the time to handle the potential rejection.

On the other hand, my father was a very outgoing person, and he loved to go out and see the sights whenever he was visiting a new town. So he and I hit different nightclubs every evening.

We would sit down at the bar and he would order me a coke with a cherry in it, because I didn't drink alcohol. He would always point out different women and say, "Now there's a nice girl for you. Why don't you go talk to her." But I was too shy to approach any of them. So my father started taking the initiative by introducing me to people. He was very proud of me for being a second-round draft pick and he would say, "Hey, I want you to meet my son, Vance Johnson. He's the new wide receiver for the Denver Broncos."

People really responded to that, and it blew my mind. Everyone in Denver loves the Broncos, and basically all I had to do was tell people my name, and they would be nice to me. So with my father's help, my confidence around strangers began to grow.

One night, I left my father at home and went out with Larry Willis, another rookie receiver, who was my roommate during that first training camp. We jumped into my Porsche and went to a nightclub. There was a long line to get in, but we didn't wait. We just walked right up to the door, told the bouncer who we were, and he let us in. No wait and no charge. It was quickly becoming part of The Vance's standard operating procedure. As we walked through the club, people kept recognizing me. I could hear them whispering, "there's Vance Johnson, there's Vance Johnson."

My name and face had been all over the media since the day I arrived in Denver. People were already starting to recognize me. Plus I had a really wild haircut that made me stand out even more.

Larry and I were just hanging out in this club talking to different people, when I saw a really beautiful woman standing near the bar. She was a tall brunette wearing really nice clothes, and she had a really pretty face. She looked sexy as hell.

I watched her for a long time, and I wanted to ask her to dance, but I was afraid. Can you imagine that? Me, Vance Johnson of the Denver Broncos, afraid to go ask a girl to dance. At the time, I had never before asked a girl to dance. Throughout high school and college, there was never a single occasion on which I went up to some girl I didn't know and asked her to dance.

So I stood there trying to get my courage up. I was telling myself "I'm Vance Johnson. All these people recognize me, and all these people envy me. This woman would probably be thrilled to dance with me."

Eventually, I convinced myself of my own greatness, and I talked myself into approaching that woman at the bar.

"Hi. How are you doing?" I said. "Would you like to dance?"

There. It was out. The hard part was done. I had gotten myself over the hump. I had asked the question. Now I would walk to the dance floor with the most beautiful woman in the club, and everyone would see me and be impressed.

She gave me an appraising glance and said, "No, thanks."

I couldn't believe it. I spent all that time trying to get enough courage to ask a girl to dance for the first time in my life, and she said, "no." I didn't know what do to then. I felt completely stupid.

When we first walked into that club, I was floating on a cloud. Everyone was recognizing me, and I felt like a king. But when she said "no" to me, it knocked me back down to reality. I was trying hard to project the confident persona of The Vance, but my ego was really fragile and any minor slight would send me spiraling back to my shy college personality.

I stood there for a second looking at this girl who had blown me off, and I was thinking that all the people in the club were going to see me walk back to my seat, and they would know that I had been rejected. I hated the feeling that I had, but I didn't know what to do. I was about to turn and walk away when she said, "But you can stay here and talk to me if you want."

Oh thank you, God. Okay. Cool. So then I figured that she must not know who I am. The first order of business was to tell her.

"What's your name?" I said.

"Angela."

"Hi Angela, my name is Vance Johnson. I'm the new wide receiver for the Denver Broncos. You've probably heard about me.

"No I haven't," she said.

"Haven't you read about me in the newspaper?" I said.

"No."

"Well, I just moved to Denver about a week ago," I said. "I drove my Porsche up from Tucson."

"Really," she said. She didn't seem impressed.

We were standing near a second floor window that overlooked the parking lot. "Yeah, that's my Porsche parked right there in front. The maroon one. I park it in the handicapped spot so no one will chip it when they open their doors."

That was classic Vance material. I was always trying to impress people. Almost from day one, I wanted people to think I was rich. I wanted them to think I was a star. I wanted them to think I was cool.

But, amazingly, after everything I had thrown out, Angela was still unimpressed.

I had told her that I was a Denver Bronco. I showed her my Porsche. I was wearing cool clothes, and my haircut was totally radical. She knew that I was famous, and she knew I had money, yet she didn't seem to care about any of that.

Well, instead of being insulted or having my pride injured, I decided that God was telling me something. I figured that since everyone else in the city was making a big fuss over me, then I should probably be with the person who didn't care about all of that.

I decided right then and there that this was the girl I was destined to marry.

I talked Angela into giving me her phone number, and she wrote it on a napkin. I was so happy. I had found Miss Right and I wasn't interested in talking to any other girls.

When I got home to my apartment, I told my Dad about the woman I had met, and he was excited for me. I decided to play it cool and wait a few days before calling her. A couple of nights later, my Dad and I went out barhopping, and I was wearing the same pants I had on the night I met Angela.

I was sitting at the bar, and I reached into my pocket and found a napkin in there. I thought it was just some trash, so I threw it into a garbage can and forgot about it. After that my father and I left to go to visit some other bars. We had a great time that night, and by the time I got home I was exhausted. I collapsed into bed and slept soundly.

Early the next morning I was laying in bed half-awake, but not quite ready to get up. I started to have a half-dream-half-daydream in which I saw myself taking the napkin out of my pocket and throwing it into the trash.

I jumped out of bed in a panic and went to wake up my father. "Dad, I threw away Angela's phone number," I screamed.

I was totally panicking. I felt like I was dying. I had met this beautiful woman, who didn't care about all of the Broncos stuff. I just knew in my heart that God had sent her to me to be my wife, and I lost her phone number.

"I'll never see her again," I said to my father.

"Yes, you will," he said. "Just go back to the club where you met her and she'll show up again."

"No, she won't," I said. "This isn't a small town like Tucson. This is a big city. I'll never find her again. Besides, I don't think she even goes out very much. I'll never find her again." I was dejected and desperate. I didn't know her last name. I didn't know where she lived or where she worked. I really didn't know anything about her except her name was Angela and her seven-digit phone number was laying in a trash can somewhere.

So my dad decided that we should go back down to the bar to see if we could find her phone number. It was late morning when we jumped into my Porsche and cruised down there. I parked in the back alley and started digging through the trash in the Dumpster. I was picking my way through all kinds of gross shit, but I didn't care. I was determined to find that napkin. When I couldn't find it in the trash bin, my father and I went into the bar. Some of the workers had shown up and I guess they were cleaning up the mess from the previous night.

We started going through the full trash cans inside the bar.

So there I was, Vance Johnson, going through the garbage where drunk people sometimes vomit, where liquor bottles and other trash have been dumped. And wouldn't you know it, I found the napkin. It was dirty and gritty and grimy, but Angela's phone number was still legible, and I thanked God for letting me find it.

At that moment, I was even more certain that I would marry her, because the odds of me finding that napkin again were a million to one. I saw it as another sign from God saying, "she's the one."

I called her that night and asked her out on a date. She said, "Yes." That was the beginning of a relationship that would ultimately result in Angela becoming my first wife.

Years later, I wished that I had left her number in the garbage where it belonged.

On the night of our date, I put on some of my coolest clothes, had my car detailed and drove out to Angela's house to pick her up for our date. (Incidentally, I was on my way to her house for this date when the officer I mentioned earlier pulled me over for doing 90 in a 55. He didn't give me a ticket). By the time I got to her house, I was feeling cocky and invincible, and I knew the date was going to go well.

I rang the doorbell, and waited. There was no answer. I kept ringing, but still no one came to the door. I couldn't believe it. After everything that I had gone through to meet her, to find her number in the trash and to finally arrange a date, Angela stood me up.

I was pissed off at her, but I took it as another sign from God that I was supposed to be with this woman, because she was clearly unaffected by the fact that I was a professional football player.

I didn't get discouraged by being stood up. I took it as a challenge. I went out to a bar by myself that night, and thought about how I was going to win Angela over.

When I talked to her later, she really didn't have any reason for standing me up, she just said she went to a club with some of her girlfriends. At the time it was cool, because there was no obligation between us. Plus, I think neither of us really trusted the other. I had planned to arrive at her house a little bit late, because I thought it was cool to make her sweat a little bit. But then when I got stopped by the cop, it made me even more late. When I didn't show up on time, I think Angela took off to meet some of her friends. She wasn't going to sit at home and wait for me to get my ass to her house.

After a while, we went on a date together, and we started seeing each other pretty regularly. As we began to date more, I learned that Angela sometimes just wouldn't show up. There were plenty of times my rookie year when I was supposed to meet her somewhere, and I would sit for hours waiting for her to show up. When she finally arrived, she would act like nothing happened. She was a very free spirit, and that's just the way she operated. I don't think it was a personal thing with me.

After training camp, I moved into a one-bedroom apartment and Angela would come visit me a lot. Meanwhile, Bettina would still call me from Arizona, and I used to pull the phone into the bathroom to talk to her whenever she called, so that Angela wouldn't hear the conversation.

About a month into the season, Bettina decided to pay me a surprise visit, so she flew to Denver and caught a cab to my house. When she arrived, I was at practice, but Angela answered the door.

The two of them got into a fight over who had a right to be in my house. Finally, Bettina said, "Well, I'm his fiancee, so you'd better get out of my apartment." Angela left, but only to get reinforcements. She came back with her sisters, and they proceeded to gang up on Bettina. They didn't beat Bettina up badly, but they hit on her a bit. She wasn't really hurt, but she was scared and bruised up. After they finished fighting, Bettina stayed at my apartment, and Angela and her sisters left.

When I got home from practice I walked in and I was surprised to see the condition of my apartment. The place was destroyed. There was shit all over the place. Lamps were knocked over. Shoes, and other clothes, and dishes were laying everywhere. The sofa was out of place, as were a couple of chairs and the dining room table.

I was even more surprised to see Bettina.

"Hey, how are you doing? It's great to see you," I said. "How did you get in here?"

"Angela let me in," she said. Then she told me everything that had happened, and started questioning me about my relationship with Angela. She couldn't understand why I had another girl in my apartment.

I really liked Bettina a lot. I thought she was a very sweet girl, but I liked Angela too, and I wasn't sure what I should do. We started arguing, and it got more and more heated with every passing minute. I was yelling at her, and she was yelling at me.

At the height of the argument, she charged at me like she was going to knock the shit out of me or scratch me or something, and I stuck my foot out to stop her. She ran right into my foot, and the blow caught her in the stomach and knocked the wind out of her. She went down to the ground and was gagging like she was going to throw up.

I was so pissed off that I didn't care if she was going to be sick or not. At the time, I thought she was wrong for visiting without telling me she was coming and for trying to tell me how to live my life. I felt that if she got hurt because of our fight, then it was her own damned fault.

But, as I watched her on the floor, I began to feel bad for hurting her. It was one of the few times during my abusive years that I really felt remorse for hurting someone. I kneeled down and hugged her and told her that I was sorry.

During the next couple of days, Angela kept calling and coming over, and Bettina and I got into more arguments. Eventually, Bettina got sick of all of it, and decided to leave. She went outside, and I watched her from a window as she waited on the sidewalk for a taxi to take her to the airport. I never saw her in Denver again.

A couple of weeks later, I called Bettina just to see how she was doing. Her brother answered the phone and told me that she had been in a car accident. I couldn't believe it. I was so worried about her that I jumped on a plane to go visit her. I sat in the hospital for a day and a half, after hearing reports that she had suffered a slipped disk in her back. Fortunately, the injury wasn't too bad, and Bettina was able to leave the hospital without having surgery. But in later years, as her back continued to bother her, I think they did operate to repair the disk.

During my visit to the hospital, her family was there. It was hard for me to deal with them, because I was pretty sure they hated me. So once I learned that Bettina would probably be okay, I left. By then, I'm pretty sure Bettina had decided that she never wanted to come back to me, and that was fine with me, because I didn't want her back. I was so convinced that God wanted me to be with Angela, that I didn't really care about Bettina anymore.

From then on, I dated Angela fairly exclusively. Every once in a while I would meet another girl and I would go to dinner with her or sleep with her, but it wasn't a regular thing. For a short time, I thought Angela was dating me exclusively, but I quickly realized that she was seeing other people too. Angela was a wild and free girl who pretty much did whatever she wanted to do. And she was a real partier who would go out nearly every night to different clubs.

Sometimes I would go to clubs with her, and it always bothered me that Angela seemed to know so many people in the "night scene." We would walk into a club and everyone would be talking to her. Guys would be walking up saying "hi," and hugging her and whispering things to her. She would just laugh and joke with everyone and have a good time. But I was miserable. I felt stupid. I felt like a stooge who was being taken for a ride.

In the short time that I had been in Denver, I had been in a lot of situations in which I really felt superior to other people. But every time I went to a club with Angela, it brought me back down to earth. It made me feel like a shy college student again who didn't go out and didn't know anyone. Instead of being the hotshot Denver Bronco, I felt like Angela was the famous one and I was just riding on her coattails. I didn't like that.

Even though I was going out every now and then and meeting new women, I didn't want Angela to be doing the same thing with guys. I wanted her to be loyal to me.

She went out a lot by herself or with her girlfriends, and she would often stay out really late. I would sometimes go to her mother's house at 2 a.m. or 3 a.m. and sit in my car and wait for her to come home. She wouldn't get in until the wee hours, and as soon as I saw her, I would drive off. I would hang around just long enough for her to see me and know that I had been waiting for her.

When I questioned her about where she had been, she always had an answer ready for me. She was always either out at all-night clubs or had stayed at the home of one of her girlfriends.

I was really attached to Angela. I didn't want to let her go, even though that's probably what I should have done.

We got into some huge arguments about her dating other guys. I was really pissed about it. I wanted her to date me exclusively. Finally, I blew up and said, "Fine, if you want to date a lot of people, we'll see who can date the most people. You just wait to see how many girls I'm going to date. We'll see who gets the most ass."

I really attacked dating with a vengeance after that. I was determined to date every woman under the sun. I was going to make Angela sorry that she wouldn't commit to me when she had the chance.

Being so famous and so popular in Denver made it easier for me to meet girls. But I still wasn't meeting or dating nearly the number that I would be in later years. At this point, I was still too shy to take full advantage of my celebrity. I really wasn't making good on my threat to Angela.

• • • • •

But, if fame changed my social confidence two or three points on a scale of 10, then the acquisition of wide receiver Mark Jackson during the 1986 NFL draft shot me right off the chart. Mark, who went to school at Purdue, was the Broncos' sixth-round pick.

I never really had any close friends when I was growing up, because I was very shy, very insecure, and I just didn't trust people. I was afraid that my peers wouldn't like me, so I kept my heart closed and tried to win people over with my athletic and artistic ability.

But when Mark got here, something clicked. I don't know what it was, but we started talking and we became friends immediately. At the time, I was the youngest receiver on the team, so with Mark's arrival, I had a buddy who was my age. We were roommates during training camp, and we quickly became inseparable. We went everywhere together. We walked together when we went to practice, weightlifting and meetings. We went to bars and nightclubs together. We became really close friends because we could talk to each other and we understood each other. I loved him like a brother.

Mark had grown up in a ghetto in Chicago, and he lived with his older sister after his parents were divorced. He went to college at Purdue and was a water boy or equipment manager his freshman year. Then he made the team as a walk-on and later earned a scholarship. He used to always tell me how much he envied me, because I had so much athletic ability and I would probably play football forever, while he had to work for everything he got.

I thought Mark was a very good receiver who ran great, crisp routes. We would often stay up late at night talking in our dorm rooms. During one talk, I basically led him through the systems of the NFL and told him what to expect during his rookie year.

"If you really want to make it, you should pay close attention to what the veterans do," I told him. "In fact, I think you should pick out one veteran player whom you think is really good, and just copy everything that he does. Only do it better than him."

And that's exactly what he did.

Going out with Mark really elevated my social confidence. Even though Mark was shy in his own way, he was a very personable guy, and he never seemed to have trouble talking to strangers. He could talk to guys or girls or old people or young people and always keep a conversation going. By hanging out with him and imitating him in some ways, I began to overcome some of my shyness, and I became more confident about my ability to talk to people.

Plus, when the two of us were together, everything came easier. We would walk into a club or a bar, and with both of us being there, we received double the recognition. People would go crazy over us. Mark wasn't as much of a publicity monger as I was. While I was always seeking out the cameras and the attention, he would generally just sit back and watch and stay in my shadow, but when the spotlight hit us, he was always ready to joke around and have a good time. We complemented each other really well.

And Mark had a lot of confidence with girls.

He made the whole game of pursuing women fun. We would walk into clubs and pick up women in less than five minutes. Mark would go up to a pretty girl and say, "Do you know who this is?" he would say pointing at me. "This is Vance Johnson. 'The' Vance Johnson. He's the stud receiver for the Denver Broncos." With that, we'd usually have the girl hooked. The next night, I would perform the introductions, with the same result. We would meet women this way all the time.

Just to make sure that we would always have some female company at night, Mark and I would call up a bunch of girls and tell them to meet us at different clubs. We'd have two girls who were waiting for us at one club at 9 p.m., and two others would be meeting us at another club at 11 p.m. and still two others would wait at a third club at 1 a.m. We would cruise from club to club meeting these women and just having a great time.

Mark and I would also have contests to see who could get the most phone numbers in one night. We'd make a $1,000 bet and run through two or three clubs collecting numbers like crazy. I think I hold the record with 22 or 23 phone numbers in one evening. That night Mark finished with about 18.

I know most guys go to a club and feel lucky if they walk away with one woman's phone number, and even then they spend the entire evening dancing with the woman, buying her drinks and talking to her.

So now you're wondering, how in the hell does a guy get 22 girls to give him their phone numbers? And how in the hell does a guy have time in one night to court that many women?

You have to spend a certain amount of time talking to a woman and buying her drinks before she'll give you her number, right? Wrong. Not when you're a high-profile professional football player. When you're in the NFL you can walk into a club, turn on your magnet, and literally draw women to you just by showing your face.

Here's the technique Mark and I used. First I would pull up to the front of the club in a convertible Porsche or Corvette and pay the valet parking attendant $100 to let me park my car right by the front door. Then Mark and I and would stand outside the car — which had VANCE82 on the license plate — and call people on my car phone. This allowed everyone who was standing in line to get a good look at us and to know that we had arrived. We'd usually get a couple of phone numbers each from women who were waiting to go into the club.

Then we'd go inside — without waiting in line or paying, of course — and give the D.J. $100 to stop the music and announce that we were in the club. So the music would stop, a spotlight would shine down on us and the D.J. would boom, "Ladies and Gentlemen, introducing, for your partying enjoyment, two of the baddest and wildest Denver Bronco players in the history of the team…Vance Johnson and Mark Jackson!!!"

Everyone would start cheering for us, and we would just stand there and wave at the crowd. After that, getting phone numbers was as easy as A-B-C. Women would basically line up to talk to us. Five or six women would just walk up and hand me their numbers, saying, "call me," or I would walk over to a pretty girl and say, "I've been watching you for quite some time now, and I think you are so beautiful. I have to go over there with my friend Mark, but I was wondering if I could get your phone number?" She'd say "yes," and in less than a minute I had met a new woman and added a new phone number to my collection.

After we had exhausted the supply of pretty women at one club, we'd jump in the convertible and go to a new club and start all over again. Using this technique, it really wasn't hard for us to end up with 18 or 19 numbers each on any one night.

The only real problem was that after we got all of these numbers, Mark and I could never put a face with a number. We could never remember what the girls looked like. So we'd be calling girls saying, "hey I can't wait to see you again, meet me at XYZ club at about 9 p.m. Oh and by the way, why don't you describe yourself for me again, so I'll be sure not to miss you."

Mark and I went out all the time together, and we'd always meet girls and go with them to their apartments and town homes to have sex. Whenever we picked up two girls and took them home, I was always really shy. I always wanted to take my girl into the privacy of a bedroom. But Mark wasn't shy at all. He'd just undress the girl right there in front of everyone and start having sex with her. I'd try to cover my embarrassment by laughing and calling him crazy.

Despite my shyness about having sex with an audience, my confidence with women was growing rapidly. After a while, I became so confident that I met girls at red lights and gas stations and convenience stores. I met them at the airport and on airplanes. I even got phone numbers from teachers at the schools I visited. And I would always follow up with the women I met. And I would always get together with them later and sleep with them.

I started to take advantage of every situation that presented itself. If I was scheduled for a two-hour autograph session at a mall, there would be thousands of people lined up to get my autograph. At first it blew my mind that all those people were there to see me. It made me feel wonderful to know that all those people admired me. But after a while, I got over being impressed, and I got back to business. I would take someone with me to sit next to me with a notebook and a pen. I would point out the pretty girls and dispatch him to go get their phone numbers. By the time the event ended, I would have dozens of numbers. But, as was the case when Mark and I had our phone-number collecting contests in the clubs, I could never put a face with a number.

I started getting mail from women all over the country who wanted to meet me and sleep with me. They'd enclose pictures of their beautiful faces, or their tits, or their asses or their pussies or their entire naked bodies. A few women even sent me videotapes of them doing strip teases and then lying down on a bed and saying, "Vance, I'm waiting for you. Call me." One woman sent me a videotape of her masturbating. When I was on radio talk shows women would call in and say that they wanted to meet me. Even married women with big fat rings on their fingers would proposition me.

I didn't really know the proper way to handle all of this. So I just went with my gut. I was like the people you see in the movies who get a lot of money, pour it onto the bed and roll around with it. I went on a rampage. I was calling women left and right and sleeping with them. I had absolutely no control, but I was loving life.

Sleeping with a lot of women may have started out as something I wanted to do to spite Angela, but it quickly became something that I did just because women were available to me, because it was a lot of fun, and because it was very gratifying to my ego.

Ironically, during all of this partying that I was doing, I think Angela was becoming a better person. She really didn't go out much or do many of the things she used to do. Of course, it could be that I didn't know what she was doing because I was never around. But, to this day, I truly believe that she was changing and trying to lead a better life.

Meanwhile, I was out raising hell.

Angela was always home on the occasions when Mark dropped me off at my house after a wild night. I was usually drunk, and Angela would be pissed off at me. She'd chase me with a frying pan or a gold club or a broom and try to hit me. She was angry because she knew I was out sleeping with other girls, but I didn't care if she was mad. I was going to do what I was going to do.

$$\bullet \ \bullet \ \bullet \ \bullet \ \bullet$$

As a Broncos' player, I was getting more attention and more notoriety everyday. I had become very famous in Denver, partly because I was always doing crazy things to get more publicity. After the Broncos beat Cleveland to get into the 1987 Super Bowl,

I decided to celebrate. I went to Westminster Mall and got my ears pierced — yes, both of them. I figured "why not? I want to be different, and having both ears pierced will definitely make me stand out," so I did it.

The best part was that while they were doing my ears, hundreds of people had gathered outside the window to watch. See, even before the needle had gone through my dangling lobes, my pierced ears were getting me a lot of attention. I loved it.

But the attention I received then paled by comparison to the reception I received at the Super Bowl in Pasadena, Calif.

When the team got off the plane, there were media everywhere. They were screaming Vance this and Vance that. They kept asking questions about every little thing. It was unbelievable. I never realized how huge an event the Super Bowl was, but suddenly I knew. And I was living it up, because I knew that it could make me famous all over the world.

We walked into the interview session on the first day of Super Bowl week, and I couldn't believe it. The place was packed from wall to wall with media. There were thousands of them. Each player had his own table for the interviews, and the reporters would basically just come up and crowd around your table and shove their microphones out and record every word you said. Later, they would broadcast your face and voice to people all over the world.

I was in heaven. I loved that kind of attention, and I knew that having a good game in the Super Bowl could make me a national hero. It could make me more famous, and that's exactly what I wanted. I wanted to become a household name like The Fridge (William Perry) or Jim McMahon. I wanted to do national commercials. I figured all of this would come true after the Super Bowl. I had been having fun since day one in the NFL, and having that kind of attention at the Super Bowl was the most fun of all.

Mark and I were playing really well on the field at the time, and we were both really flamboyant, and I think the media knew they could count on us to say some crazy things during interviews.

During the week before the big game, Mark and I had dinner with people from *Sports Illustrated*, we did an interview on the *Today* Show, and I was also on *Nightline* with Ted Koppel.

It was cool to be on the Koppel show, because I was sitting opposite Dexter Manley during the interview. I was on national television with a great media star, and a great football player. I really felt like I had made it to the top. And this is just a little thing, but every time Ted Koppel said my name I felt a little better. It was weird to be sitting with someone like him and to have him call me by name and ask me questions. It was totally flattering.

Although John Elway was easily the most popular player on the team, he wasn't even close to being the most flamboyant. He didn't have crazy haircuts, crazy cars and crazy attitudes. He didn't say wild things in the paper. He didn't do a whole lot to try to get attention drawn to himself.

He wasn't the type of interview that the networks were looking for. They wanted someone who wasn't afraid to go out on a limb. They wanted someone who could be counted on to say anything at any time. They wanted someone unpredictable and dangerous.

They wanted The Vance.

And I didn't let them down. During interviews I was always tried to be wild, crazy, sarcastic or intelligent. I was always changing my approach.

Probably the most fun show I did during Super Bowl week was the *Late Show* starring Joan Rivers. During that show, Joan asked me about my sex life, and I didn't hold anything back. On national television I said that my sex life was great. I talked about how I loved to have sex the night before a game because it helped me play better. At the time, I thought it was really cool to be talking about sex like that. I thought everyone would be impressed by my sexual conquests, and a lot of women who were watching were going to want to have sex with me. In fact, I was sort of hoping that a beautiful, rich woman would see me and want to be with me.

I wanted her to be rich so she wouldn't want to sue me later.

During that interview with Joan Rivers, I also said, "I want to be famous as hell. I want to be famous so bad it hurts. And I'll do anything legally possible to be famous."

Although I would later change my tune about that, I meant it at the time. This was all a big adventure to me. More fame seemed better than less fame, so that's what I was shooting for.

I wanted to do commercials, and make a lot of money. I wanted people to go crazy when they saw me in person, they way people used to get when they saw the Beatles, or the way people still get when they see Michael Jackson.

Joan and I laughed a lot during that show, and toward the end she told me that she really enjoyed meeting me and she would never forget me. It really made me feel good to hear something like that coming from Joan Rivers. I thought I was on my way to becoming a big shot.

6

The First Marriage

Angela and I were living together by this time, and our relationship was pretty rocky because both of us were pretty much doing our own things. But despite all of our problems, I was not reacting to her in a violent way. I had never been physically abusive to Angela.

Often when we got into verbal fights, Angela would leave and go to her mother's house, which was only a few miles away.

One day I came home and found that Angela was gone, and she had taken a lot of her belongings with her. Since she would often leave for one reason or another, I didn't think about it much at first. I figured she would come back when she was ready. It took me a few hours to realize that this time, in addition to her property, she had taken every dime out of my bank account. Since Angela and I had been living together for so long, and we were eventually planning to get married, I had made her a co-signer on my bank account. At that point in my life, money didn't mean much to me. It was just something to be earned and spent. I was making a lot of it, and I was spending a lot of it. Angela was spending some of my money, too, but I didn't really care.

But when Angela disappeared, she had all of my money with her — about $50,000 — and I was pissed. How the hell was I going to live the high life without any cash? That bitch stole my money, and I wanted the shit back.

I called her mother's house, but Angela wasn't there. I called a bunch of her friends, but no one had seen her. I could not imagine where she might have gone, so I didn't know where to start looking. I was in a rage, and the person I wanted to take it out on was not available.

That night, Angela called me from a friend's house in Houston or Dallas to tell me that she was pregnant. She had gone to Texas to have an abortion.

The minute she said she was pregnant, I forgot about the money. All I could think about was my child. I pleaded with her not to do it. I begged her not to kill our child. She was crying on the phone and saying that she had to do it. We went back and forth on this for hours. Finally she agreed to keep the baby on one condition: I had to marry her.

I agreed and made reservations on the next flight down to Texas.

Then I left my apartment to do something that I had never done before in my life — drink some alcohol. I was so upset about everything, that I thought that alcohol might help me. In the movies people always drank to "settle their nerves" and mine were going haywire.

I had never even had a sip of alcohol before then. When I was growing up, my dad drank all the time, and his friends all drank all the time. Occasionally my dad would take me to a bar with him to kick all of his friend's asses on the pool table, so that he could brag about how talented I was.

These men would always talk to me, and their voices would be slurred and they'd spit liquor in my face as they talked. I hated it.

And for some reason, all of the people who drank had really big guts, and I definitely wasn't into that. So I decided early in my life that I was never going to drink alcohol.

But after I got off the phone with Angela that day, I was in shock.

My girlfriend was pregnant, and she was thinking about having an abortion, which terrified me; I was about to get married to save the child; my girlfriend had taken all of my money out of my bank account.

A bottle of booze seemed like the right thing to do at the time.

I went to a liquor store near my house and asked the clerk for something good to drink that was kind of mild.

He said, "Well, we have this new stuff called Hot Shot, and people have been saying that it tastes like a cinnamon schnapps."

I didn't know what a schnapps was, but I thought the cinnamon part sounded good so I said, "Okay, let me have a bottle of that."

My first tentative sip of alcohol tasted pretty good. This stuff really did taste like cinnamon, and I couldn't even taste the alcohol in it. I drank about 16 ounces in a very short time, and it didn't bother me at all. So I popped open another one. And then another one.

I felt it later.

I drank because I didn't want Angela to kill my son. I drank because I was depressed. I was unhappy. I thought my life was horrible, and I was a horrible person. I already had two children, and I thought everyone would think I was a bad person if I had another one.

The thing that was weird about drinking alcohol for me was that it made me feel better and worse at the same time. When the liquor got inside of me it made me feel numb to the pain in my heart. But before then, I had never had a drink, and I was always proud of myself for not drinking. I compared myself to guys like Steve Sewell on the team who didn't drink alcohol. After I took that first drink, I felt bad for losing my alcohol virginity. Guilt about that just added to my pain, so I kept drinking to numb it.

On the plane I was drunk as hell, but I praying to God in heaven that I would be able to keep Angela from getting an abortion.

She picked me up at the airport, and I was so happy when she told me that she was still pregnant. We decided to go to Las Vegas at once to get married, but before we left I said, "I want you to go get all my fucking money out of the bank."

I waited in the rental car while Angela went into the bank to get the money. She came out and said, "they're going to have to give me a cashier's check because it's so much money.

"Hell no," I said. "I want my shit in cash."

So she went back inside and a few minutes later, came out carrying three or four of those little bags that they load onto armored trucks. We put the money into a suitcase and left for Vegas.

When we got there, I started gambling. I was sitting at the craps table playing the field bet. If you know anything about craps then you know that you should never play the field because you have to hit 11s or 2s or 12s or something like that to win money, and the dice always come up 6, 7 or 8. But I was playing the field bet because it seemed like the thing to do at the time.

Since that first bottle of Hot Shot, I had not stopped drinking. I didn't know where Angela was, but I figured she was up in the room getting drunk, too. I was losing money faster than I could keep track, and by the time the evening was over, I had lost the entire $50,000 on the craps and black jack tables.

When I woke up the next morning, I was funky. I stank like hell, and I was still wearing the T-shirt and jeans from the day before. Angela had on a pair of shorts and a shirt, and we went down to the lobby for the limo ride to the church where we were getting married. I think the limo ride plus the ceremony cost $20, but all I had left after the previous night's gambling was $12. I had to borrow $8 from some random guy in Vegas in order to get married to Angela.

We were in line with a bunch of other couples for the ceremony. A lady opened a curtain, pushed a button to start the wedding music. Then that same lady moved into position to serve as the witness who would sign our marriage licenses. It was all very low class.We didn't even have rings to exchange, but that little chapel was prepared for everything. They had a wide selection of bubblegum machine rings, so we picked out two of those.

We walked out of that parlor as Mr. and Mrs. Vance and Angela Johnson. We had no money in our pockets, no ride to the airport and no hope of pawning the plastic rings on our fingers. But we were married, and we were going to have a child and that was all that mattered.

We walked to a nearby hotel and rode their shuttle van to the airport.

Although I would later regret marrying Angela, I will never regret the decisions that I made at that time, because my little boy, Vaughn Edward Johnson, became the apple of my eye. I love him dearly, and I think I will always feel especially close to him, because I saved his life.

• • • • •

After Angela and I returned from Vegas, I called my mother and told her that I was married, but during the first few months very few people knew that we were married. It wasn't a big secret or anything, we just didn't broadcast it all over radio and television. A couple of weeks after the wedding, I was in the showers at the Broncos' facility when one of my teammates looked over at me and said, "How's our girlfriend?"

I didn't know what he was talking about. "Our girlfriend. What do you mean?"

"Aren't you going out with a girl named Angela?" he said.

"Yeah. Why?"

"Because she's a big freak, man. She's a super-freak."

"What do you mean by that?" I said. I couldn't believe my ears. A freak was what players called all of the groupies. All of the women who made themselves available to NFL players and other celebrities. During my first year, I had my share of experiences with freaks, and I had heard plenty of conversations about them in the locker room. But now this man was talking about my wife and it was a different story.

But he didn't know Angela was my wife, and I didn't tell him. I wanted to hear what he was going to say.

"Man, she's one of the biggest freaks in town."

When I said I didn't believe him, he told me to ask another player about her.

When I got out of the shower, I approached the other player and asked him if he had ever slept with Angela.

"Angie?" he said. "Yeah, I used to call her at 3 or 4 in the morning, whenever I wanted to get laid. She would come over and the whole time she was taking off her clothes, she'd be saying, 'I don't know if I should be doing this'."

This can't be true, I thought. This is my wife! I know that we were both unfaithful to each other when we were dating. But I didn't think she was sleeping with any of my teammates. I didn't think I would ever hear her name come up in conversation in the locker room.

I was devastated.

I went back to the first player and asked him to prove to me that he had slept with Angela. He told me her favorite position, and he was right. He described marks on her body and other details about her that he could never have known unless he had been with her. Everything he said was true. He told me the type of language Angela used and the words that she would say when she was having sex, and he was right.

I was sitting there listening to this man, and I was boiling. I felt so embarrassed and stupid. One of my teammates was telling me all these things about my wife that only I should know.

When Angela and I had first started dating, I had asked her if she had ever dated any of the other players. She said, "no." That was something that was very important to me, because I never wanted to hear the name in the locker room.

I still didn't believe that Angela fell into the category of a freak, but I believed that she had slept with two of my teammates.

I went home that day, and I was really quiet. I didn't want to talk to Angela about anything. She could tell something was bothering me. She wanted to know what was wrong, but I kept my tongue. I was fuming inside, but I didn't know how to handle the situation, so I didn't say anything.

I had grilled the two players for information. I knew approximate dates. I knew a lot more than I wanted to know. I believed that Angela was with my teammates on some of those long nights when I was sitting outside of her mother's house waiting for her to come home.

I kept this bottled up inside of me for three or four days before I finally decided to confront her about it.

She denied all of it. She said she had never even met the two players before. But I knew she was lying. There was no way those guys could know all of those things unless they had slept with her.

We argued about it for a long time, and finally I blew up. I grabbed her and shook her violently while I yelled at her that I knew she was lying and that I knew she had fucked my teammates. I shoved her against the wall and against a closet door, and I kept screaming at her.

Then she confessed and said that she had been to bed with them. Even though I wanted her to tell me the truth, hearing it from her lips just made me even more angry. I was so mad that I thought I had a right to hurt her. I started slapping her, but slapping her just wasn't enough. So I pushed her and she fell into the closet. But that wasn't enough. I just kept screaming, "Why? Why? Why?"

So I pushed her again, and she fell over the bed and onto the floor. Then appeared to pass out. She was lying on the floor with her eyes closed and I panicked. I said, "Oh my God! I killed her."

I checked her pulse and tried to see if she was breathing, and I could tell that she was alive. So then I tried to revive her. I carried her into the bathroom and laid her on the floor. I turned on the faucets in the sink, cupped my hands under the stream and dumped water onto her face. But it wasn't working. She wasn't coming around, and I thought it was because I couldn't get enough water out of the sink to revive her. Every time I carried my hands away from the stream, the water slipped through the cracks of my fingers, so that only a few drops hit her face.

So I reached over and stuck my hands into the toilet and splashed a big wave of water onto her face. I just kept pushing my hands into the toilet and dashing water onto her face until she was revived.

I didn't think about how gross that was, I just did it. I wanted to revive her and that seemed like the only way to do it.

When she finally came to, she looked from me to the toilet to the water that was on her and said, "You are fucking crazy."

That off-season we moved into an apartment in Tucson just to get away from everything. It felt good to be away from people in Denver and the whole situation with the other players. We flew to California to visit friends and just spent a lot of time together trying to repair our marriage.

But it wasn't working. I was really hurt by her sleeping with my teammates, and that pain turned into mental and physical abuse against her. Every time I looked at her I wanted to hurt her. I wanted to take the emotional pain that I was feeling and turn it into physical pain for Angela. I wanted to push her, to punch her, to shake her. And I did a lot of those things. I was very angry, and I was extremely abusive to Angela.

By the time we got back to Denver, our relationship was pretty much ruined. I told her not to count on me ever being home, because I was going to go out every night to pick up women. I was going to get a lot of "ass," and there was nothing that she could do about it.

"If I have to live with this shit, then you have to live with it, too," I said. "You just wait to see how many people I'm going to be dating. I'm going to have more women than you can imagine. I have to go to work every day and see these guys that you slept with, so everywhere you go there's going to be a woman there whom I have slept with."

The day we got back to Denver, I started going out. I was a lot more successful at meeting women, because I used alcohol to blot out my shyness. I would always be really nervous when I went into a club, but I would just go to the bar and get a couple of drinks really fast, and that would settle me down. I'd be a lot more relaxed and confident, which made talking to girls a lot easier.

I began to develop a lot of techniques for meeting women. When I went into a nightclub, people always recognized me, and if they didn't I would fall back on the DJ introduction routine to make sure everyone knew who I was. I'd go into the club, get a couple of drinks and down them really fast. Then I'd get a rum and coke to carry with me and stand somewhere with my drink surveying the crowd. Women would always be looking at me. Some would smile at me, some wouldn't. Some would be on the dance floor dancing suggestively and looking at me. Some would make sexual gestures at me. Then one or two or three of them would just walk up to me and whisper "I want to fuck you." Or they'd grab my ass or something like that. That was the type of woman I would pick out, if I wanted to take someone home and have sex that night.

I rarely ever worked hard at meeting the type of woman who was willing to sleep with me immediately. That type of woman usually took the initiative in making her intentions known. At certain times, just having sex with someone was very attractive to me. Usually when I was feeling pain about things that had happened in my life, I would want to go out and screw someone. I might start thinking about everything that happened with Angela, or some other women may be suing me again. Sometimes, I'd just want to say, "fuck it." Since I'm getting used, I'm just going to use everybody, too.

Other times, I would go into a club looking for romance. But a lot of times, I'd be after both things at once. I wanted to have sex with someone almost every night, but I also wanted to find women to date romantically.

After I entered the nightclub and had met an "easy" woman, I would usually leave her and start looking for a "Star." Star was the term I used for pretty women who had nice bodies and nice personalities. I'd try to meet them, talk to them and get their phone numbers. After I got a numbers, I would go find the "easy" girl who wanted to have sex with me, and we'd make plans to go somewhere together.

My "Stars" were the women I worked the hardest to meet. My typical star would definitely be white. I have always been attracted to white women, and I don't know exactly why. She would have blonde hair with really pretty eyes. She'd be kind of shy, and she definitely wouldn't dance with any black guys. Actually, that was the number one rule. After Angela, I never wanted to have any woman who was messing with other black guys. I wanted to be the only brother she saw.

One night in a club in Aurora, I spotted a tall, pretty girl with long blonde hair. She had a nice body, and she was standing with a couple of her girlfriends. She looked shy to me, and that was really attractive. Even though I was being a slut and sleeping with a bunch of girls, I never wanted a girl who was messing with a lot of guys. I know that sounds crazy and hypocritical, but that's the way I used to think. I thought it was okay for a guy to have a lot of lovers, but it was wrong for a woman to do the same thing.

I approached this girl and introduced myself. She said her name was Michelle, but other than that she really wasn't all that receptive to me. So I walked away. I didn't feel rejected by her, I felt challenged. At that time in my life, I believed I could make any woman like me if I worked hard enough at it. So when I was faced with this type of challenge, I would go sit in a corner and develop a plan of attack. It was fun for me.

That night I went to the DJ's booth and gave him $20 to dedicate a song from me to Michelle. He put on a really sexy song, and shined a spotlight on the girl.

"Vance Johnson would like to dedicate this song to you, Michelle, because you are so beautiful." She was standing there with everyone's attention focused on her, and I could tell that she was both embarrassed and excited. She just lit up. I walked over to ask her to dance and she said, "yes." I got her phone number, called her later, and we went on a few dates.

After that, I used that same technique pretty often.

Another time, I saw a girl I wanted to meet, but when I approached her, she didn't seem interested. She flat wouldn't talk to me. I walked away trying to formulate a plan. If you've been into nightclubs, you know that there are always three or four people walking around carrying baskets full of individual roses. These rose vendors sell a lot of flowers simply by putting pressure on guys.

A typical rose seller will walk up to a guy who is talking to a woman and say, "Sir, would you like to buy a rose for the beautiful lady?"

A lot of times the guy is really reluctant to say "no," because he doesn't want to hurt the girl's feelings by suggesting that she's not worth a $3 rose. So, he buys a flower.

These vendors never had trouble selling to me. I was always buying flowers.

On this particular night, after I'd been rebuffed by that girl, I sought out every rose vendor in the club. Once I got them together, I bought every single rose that they had — including the baskets — and asked them to deliver them to the girl I liked.

They walked over and handed her all of these flowers. She had 300 or 400 roses. And everyone around her was looking at her. She was the center of attention. There was a basket in each of her hands, and two at her feet. Women love flowers, and I'm sure we've all seen the reaction a woman has when you buy her one flower or a dozen flowers. So you can imagine how she might react to several hundreds roses. This girl was smiling so big I thought her face was going to crack. I could tell that she felt totally flattered and really special.

She came over to talk to me, and I said, "I just think you are really beautiful, and I wanted to get you a rose. But the more I looked at you, the more I realized that one rose wasn't enough. And one basket of roses wasn't enough. So I just got every rose in this entire club, because that's the only way I could represent how beautiful I think you are."

Although it sounds like a total ploy to get her into bed, that's not why I did it. I really did think she was beautiful, and I really did want to make her feel good. Like most people, I get more pleasure out of doing something nice for someone than I do from doing something mean. It made my heart feel good to see this woman's reaction to all of those flowers. I'm sure that she'll remember that night for the rest of her life.

The flower routine became another strategy that I would often use when I wanted to win a girl over.

• • • • •

There was a woman who used to park outside the Broncos' facility every day and watch the players leave. She would often wave at me, or call my name, but I didn't pay much attention. Then she started leaving notes on my car. She even started leaving roses for me on the hood of my car. One day as I was walking out, I saw her sitting in her usual spot, so I waved to her, got into my car and went home.

When I got into the house, I saw Angela looking out the window.

"What are you doing?" I said. She said there was someone out front.

I looked out and saw that the girl from the facility had followed me home. So I went outside and talked to the woman for a few minutes. It's embarrassing to admit now, but I got her phone number while my wife watched from inside the house.

A couple of weeks later, Mark, Ricky and I were out partying at a club called Neo in Aurora. It was real late. I was drunk, and I needed to get home. But instead of trying to get home, I was racking my brain trying to think of any girls I knew in the area who would be receptive to a little late-night rendezvous. Then I remembered that I had a phone number in my glove compartment for the girl who had followed me home from the facility.

I called her and she gave me directions to her house. When I arrived, she led me into her bedroom, took off my clothes and climbed on top of me. We had sex for only a couple of minutes before I finished. I got up, dressed and left. I really hated myself that night, because I was so drunk that I didn't really know what I was doing. It was rare for me to get drunk to the point that I didn't really remember what had happened. But that's the condition I was in that night.

I never called her again.

Two years later, I was working out in the Broncos' weight room when Ricky and Mark came in and said there was a woman sitting outside in a truck. She had a little boy who looked just like me. I thought they were joking, but a couple of weeks later I got a letter from this girl saying that she wanted to talk to me about our child.

After that, I saw her a few times sitting outside of the facility, but I never went over to talk to her. One day as I was leaving, she followed me, so after about a mile, I pulled over and walked back to her car. I looked in the back seat and saw the little boy. As soon as I saw him, I knew he was my child. But I still didn't understand why this woman was coming to me now after all this time had passed.

"Why are you doing this?" I said.

"Because I'm getting a divorce, and I need money to take care of my child," she said. "I met with an attorney, and he said I could get $2,500 a month from you."

"It doesn't cost $2,500 a month to take care of a child," I said.

"I know, but that's what the attorney said I could get," she said. "Maybe we can come up with an agreement or something so you won't have to pay that much."

I just looked at her and I knew she was just like all the rest. "I guess you hit the jackpot, didn't you?" I said, and sadly walked back to my car and drove home.

The woman was married and living on welfare, but her husband was leaving her because he found out that she was cheating on him. Apparently her husband, who was Hispanic, initially thought my child was his. But the kid's skin was too dark and as time passed, it became clear to the husband that he was not the father.

Then the investigation started.

After I was served with court papers, I coughed up $500 to get DNA testing done. Despite the fact that my son looked just like me, it seemed crazy to me to think that I could have fathered a child when I spent only a few minutes with the mother. I wanted to make sure that the boy was mine.

The results showed that there was a 99.9 percent probability that he was my son. I said, "Okay. He's my son, and I'm going to take care of him."

I love all of my children, and I am more than willing to pay for their support. But this woman wanted $2,500 a month, and that seemed ridiculous to me.

We eventually went to court to have this matter settled. My attorney started to give me a hard time when the woman showed up. She was wearing a tight, black miniskirt, with a shiny, black top that was v-cut damn near to her navel. She had really big tits and they were hanging out. At one point, just before the hearing started, she looked over at me, squeezed her arms together so that her tits nearly popped out of her shirt and said, "Vance, please don't be mad at me."

Remember earlier in 1994 when Michael Jackson had to go to court in Denver to defend himself against a woman who claimed he stole her song Dangerous? Remember when the judge told her to go home and change into "something more appropriate for court" after he took one look at her tight, black, leather outfit? That's the type of outfit this woman was wearing.

Sitting in that court room, I was embarrassed to admit that I had had sex with her. But that was part of my life at the time. I was always doing things that I was later embarrassed about. Unfortunately, it took me a long time to learn that I should try to get control of my life, so that I didn't continually end up in situation like this.

The judge order me to give her $20,000 in back pay and $1,300 a month for as long as I am a professional football player. After I retire, the amount will be reduced.

So this woman went from being on welfare to getting a fat check from me every month. Like I said earlier: she hit the jackpot.

• • • • •

Despite all of my craziness, I still worked hard to be a good role model for kids. I was always talking at schools, signing autographs and visiting kids in the hospital. I always tried to be someone that kids could look up to. But it was tough. There was so much chaos in my life behind the scenes that I had a hard time keeping everything behind the curtain all of the time. Sometimes the chaotic side of me would come peeking out, and I'd have to run over and try to close the curtains all the way.

One time during the 1987 season, I got arrested for failing to appear in court for a traffic ticket. I was supposed to go to court in August, but the Broncos were in London at the time for an American Bowl preseason game, so I missed my appearance. Then I flat forgot about the ticket.

Well, in December the cops caught up with me and took me to jail. It was no big deal really. I had to go to the police station to pay the fine. But then the media grabbed the story and blew the whole thing out of proportion. They made it sound like I had committed murder or that I was a drug dealer or something.

Both Denver newspapers ran stories about my arrest. One of the Denver TV stations ran a trailer at the bottom of the screen that said, "Vance Johnson thrown in the slammer, details at 10." I couldn't believe it. They were making my arrest seem much worse than it was. It bothered me to think that there were little kids out there watching TV at 7 p.m. who would see that little note that said, "Vance Johnson thrown in the slammer." Those kids aren't going to be awake at 10 p.m. when the news comes on and they learn that I was arrested for not paying a traffic ticket. As far as kids are concerned I may as well have been a convicted felon. A bunch of kids probably went to school the next day and said, "Did you hear what happened to Vance Johnson? He got thrown in the slammer."

I was very disappointed in myself for letting that happen, but I was also disappointed in the media, for the way they delivered the news. I thought they were irresponsible.

Besides, it really wasn't that big a story. They only covered it because I was a Denver Bronco. If the average person goes to the dentist and has a cavity to be filled, who cares? But if the president goes in and has a cavity, it will be reported in every newspaper in the free world. Reporters will be standing outside the dentist office saying, "Mr. President, how big was the cavity? Mr. President, what type of filling did you get, metal or gold? Mr. President, did your insurance cover the entire dental bill or did you have to pay part of it. Mr. President, how many shots of Novicain did you get?"

The media does that to a certain extent with all famous people. They report every little thing as if it were the most important event in the world. Lots of people fail to pay traffic tickets, but when I did it, it was big news. And when a television station says, "Vance Johnson thrown in the slammer," I become a convicted felon in the minds of many people before they even have a chance to hear the whole story.

• • • • •

During the off-season that year, a lot of the players attended one of the many dinners that are held in the city every year. A lot of business people always attended these types of affairs, so I thought it would be a fun event for Angela and I.

When we checked in at the door, an attendant gave us name tags and told us that we were assigned to table 54 or something like that. We were walking through this big ballroom looking for our table when we ran into a couple of guys from the team who were standing with their wives. They were the two guys who said that Angela had slept with them. There was no way that we could just walk past them without stopping to speak.

I looked at them and they looked at me, and we all held our breaths wondering what was going to happen.

I was completely embarrassed and pissed off. I said hello to everyone and introduced them to my wife. Through clenched teeth I said, "I don't know if you guys have met my wife." They said "no" and shook her hand. I stood there seething, and I could tell that the two guys were nervous because they weren't saying much. I was so mad that I was tempted to say to one of the other wives, "That's a very nice dress you're wearing. By the way, did you know your husband was fucking my wife?"

But I didn't say anything. Finally I couldn't take it anymore. I said goodbye to everyone, and Angela and I left the party. That night, I decided to divorce Angela.

I told her that I wanted her out of my house before the end of training camp.

"You can have everything, except that house, my clothes and anything else that was clearly mine," I said. "Just get the fuck out."

We got into a lot of fights on the phone during camp because she threatened to clean out the house and take my stuff too. One night after curfew, she called me and said that she was moving out right then and she was taking everything.

I was hit with an impulse reaction that was pretty typical for me at that time. I didn't think anything through, I just jumped out of bed and put some clothes on. Then I threw a sheet over my head and raced out the front door past the security guard. I knew that if he couldn't see me, he couldn't report to Coach Dan Reeves that I had left the dorm in the middle of the night. I jumped into my Porsche and drove about 150 mph all the way to my house in Westminster, a suburb of Denver. When I got there I saw Angela and her sister loading up a truck, and they had a lot of my personal stuff.

I jumped out of the car and said, "Surprise. I'm home."

She and her sister were standing there with a bunch of stuff in their hands, and when they saw me, they were so shocked that they dropped the shit. Angela ran into the house, but her sister just stood there yelling at me.

She said, "You ain't gonna do nothing to me. You ain't my man. You ain't my man. You can't do nothing to me."

I walked up to her and pushed her to the ground, and told her to shut up. Then I went into the house looking for Angela. Inside we got into a big argument, and I finally went out to their truck and started taking my stuff into the house. I was there most of the night, and eventually things started to calm down a bit. By the time I left, early that morning — I had to get back to Greeley in time for the morning practice — everything had really cooled down. She continued to move out, but I wasn't worried about her taking my stuff after that.

I was relieved to know that Angela was out of my house.

The Second Marriage

A few days after Angela's departure from my home, I was walking across the University of Northern Colorado campus — where Broncos' training camp is held — with one of the offensive linemen. We saw two gorgeous women lying in the sun wearing bikinis. One of them was incredibly beautiful, and I really wanted to meet her. There was a young student who was always hanging around the players, and he always seemed to want to do things for us. I grabbed this guy and told him to go talk to the girls for me. I can't remember his name, but he raced over to where they were lying, and invited them to come over to me and the offensive lineman to be introduced.

When he conveyed the message, the girls looked over at us, and whispered to each other. Then they stood up, wrapped their towels around their bodies, and walked over to where we were standing.

The one I liked was even more beautiful at close range. Her name was Chri (pronounced SHREE). She was about 5-feet-10 — my height — and she had soft green eyes, long blonde hair and really fair skin. After talking to her for a few minutes, I learned that she was a really sweet person, too. I got her phone number and promised to call her. As they were walking away, Chri's towel fell off, and I saw that her body was as beautiful as her face.

I went to find Mark, and I introduced him to Chri's friend so that we could double date. Since the girls were not old enough to go into clubs (they were both 18), our first date consisted of a short walk on the University of Northern Colorado campus, which ended with the four of us standing outside the players' dorm talking. A lot of the other guys walked past and saw us with these girls. Later, in the locker room, everyone remarked on how beautiful the girls were, and asked how we managed to meet them.

It wasn't until years later that I realized it, but Chri was sort of a trophy for me, at least in the beginning. I had this notion that having a pretty woman on my arm would make people believe that I was popular and successful. So when guys made comments about her beauty, I took it all in with a sense of pride. It made me feel good to know that they envied me.

Chri and I started to see more and more of each other, but there was nothing sexual about our relationship. It was weird. For the first time in my career, I was spending a lot of time with a beautiful woman, but I was not sleeping with her. There was no hugging, no kissing, no nothing. Plus, when we first met she told me that she knew my name, but she really didn't know anything about me. And the more we talked and the more time we spent together, I realized that she loved me a lot more than she loved the Broncos. She just wanted to talk to me and be my friend.

I was falling madly in love with Chri. I told her about my separation from Angela, and that I would be getting divorced soon. I really wanted to be with Chri, but at the end of the summer, we had to say goodbye. She left Colorado to live with her sister in Florida.

I was very disappointed. I gave her my car phone number and told her to call me if she ever wanted to talk. I always gave women my car phone number, because I was a married man and I couldn't have them calling me at my house. Of course, industrious women would always get access to my unlisted home phone number, so during my chaotic days, I would get a lot of calls from women at home. I'd usually change my phone number about once a month.

After Chri left, I kept waiting for her to call me, but she never did. Months passed and there was still no word from Chri. I figured I would never see or hear from her again.

During that same training camp, Angela came up to Greeley one day to talk and try to work things out with me. She got a motel room, and I went to visit her and talk. We ended up having sex that night, and that's when she became pregnant with our second son, Vincent. He's a beautiful little boy.

• • • • •

After training camp, I moved back into my house and lived there alone. Although, Angela and I were separated, I still saw her whenever I went to visit Vaughn, which was often. But Angela was pissed off at me, so she started denying my visitation with Vaughn because she knew that would hurt me. Plus, because I was such an abusive person, she was afraid to be near me.

But I missed my son, and I was determined to see him, so on the nights that Angela went out with her friends, I often sat outside her house to wait for her to come home just so I could get a peek at Vaughn — she picked him up from the babysitter's house on her way home.

One day, I went to her house when her mother was there, and I said, "fuck this," I wanted to spend time with my son, so I just picked him up and carried him out of the house. I had done this on several other occasions, but apparently Angela had recently gone to court to get a restraining order against me. It said I was a dangerous individual, and that I should not be allowed to spend time alone with my son.

So Angela called the police, and she came with them to my house later that day. I explained to the cop that I loved my son, and I just wasn't spending enough time with him. The cop listened to my side of the story and was sympathetic. It turned out that the cop had just gone through a divorce and he knew how I felt. So the police checked Angela's record, discovered that she had an outstanding warrant for a traffic ticket or something, and they arrested her. They actually put handcuffs on her right there in the front lawn and took her to jail.

I was ecstatic. Unfortunately, the restraining order was still valid, so I had to give Vaughn to Angela's mother.

• • • • •

During all of this, Mark and I were still partying hard. We were meeting girls everywhere we went, and we were having a blast. We took girls home every night, and we rarely saw the same women twice. One night we were at a strip club, and I started talking to one of the dancers. I ended up going home with her, and she turned out to be one of the wildest people I have ever met in my life. I was lying on her bed while she was making a phone call. I leaned over to the nightstand to get a scrap of paper, and when I opened the drawer, I could not believe all of the sexual paraphernalia she had in there. There were dildos, vibrators, ben wa balls, sex oils and a bunch of other toys. She had so much heavy-duty equipment, that I was actually afraid of this girl. I didn't think I would be able to keep up with her. You can imagine the kind of wild things we did that night.

A few days later, I went to a Denver radio station for an interview and got a phone number from a woman who worked there. I called her to set up a date, and she offered to cook dinner for me. That's cool, I thought. She was a nice, professional girl, so I figured that would be one of the nights that I didn't have sex. I went to her house and dinner was great. But after we finished eating, she disappeared into the bedroom.

"Vance, could you come in here for a second," she said from the other room.

I walked in and was totally shocked. The overhead light was off, but she had candles lit everywhere. And she was wearing a tiger outfit! She started growling at me while she peeled my clothes off.

"This is only going to happen once, so let's make the best of it," she said.

I was in shock. I couldn't believe the transformation this woman had made. In less than two minutes, she had gone from being a sweet girl to being a tigress.

That was another one of those wild nights.

• • • • •

Even though I wasn't well-versed in the long-term effects of alcohol on the body, I did know that if I drank right before I got into my car, I might get into an accident and kill someone. So I tried to make sure I never drove drunk. I would generally do all of my drinking the minute I got to the first nightclub. I'd have two or three or four drinks really fast to loosen me up, then I'd just drink cokes the rest of the night. By the time I left, I was sober enough to drive.

Unfortunately, Mark and I started barhopping a lot, so there were a few occasions when I was behind the wheel when I shouldn't have been. I never got pulled over by the cops though. But I did have one close call. After going out and drinking one night, I jumped into the car to take my father to the airport. A friend of mine — I'll call him Jimmy — went with us. On our way back from the airport when disaster struck. Some guy came flying down the highway at about 100 mph and ran right into the back end of my Porsche. I was swerving on the road, drunk as hell, trying to stay in control. I finally got the car pulled onto the shoulder, and ran to catch the guy who had hit us. His car had run off the road.

Someone called the cops, and soon an ambulance came and took all three of us to the hospital. I was lying on a gurney in the hospital, and I knew that I was drunk. I also knew that they were probably going to check my blood to see how drunk I was. I didn't want to get a DWI, so I crooked my finger and asked one of the staff members to come down to whispering level.

"Are the police here?" I said.

"Yes," the person replied.

"Are they going to do a test for alcohol?" I said.

"Yes," the attendant said. "They need to take some blood to check your blood-alcohol level because you do have alcohol on your breath."

I sat there for a minute digesting that. "Is there any way we can make this thing last longer, so they won't get me while I'm drunk?" I said. "Because I think I am drunk."

The attendant looked at me for a second, then rolled me into an X-ray room on the top floor of the hospital and left me there.

The cops were getting pissed because they knew I had been drinking and they wanted to do the test as quickly as possible. The hospital staff apparently told them that I was having some tests done, and the cops couldn't take any blood from me until the medical people were sure that I was okay.

Three hours after the accident they brought me back down and took my blood. The cops were really pissed off by the delay, but there was nothing they could do about it. After a three-hour delay my blood-alcohol level still tested at .053. The cops called about a week later to tell me that I was driving impaired, but they couldn't charge me with anything.

If blood had been drawn for them immediately after I arrived at the hospital, I'm positive that I would have gotten a DWI.

That was just another incident that heightened my sense of invincibility. I believed that I could do anything I wanted to do, and people all over the city were helping me cover my mistakes.

• • • • •

Earlier, I mentioned all of the free items, discounts and other preferential treatment I received because I was a Denver Bronco. There were free meals at restaurants, free movies, discounts on clothing, free haircuts, free this, free that. I had it all.

Well, I neglected to mention that there were a couple of occasions when I did not get "comped." In fact, on these occasions, I got my ass embarrassed.

It didn't take me long to get used to the special treatment I received. Within a matter of months, I was completely spoiled. When I went to restaurants, I expected to be seated immediately, and I expected to get free food. On the rare occasions that I suffered a brief 5-minute delay in getting a table or if the manager did not offer to cover my tab, I was always furious. At the time, I would think, "Don't they realize how lucky they are to have The Vance in their restaurant. I'm helping their business. People were coming to eat there on the off chance that they might see me."

One day Angela and I were eating dinner at a Chile's restaurant in North Denver. This restaurant was fairly close to our house, so we went there quite a bit. But in all the times that we had visited, the manager had never offered to pick up my tab.

"What the hell kind of bullshit is this?" I asked Angela when the check came. "As much as we come in here, you'd think they'd hook us up with a couple of free meals every once in a while."

I called our waiter and asked him to fetch the manager. I figured I would just have a little talk with the guy to set him straight and everything would be cool.

The manager came over, and I ripped into him. I was loud-talking and cussing at him and asking him if he had any idea what it means to have a celebrity in his restaurant.

"You're running a business here, and I'm doing you a favor by coming in here to eat," I said. "You could at least return the favor by giving me some free food every once in a while."

The manager apologized over and over again for not recognizing me, and he thanked me for being a customer at his restaurant.

"Now we're getting somewhere," I thought.

But, to my surprise, he did not offer to pick up our dinner tab. After that entire ordeal of me telling him how lucky he was to have me in his store, he didn't pay for my meal. I couldn't believe it.

"Tell you what," he said. "I'll have the waitress bring you a milk shake, on the house."

It was a very humiliating experience. I never went back to the restaurant.

On another occasion, Angela and I went to the movie theater in the Westminster Mall, and as usual we walked right past the ticket taker and into the movie of our choice. This was during the season, and I'd had a really good game that week. We walked into the theater about 10 minutes before the movie was scheduled to start, so the lights were still on. Everybody recognized me and started clapping. They were giving me a damned standing ovation in the movie theater, and I was loving it. Everybody loved The Vance.

I waved to the crowd, and Angela and I found a couple of seats in the middle of the theater. A couple of minutes later, a guy wearing a theater uniform came in, worked his way down the isle in front of us until he stopped right in front of me.

I thought he was about to ask me for an autograph, so I smiled at him, and waited for the question.

"Excuse me Mr. Johnson," he said. "You didn't pay for your movie tickets."

"What?" I said, caught off guard.

"You need to pay for your movie tickets," he said.

So there I was looking at this guy, and he was looking at me, and I knew he was serious. Everyone around me had heard what he said, and people started to murmur.

"What a jerk," someone said. "He didn't pay for his tickets."

Quickly the word was spreading through the theater.

"Oh, my mistake," I said. But I was too embarrassed to get up, walk past all of those people and go pay for the tickets. Angela saved me by offering to go pay.

I sat there munching on popcorn as people kept staring at me and talking about me. I think some of them wished that they could take back the standing ovation they had given me. I wished I could crawl into a hole.

But that day, and the day in the Chile's Restaurant represented the few times that my arrogance back-fired on me in front of a crowd of people. Usually, when The Vance asserted himself, people let him do whatever he wanted. And if there was any resistance at first, I'd put on my full-court-press attitude and quickly overcome any obstacle.

I was a spoiled brat, and probably what I needed more than anything was for people to treat me like a normal person, like those restaurant and theater managers did.

• • • • •

I was cruising in my car one afternoon when the phone rang. It was Chri. My heart dropped. It had been 11 months since she left, and I had not heard one word from her at all. I was already deeply in love with her, but I had already resigned myself to the fact that I would probably never see her again. I was shocked to hear her voice.

"I just called to say that I'm back in town," she said.

I couldn't wait to see her.

Even though Angela and I were separated, I didn't want to bring other women to the house until we were divorced. So most of the time, Chri and I would go bowling or go see a movie or do other things like that. Nothing sexual would ever happen between us. I started spending most of my time with Chri, but I also wanted to see my son, Vaughn. It became increasingly difficult for me to juggle all of the time involved, so I asked Angela to move back into the townhouse, so that I could see Vaughn more regularly.

But eventually, I decided that I wanted to be with Chri and that I would try to get legal custody of my son one day. I brought Chri to the house, and Angela stood on the steps and asked me if I loved Chri. I said, "Yes. I love her and I want to be with her." I agreed to let Angela have the townhouse, and Chri and I moved into a different townhouse together.

Despite all appearances to be reasonable and to just let things go, Angela was pissed off about my being with Chri and couldn't stop thinking about her. One day just a few days before the divorce was final, Angela and her sisters jumped Chri as Chri was pulling into the garage at our new townhouse. Chri saw the women coming toward her, and she tried to hurry into the garage and close the door. But Angela dove under the garage door and stopped it with her body. Then she grabbed Chri by the hair and she and her sisters started to beat up Chri.

They were yelling and screaming that this was a married man's house, and Chri's fucking ass shouldn't be there. They didn't really hurt her, but it scared the shit out of Chri. But we didn't call the police, because it was just a few days before the divorce would be final, and I just wanted to get everything over with. Plus, I knew that I would look like shit in the newspaper if the reporters wrote that Vance Johnson's wife had beaten up his girlfriend. Chri wanted to press charges, but I talked her out of it because I didn't want any public attention for the crazy shit that was going on in my life.

Meanwhile, I was really in love with Chri. Ours could have been a story-book relationship, if I hadn't fucked everything up. She was completely opposite from the girls that I had dated in the past. In addition to being beautiful, she was a wonderful person who came from a great family. She was exactly the type of person that I wanted to be in a relationship with.

But by the time we met, I was too far gone into living the life of The Vance. Even though I loved her, I couldn't — or wouldn't — stop doing the things that I was doing. I tried though. I cut down on my partying and started spending more time with

Chri. But when I did go out, I was still collecting phone numbers and I was still sleeping with other women. I couldn't control it.

Despite my inability to be monogamous, Chri and I were going strong when my divorce from Angela was completed a few weeks before the Broncos went to the Super Bowl in January 1989. We were in great spirits when we left Denver to go to the big game.

But when Chri and I returned from the Super Bowl, the shit really hit the fan. As we walked through the airport, people kept staring at us. During my years with the Broncos, I had become used to having people recognize me, but this was different. People actually seemed to be glaring at me like they were angry. Even though we had just lost the Super Bowl, I didn't think people would be pissed off at me personally. I couldn't figure out what was going on. Then I looked over to my right and saw a long line of *Rocky Mountain News* paper racks. On the cover in big bold print was the headline, "Men Who Beat Women." Under the headline was a big picture of me. I couldn't believe it. I stood there in shock for a moment, then I grabbed Chri's hand and we walked quickly out of the terminal.

I went into hiding after that. I couldn't believe they had used a picture of me with that article. I couldn't face anyone. I couldn't even bring myself to read the article. In fact, I never saw the article until I started writing this book.

So here is a reprint of the article:

MEN WHO BEAT WOMEN:
VANCE JOHNSON, STAR RECEIVER FOR THE BRONCOS, IS FAR FROM A HERO TO THREE WOMEN WHO KNEW HIM WELL.
"HE HAS HURT SO MANY WOMEN," SAID THE MOTHER OF ONE OF HIS CHILDREN. JOHNSON DENIES HE'S HIT ANY WOMEN; THEY SAY IT'S TIME THE PUBLIC LEARNED THE TRUTH

Off the playing field, when he's not wearing his orange football jersey No. 82, Vance Johnson has cultivated the image of a talented portrait artist and compassionate citizen who is willing to lend his time and celebrity name to charity causes.

But according to his ex-wife and two former girlfriends, the Denver Broncos star receiver is not the man he seems to be.

Vance Johnson, they say, batters the women he loves.

He denies it.

"Everyone loves him because he catches the football, but he has hurt so many women," says Lisa L. Edgar, who lived with Johnson in 1984 and has custody of the couple's 4-year-old son, Vance Jr. "I'm not a vindictive person . . . but what he did was wrong. He's a violent person . . . and I'll never let anybody treat me like that again."

In separate interviews with the *Rocky Mountain News* the three women said they were threatened and beaten by Johnson throughout their relationships.

A fourth woman who took Johnson to court over an assault-related incident in Arizona declined to be interviewed.

Johnson said his accusers are trying to "get back" at him because they are bitter that he ended relationships with them.

"I never beat anyone," Johnson said. "Everybody has been slapped around a bit in their life . . . but I haven't beat up anyone — ever."

But Lisa Edgar, Ana Maria Zuniga and Johnson's ex-wife, Angela, describe several battering incidents. Zuniga said she was punched repeatedly, grabbed by the throat and thrown. Both Edgar and Angela Johnson said they were hit or slapped and pushed down stairs when they were pregnant. All three women said Johnson destroyed their clothes during rages.

"It was terrifying," said Angela Johnson, who divorced the 26-year-old football player last fall and retains custody of their two sons, ages 2 years and 9 months. "If I tried to fight back, that would make him madder."

Zuniga, a girlfriend from high school, said Vance Johnson had a Jekyll-and-Hyde personality. "He could be so sweet . . . and then he would explode," Zuniga said. "You would never know what set him off."

In one of the most violent episodes during their 2 1/2-year marriage, Angela Johnson said Vance Johnson put a .22-caliber handgun to her head and threatened to pull the trigger. Another evening, she said, he dragged her down the stairs by her hair. In yet another brawl, she said, the two fought until she blacked out. She said Johnson revived her by splashing her with water from the toilet bowl.

In Colorado, police were called frequently to Vance and Angela Johnson's Arvada townhouse to help settle domestic disputes. The *News* obtained five police reports, dated from

December 1986 to November 1988, in which officers were called to investigate disturbances at the townhouse and a relative's nearby home, where Angela Johnson said she would often go to escape her husband's violent tantrums.

In each case, the police reported the parties showed no visible injuries and that Johnson did not want her husband arrested.

"He was always worried I would call the cops and show the bruises," said Johnson. "I would never call the police because I had been beat up. I would call because . . . I wanted to get the hell out of there."

After one particularly brutal beating, in which she claims Johnson gave her a black eye, her father took a photograph of her face to show police. The police, however, were never contacted.

"Just the thought of the police getting involved, she felt it would make it worse for her," said Barbara Stacionis, Angela Johnson's mother. "That's how much he intimidated her."

According to experts, battered women typically do not call police.

"It doesn't take long for a battered woman to learn that calling the police will result in another beating," Denver author Lenore Walker writes in *The Battered Woman*.

Angela Johnson's statements to police that she was in no danger contradict a November 1988 restraining order issued by an Adams County judge requiring Vance Johnson to stay away from his estranged wife.

In the restraining papers, Angela Johnson said her husband "has a history of mentally and physically abusing" her throughout their marriage. She referred to a Nov. 6, 1988, confrontation in which she said Johnson, in an argument over the custody of their 2-year-old son, smashed the windshield of her Chevrolet Blazer with a golf club and then threatened to "kill and stab" her sister.

In Arizona, Johnson was held in February 1986 by the Pima County sheriff in Tucson for attempted assault. According to the sheriff's report, Johnson broke down the door of an ex-girlfriend's apartment in Tucson and threatened her with a golf club before leaving.

In a plea bargain, Johnson pleaded no contest to a misdemeanor trespassing charge and was fined $200 and sentenced to six months of unsupervised probation. The victim, Bettina Gaona, also filed a $100,000 lawsuit against Johnson. Records show the case was dismissed in 1987 when Johnson agreed to an undisclosed out-of-court settlement.

Asked about the case, Johnson said it wasn't serious. "That was a whole misunderstanding, and no one was injured," he said. "Bettina and I are friends again . . . I don't want to talk about it."

Edgar, 23, cites an earlier incident at the same Tucson apartment in which she said she was the victim. Edgar said she was six months pregnant and had gone to the apartment to talk to Johnson about the pregnancy.

An argument ensued and Johnson, she said, pushed her down the stairs. Edgar said she was rushed to the hospital for treatment of internal bleeding but that the baby wasn't harmed. Months later, she said, Johnson threw her to the ground again.

"My family never knew how extensive (the beatings) were," said Edgar, the daughter of a retired Army colonel. "It was a hard time in my life. I was 17 and he was my first boyfriend. I fell in love with him — he was so charming."

Edgar said the relationship dissolved when she became pregnant. She blames herself for not standing up to Johnson when he became physically and verbally abusive.

"It wasn't just physical. It was mental, too. He would wear you down. I didn't look right or I wasn't dressing nice enough. I was young and he made me feel it was my fault. It was just his way, I guess, of taking out his anger."

Zuniga — the mother of Johnson's 6-year-old daughter — said she began dating Johnson when he was a senior attending Cholla High School in the late 1970s. But it wasn't until 1982, when Johnson was playing football for the University of Arizona, that she claims Johnson started beating her.

"He was reading my high school yearbook and he got upset over some comments some guys had written on the pages," Zuniga, now 25, said. "He just turned about and hit me. He didn't say anything, and I didn't expect it. It was silly."

Gradually, she said, the attacks grew worse.

"He knew where to hit you — where it wouldn't show," she said. "His favorite place was on the shoulder and arms — never the face." Sometimes she would hit back. "You are forced to act that way ... but the more I hit him, the more he would hit me, so I usually just sat and waited for him to get done."

Even after the couple broke up in the summer of 1983, Zuniga said, Johnson continued to harass her.

In 1984, Zuniga said, she was on her way out of the copy print store where she worked when Johnson appeared from around the corner and, in full view of customers, grabbed her by the neck and threw her against the door.

Edgar also remembers the confrontation. She was sitting in Johnson's car, watching from the parking lot. "That was the first time I ever saw him do something like that," Edgar said. "He had taken me with him ... and when he came back to the car he said, "If you ever get out of line, the same thing will happen to you."

Zuniga said she dreaded leaving her office at night, fearing that Johnson would be waiting for her in the parking lot. "It wasn't until I threatened to go to the newspapers that he stopped," she said.

"I lived with my aunt for a while ... and I used to wake up screaming, 'He's going to kill me!'"

Angela Johnson, 25, who moved into Vance Johnson's Arvada Townhouse in September 1985, five months after they first met in a Denver nightclub, said Johnson had an intoxicating effect on women.

"He would tell me how much he loved me. I believed him," she said.

"Even before their marriage in March 1987, she said the two had violent spats. "At first he used to cry and say he was sorry," she said. "But later he would act like nothing happened ... "

It was the hitting, though that scared her the most — an unexpected slap on the face. A punch on the arm. A shove against the wall. "I don't consider myself the classic battered wife," Angela Johnson said. "Vance wouldn't come home every night and just beat on me. But he could be very violent when I would stand up for myself."

Most of their arguments, she said, were about him seeing other women.

One time, she said Johnson became so enraged over her accusations that he took a butcher knife to her entire wardrobe.

> Edgar, Zuniga and Angela Johnson say they are incensed
> by media reports portraying Vance Johnson as a football
> hero and model citizen who has been burned by women
> after his fame and fortune.
>
> "That's just not true," Edgar said. "We knew him when
> he was nothing."
>
> Zuniga said she no longer feels any bitterness towards
> Johnson but fears for his next victim. "What I've said is going
> to make a lot of people angry . . . but it's not revenge. It's
> 'Vance, you need help.'"
>
> Said Angela Johnson, "I put up with so much — It was
> always, 'Vance Johnson is such a great guy.'
>
> "I'm not going to cover up for him any more."

Even today it blows my mind to read all of the things they said about me.

For days after the article came out I refused to answer any phone calls. I refused to talk to the media. I refused to talk to anyone. That article destroyed me emotionally. As The Vance, I thrived on being the center of attention, but I also desperately needed to be respected. After that article I was certainly the center of attention, but I wasn't respected by anyone. I couldn't take it.

And despite the quotes that they had from me in that article, I was completely taken by surprise by the story. I think they took my comments from previous interviews or from stories about other things that had happened in my life and weaved them into the "Men Who Beat Women" article.

When this story hit the streets, I was destroyed. I was miserable. I couldn't believe this was happening to me. When the murder charges were filed against O.J. Simpson in June 1994, I could understand his pain. People who don't live public lives, can never understand how devastating a newspaper or television report can be. As soon as negative news is released by the media, everyone in the community forms an opinion about you.

Try to put yourself in that position.

Imagine that you are sitting in your living room picking your nose one day. You are really digging deep up there. Your index finger is buried in your right nostril all the way to the third knuckle. Now suppose a television crew happens to be filming the entire scene through a window. Then the station broadcasts the scene on the evening news. They tell everyone your name and address and even what type of car you drive.

Wouldn't you be embarrassed to go to work the next day? Surely some or all of your co-workers would have seen the broadcast. Wouldn't you be reluctant to go to your health club? Probably some of the members recognized you from the newscast.

All of your friends would know it was you and you would be embarrassed.

Even the district attorney tries to use to the newspaper as a deterrent to people. I've seen those ads that they use to list the names of people who receive DWI tickets. They've even started publishing the names of men who solicit prostitutes. They're doing all of this stuff to scare people, because no one wants to see their name in the newspaper for something bad like that.

It's humiliating

Well imagine that you are a famous person. Everyone knows who you are. It's a rare day when 10 people don't ask you for your autograph. When you walk into a restaurant, a department store or a movie theater the place starts to buzz. You are very recognizable.

Then a newspaper article comes out with your picture on it saying that you abuse women. Suddenly everyone looks at you a little bit differently. People used to look at you with admiration — now they view you with contempt.

That's why I could understand why O.J. Simpson might have felt suicidal when fingers started pointing toward him in his wife's death. He has spent most of his life being a national hero. Everyone liked him. He was successful, and he was nice. Then he was accused of murder and the entire country seemed to turn against him. The image that he had built up over all of those years came tumbling down.

Plus his ex-wife, whom he still loved, was dead. And I can't even imagine what it would feel like to have people call me a murderer. To have the entire country think that I murdered my ex-wife would be tough.

O.J.'s life as he knew it was destroyed.

That's how I felt after the "Men Who Beat Women" article. I immediately thought that everyone was staring at me. I was afraid to drive my car. I didn't want to go out to eat. I didn't want to go see a movie. I didn't want to do anything that would put me in public. I was scared to death about what people were thinking of me.

One of the most painful things that happened was when the Denver Children's Home called me and said that they no longer wanted my support.

The Children's Home is a safe haven for kids who have been physically or emotionally abused, sexually assaulted or abandoned. It's a place for them to grow up and get over some of the trauma in their lives. I first visited the home during my rookie year, and I was immediately hooked. I felt so close to the kids. I could identify with what they were going through, and I wanted to help them. I gave a lot of money to the home, and I would often go by and play with the kids or eat dinner with them.

Although I was doing a lot of terrible things in my personal life, those kids didn't know about it. They loved me, and they looked up to me, and they believed in me. They thought I was a good person. And I always felt like a good person when I was with them.

But after that article, I was no longer allowed to come visit. I was no longer welcome at the Denver Children's Home, and that hurt me worse than anything. I felt like a loser, because I had ruined one of the few good things in my life. All those kids were in the home because they had been abused by someone. And then, because of that article, all of those kids knew that I was an abusive person, too. They knew that I hurt people, and that I needed help. I wasn't their role model anymore. I was just another adult who had disappointed them.

I was devastated.

I hope someone from the Denver Children's Home reads this book, and knows that I have changed my life. I want all those kids to know that I love them and that I'm sorry I let them down. I want them to know that I have taken responsibility for my actions, and I am trying to change my life. I want them to know that they can look up to me again. I promise to be a good role model for them.

About 10 days after the article came out, I was finally able to talk to the media. I went on a Denver radio show and, for an hour, I basically denied any charges that had been made against me. I told them that my ex-wife and former girlfriends were just angry because I wasn't with them anymore. I said they were trying to ruin my life.

Unfortunately, most of the things they said in that article were true. A few of the incidents weren't true, but the basic message of the article was that I was an abusive person — and that was entirely true. I was verbally, physically and emotionally abusive to the women who were quoted in the article. However, for the record, I would like to correct two things. First, Angela and I never owned any guns, so I never put a gun to her head and threatened to pull the trigger. Second, yes, I did smash the windshield of Angela's Chevrolet Blazer, but not the way it sounds in the article. The story creates the impression that Angela and my son were sitting inside the truck when I hit it. That's not true. Although I was very abusive to Angela, I would never jeopardize my son's safety like that. No one was in the car. It was late one night after Angela and I had been fighting. I stormed out of the house to go for a walk and saw the truck parked on the corner. I was really pissed off, so I decided to take out my anger on the truck. I picked up a brick, reared back and threw it as hard as I could into the windshield. It was a pretty stupid and expensive thing for me to do, but I didn't care.

There are other specific things in the article that weren't true, but I'm not going to try to dilute the basic facts. I was an abusive person. I had a problem, and I desperately needed help.

Today, I can admit and take responsibility for the abusive things that I did in my former relationships, but at the time, I denied everything.

My denial was so deep that I put an attorney on retainer and hired a private investigator to interview my former lovers and find out if I was an abusive man. I was going to use the results in a lawsuit against the *Rocky Mountain News*. This investigator went around and talked to about 12 different girls that I had dated and of those, I think Ana, down in Arizona, was the only person who said that I was ever abusive.

That made me feel good. It enhanced my feeling that I was a victim in this case. That the *Rocky Mountain News* had falsely accused me. That there was some conspiracy to try to ruin me. I fully planned to launch a lawsuit against the *News* for libel but — as you'll learn when you read the chapter titled, "Where did all my money go?" — I didn't have enough cash.

I was a spending fool, who squandered every penny just about as quickly as I earned it. Getting an attorney on retainer and paying for a private investigator cost me about $10,000 or $12,000, and I simply could not afford to continue. The reality for me was that I could file suit. Then a trial could take forever to start. Then the *Rocky Mountain News* could appeal the judgement, and drag the thing out for years. I couldn't afford to finance the lawsuit, so I dropped the idea.

But my feelings were still deeply hurt, and I was still terrified about what people were going to think about me since the domestic abuse bomb had been dropped.

Since my rookie year, I'd been a real media hound, and I never saw a camera or a poised pen that I didn't like. But after that article, I cut off all contact with the media. The story came out in February 1990, and after making those initial denials on the radio a couple weeks later, I didn't talk to another reporter until training camp started in July that year.

Instead, Chri and I escaped to Arizona to get away from the commotion and to let things die down a bit. At this point, Chri and I had not had very many physical fights, even though we did argue a lot. In Arizona, we spent a lot of time together, and she told me how much she loved me and that she wanted to spend the rest of her life with me.

We decided to get married. I loved Chri and I thought that marrying her would erase some of the pain that I was feeling from my relationship with Angela.

We went to Hawaii for a pre-honeymoon, and we were having a pretty good time. We were getting drunk at night, laying out on boats during the day, taking a lot pictures and running on the beach. It was the perfect vacation — until I started to get jealous.

Chri was a really beautiful woman, and she looked stunning in a bikini. So when we were at the beach, guys would be staring at her, and it pissed me off. I think part of the problem was that we weren't in Denver anymore and all of the people on the beach didn't know that I was The Vance. If they had known I was Vance Johnson of the Denver Broncos, it probably wouldn't have bothered me to have them looking at Chri. I would have figured they were just jealous of me because I was with such a beautiful woman, but since they didn't know who I was, I felt very insecure. So much of my confidence was tied up in being a Bronco and being recognized in the community, that I didn't have much confidence on those isolated beaches in Hawaii.

As more and more guys stared at Chri, I got more and more pissed off. Finally, one evening in our hotel room, I started an argument with Chri. I was mad at all those men, but I was taking it out on her. I accused her of flirting with other guys. I accused her of trying to be extra sexy, of wiggling more than she should have when she walked, of being too seductive when she was lying on her beach towel. Basically, I accused her of any stupid thing I could think of, because I was so insecure.

We were yelling and screaming and at one point she pushed me, so I pushed her back. She tripped over something, fell and hit her head on the corner of the dresser. She had a big scratch on the back of her head, and she started crying. I apologized for hurting her. I really felt bad.

After the "Men Who Beat Women" article, Chri had defended me. She told me and anyone else who asked that I was not an abusive man. But that night, she told me that I really did have a problem with abuse.

"You shouldn't have done that," she said. "Guys shouldn't hit girls."

I wasn't prepared to admit my problem to her or anyone, so I shot back, "Well, girls shouldn't hit guys either, and you hit me first."

When we got back to Colorado during the summer of 1990, Chri and I started planning for our wedding which we scheduled for the summer of 1991.

But then we started arguing, and Chri didn't believe that I was really going to marry her. I kept telling her that I was committed, but she didn't believe me. So finally I went and got a marriage license to show her that I wanted to get married.

About a week or two after we got our license, we went to a golf tournament in Fort Collins with a bunch of friends. We were all having a great time at this tournament, and we were all drunk.

Then my friend said, "Hey. I have a great idea. Why don't the two of you just go and get married?" It was kind of like a dare. Chri said I looked at each other, and she said she would do it if I would do it. I said, I would do it if she would do it. So everyone said, "Great! We're going to have a wedding." I called my dad in Denver and asked him to drive up with the marriage license. My friend called one of his buddies who was a judge, and we all jumped into our cars to go to the judge's house.

In the car, my friend told me that I didn't have to go through with this right now. "It was just a joke, Vance. You should think about it and do it in a week or two," he said. But I was in love with Chri and I was planning to marry her soon anyway. "What's the difference between now and a few months from now?" I said.

We got married on July 16, 1990. We spent our wedding night in a hotel in Fort Collins, but we were both too drunk to consummate the marriage. I didn't care. The next day, I was really happy that we had done it. We talked about having kids, and we started trying to have kids right away. I love all of my kids dearly, but I was excited about having a child with Chri, because it would be the first time in my life that I made a conscious decision to have a child with a woman that I loved.

Our marriage also took a lot of the sting out of the "Men Who Beat Women" article. Chri is a really beautiful, intelligent person, and she went on television and radio interviews and said all of the allegations that were made about me were lies. She said, "if this man was abusive, then I wouldn't be marrying him."

People looked at this beautiful young woman who was saying "I love Vance Johnson, and I know he is not an abusive person," and they believed her. Through her efforts, a lot of the talk about my abuse problem died down.

Chri knew I was an abusive person, but she defended me because she loved me. At the time I loved her for doing it, but now that I look back, I realize that she became an enabler for me. I needed to change, but instead I just became a progressively worse person. And the worse part is that I was still abusing Chri.

But I loved her dearly and I wanted to change my life for her. Even before our wedding, I cut down on my partying. I wasn't going out with Mark quite as much. I was still seeing a couple of girls on the side, but I promised myself that after we got married, I was going to be faithful.

The Broncos' 1990 training camp started up a couple of weeks after our wedding. As I loaded up my car for the drive to Greeley, Colo., I decided that I would never have an affair on Chri. I was going to be a good husband. I was going to be a good person. I was going to change my ways. I wasn't going to do anything that would hurt my sweet, young, innocent, wonderful Chri.

A few days into camp, I was lying in my dorm room asleep late one night when someone knocked on my door. Mark Jackson was my roommate in the dorm suite. We each had our own bedrooms, and we shared a bathroom, a living room and a kitchen. It was like a small two-bedroom apartment. I got out of bed to answer the door. When I opened it, I saw a blonde girl who worked on the University of Northern Colorado campus. I had seen her around before, but I'd never really talked to her. She was a tall, pretty blonde woman.

"What are you doing here?" I said.

"I just came by to say 'what's up?'" she said.

"Well, you really shouldn't be up here," I said.

"I know, but it's past curfew and if I leave now I'll have to go past the front desk. I'll get in a lot of trouble," she said.

So I invited her in, and we started talking. I was chanting a prayer to myself, "I will not cheat. I will not cheat. I will not cheat." I was determined not to fall into this trap. I was not going to go back on my promise to myself. I was not going to betray Chri's trust.

It was late, and I was tired, so I went to bed, and invited her to sleep on the other bed in my bedroom. We lay across the room from each other still talking a little bit every now and then. I was starting to fall asleep, and I was proud of myself for resisting the temptation to have sex with her. But when she walked over to my bed and laid down beside me, I didn't tell her to leave. Even though I knew it was a mistake, I figured there was no harm in sleeping in the same bed with her as long as nothing happened. We fell asleep in each other's arms.

I woke up in the middle of the night and saw her blonde hair spread out over the pillow. In the half-awake, half-asleep state that I was in, I thought it was Chri. I kissed her back and her neck. She rolled over and got on top of me, and we started to have sex. We reached orgasm at the same time, and I looked into her face . . . and I saw that it wasn't Chri.

I felt sick to my stomach. After promising myself that I wouldn't cheat, I'd had an affair. After marrying a wonderful woman, I'd had an affair. After trying to be a good husband and a good person, I'd had an affair only two weeks after my wedding.

I felt like the worst person on the planet. I didn't think Chri would ever forgive me. I didn't think God would ever forgive me. I didn't think I deserved forgiveness.

But after that night, I said fuck it. It's not worth my time to try to stop having affairs. I can't control it. It's just part of me. I have to be with a lot of women. That's who I am. If Chri doesn't like it, then maybe she married the wrong guy.

I never had sex with that blonde-haired late-night visitor again.

But I did have some communication with her. A few months after that night she filed a paternity suit against me. Our one night together had made me a father for the sixth time.

In court, the judge ordered me to pay her $1,500 a month in child support for as long as I am in the NFL.

Unfortunately, there is so much hostility between the mother and me that I rarely get to see my child.

• • • • •

After training camp, I moved back into the house with Chri, and I continued to have affairs on her. Whenever an opportunity to have an affair came along, I took it. I don't know why I couldn't be faithful to Chri, because I loved her greatly. I just didn't have the desire in my heart to be faithful.

One night Mark and I went to a bar to hang out, drink and hopefully, meet a couple of girls. We hadn't been there very long when we spotted two cute girls sitting together drinking and laughing. We went over and started talking to them and they were drunk as hell. We high-fived each other and said, "Well, we got two tonight." The four of us kept talking and drinking and eventually they asked us to come back to their townhouse with them.

We said, "cool."

When we got to their place, Mark and his girl immediately started having sex. He started to peel off her clothes right in front of me and my girl, and then the two of them disappeared into a bedroom. The girl I was with took my hand and led me into her bedroom. We talked for a little while, and I was surprised by how much she knew about me. She knew my wife's name. She knew my kids' names. She knew I was an artist, and she knew where I attended college.

She knew all kinds of stuff about me, and I thought that was cool. I said, "If you know all that, then you know what I want, too." She started taking her clothes off.

We started having sex, and after I orgasmed she looked at me and said, "Are you done?" I said, "Yeah," and rolled off of her.

She got up and walked out of the room. I thought she was going to the rest room or something, but about five minutes later, Mark came into the room and said, "What the hell is going on, man?"

"What do you mean?" I said.

"The girls just left," he said. "What happened?"

"Shit, I don't know," I said.

So we sat and waited for them to return. After about an hour they still had not returned, so we decided to leave.

The next day, the girl called to say that she was going to tell the media that I'd had sex with her. I couldn't understand why she would want to do that, but she quickly came to the point of the matter. She wanted money.

She knew that I had gotten married about a month before I slept with her, and she was threatening to go to the media and tell them about my affair with her. I didn't want that to happen. Part of me wanted to protect Chri from the truth, because I knew it would destroy her. Part of me wanted to protect myself, too. The "Men Who Beat Women" was probably still on people's minds. Chri had just finished going on television and radio and telling all of Denver that I was not an abusive man. I could only imagine what people would think of me if they saw an article in the paper headlined: "Vance Johnson Cheats On Wife." I felt that would destroy whatever fragment of a good reputation I had left in Denver.

The next contact I had with that girl was through her lawyer. She wanted to negotiate a settlement with me. I hired a lawyer, and the two attorneys hammered out a deal. I had to give the girl $20,000.

The deal we ended up with was that I had to pay her $5,000 a year for the next four years. I think she originally wanted the money all up front, but I didn't have it. The way I was blowing through money, and suffering through tax liens (which I'll explain later), I just didn't have enough cash to comfortably pay her $20,000 all at once. She was a college student, so the deal we struck was that she would get her money every year when it was time to enroll in school.

She was basically the first recipient of the Vance Johnson Scholarship Fund.

This fit the general pattern of events in my life.

I was learning that women always wanted my money. No matter what else was going on, they looked at me and their eyes started to flash dollar signs, because they knew that they were going to get paid one way or another.

•••••

I was being even more physically and emotionally abusive to Chri. As time passed, I became worse and worse. Once we got into a big fight and she kicked me. I grabbed an empty cassette tape case and threw it at the television screen to scare her. But it ricocheted off and cut her leg. She was yelling and screaming and crying.

One thing about Chri that drove me crazy was that she would cry for hours. If she got upset about something she would just lie down on the bed and cry. It drove me nuts. We'd get into a verbal fight and I'd yell and scream at her, and she would start crying. She wouldn't stop crying until three or four hours later. And it wasn't a soft whimper accompanied by an occasional tear streaming down the side of her face. She would flat out bawl. Looking back now, I feel really bad that I caused Chri so much pain, but at the time, I would just get pissed off at her for crying so much.

The night that I scraped her leg with the cassette case, she had been in bed crying for several hours. I kept yelling at her to shut up. But every time I screamed at her, it made her cry even louder. Finally, I couldn't take it anymore. I ran into the bedroom with some paper, and shoved it into her mouth to muffle her crying.

I'm embarrassed to admit that, but I really did it. And that was a fairly typical night in our relationship. She was such a sweet person, but I wasn't very nice to her. I was very physically and emotionally abusive to her.

One day we got into a big argument, and she threatened to call the police. I was really afraid of the police — and she knew it — so I begged her not to call them. She said she wanted to leave the house, so she called her father and he came over and helped her pack up her clothes and move out. Her parents hated me.

Several days later, she asked me to come pick her up because she missed me and wanted to come home.

In our attempts to have a happy home, we even went out and bought a really nice Rotweiller named Viper. I've heard that dogs are really good judges of character. When someone who has bad intentions comes around, a dog can sense it, and he'll start growling or barking because he wants to protect you, or he'll go hide because he's afraid. Viper was a beautiful dog, but he was such a great judge of character that we had to get rid of him. He was terrified of me, and he would always go hide when I came around. I screamed at him, and I screamed at Chri and all of the noise scared him. He would always run out of the room when I came in, or he would hide under the back porch. At one point, he spent several days in the crawl space under the house, because he was afraid to come out. Chri would have to go out back on her hands and knees and try to slide some food under the house, just so the dog could eat. We had to get rid of him because he was clearly not happy or healthy. It made me feel terrible to think that even a damned dog was afraid of me.

But that's how bad I had become. I was a terror. I was a jerk. I was an abusive person, and I didn't really care who I affected.

During January of 1991, Chri went to visit her grandparents, who live in a small town in Iowa. I never went to Iowa with Chri because her grandparents didn't like me. They were disappointed that Chri had married a black guy and even more upset that I was such a mean person to Chri. So while my wife was in Iowa, I went to Arizona to visit my family.

Meanwhile, Mark was in Denver cruising in my Mercedes and was supposed to pick me up at the airport when I got back, because we were going out to party. On the flight to Denver, I had a window seat and I had fallen asleep. An older black couple was sharing my row, and partway through the flight, the woman, who was sitting right next to me, woke me up.

"I don't know what you're thinking about, but you're burning up over there," she said. "Are you having problems?"

I looked at her, and said, "What are you, psychic?"

"Actually, I am," she said. "You need to be careful on this trip home because someone is going to try to kill you."

I don't believe in psychics, so I laughed at her. "Okay, if you're so psychic tell me about her," I said, pulling a picture of Chri out of my wallet.

She took the picture in her hand and said, "Your wife is a lot like your mother."

"You're right," I said.

"One day she's going to hurt you more than anyone in your life," the woman said.

Whatever. I figured she was wrong about Chri hurting me, because Chri was such a sweet person. She would never do anything to hurt me, so I just put it all out of my mind.

Mark picked me up at the airport and we went straight to a strip bar. We were boozing it up, talking to the girls and having a good time. I had been talking to one of the women for quite a while, and I made plans to go home with her that night. We talked for a long time then she left to go to the restroom. While she was gone, a big white guy walked up to me.

"What are you doing?" he said.

"I'm just hanging out," I said. "Talking to this girl. I think I'm going to take her home tonight." I figured he would be impressed by the fact that I was going to have sex with that pretty girl that everyone else was ogling. I was wrong.

"You aren't taking her anywhere," he said. "That's my wife." He pulled open his jacket, and I could see a gun in there. I got scared in a hurry.

I looked over my shoulder and there was another guy standing behind me blocking my way. I looked back at the first guy then walked between two tables and got away from them. I hurried through the bar until I found Mark. I told him I had to leave because these guys were hassling me. I told him to pick me up at another strip bar located down the street. He said "okay," and I raced out of the club. The two guys tried to cut me off by the door, but the place was crowded, and I darted around a group of people to get outside.

There was a blizzard in Denver that night. Snow was piled deep on the ground, ice was everywhere and more flakes were falling every minute. The two guys followed me outside and jumped into their pickup truck.

I didn't even have a coat on. I was in short sleeves, but I didn't feel the cold. I was loaded full of booze, and my adrenaline was pumping. I took off running down the street. I don't know how I kept from slipping on the ice. I guess fear kept me on my feet. I was Speedy Gonzalez high-tailing it down the street, and nobody was going to catch me. I only looked back once, and I saw the guys in the truck were slipping and sliding all over the road trying to catch up with me. I ran into the parking lot at the other strip club and hid behind some cars. When Mark pulled up in my Mercedes a few minutes later, I jumped in the passenger seat and we took off.

I told him about the woman on the airplane who said someone was going to try to kill me, and we both laughed because we were amazed. I'd never believed in psychics, but she made a believer out of me.

We went to a nightclub, picked up a couple of girls and took them home to have sex with them. We had sex in the new house that I'd had built for Chri. It had just been completed, and we hadn't quite moved in yet. There I was having sex with another woman in our new house.

I had a problem.

• • • • •

Finally, Chri decided she'd had enough abuse. She left me. To this day, I regret the way that I treated Chri, because she was probably the nicest person I had ever been with at that point in my life. Even though I tried to stop myself, I continued to use her and abuse her. I didn't treat her the way a wife should be treated, and that is why the relationship crashed.

After she left, I realized just how bad I had become. I wanted her back. I wanted to stop being an abusive person. I wanted to stop having affairs. I wanted to completely change my life, but I wasn't sure how. I felt like a complete failure. Marriage was supposed to be forever, and there I was on the brink of another divorce. I didn't want to be a failure. I wanted things to work. Chri and I talked about getting back together, but by then I think she had already been through too much with me. She was too shell-shocked to deal with me.

I was really upset about Chri leaving me, because I knew it was all my fault. I knew that I had been a terrible person, and I had forced her to leave. I desperately wanted to prove that I could be a good person. I wanted to change my life.

Deep down, I knew I was to blame, and I felt completely numb. I was sitting in my 7,000-square-foot house with a Porsche, a Mercedes and a Corvette in the garage, and I was miserable.

I was sitting in my bedroom with music blasting, and I was drinking glass after glass of Tanqueray. I wanted to drink myself to death. I wished I had a gun, because I wanted to shoot myself. Instead, I broke the glass on the edge of the counter in the bathroom and sat on the floor making scratches on my wrists.

There I was, Mr. Bad Ass football player who never feels any pain. Mr. Tough Guy who never cries, even when he's injured on the football field. I said, "Go ahead Vance, slit your wrists. It won't hurt, and you can just lay here and bleed. Your whole life has been destroyed. You lost another wife. You're just a terrible person. What do you have to live for? The world would be better without you."

I was sitting on the floor thinking that I was going to do it. I'd made a couple of scratches on my wrists, but nothing that was bleeding very much. Finally, I hit a vein in my left arm that started to bleed pretty good. Then I started to get scared. I grabbed a towel and tried to stop the bleeding. I wanted to die, but at the same time, I didn't want to die.

Then our psychologist — I'll call him Dr. Rakowski — called the house. He was the marriage counselor that Chri and I were seeing before we split up. Dr. Rakowski knew Chri and I were going through a really tough emotional period, so he occasionally called our house between sessions just to see how we were doing.

Earlier that day Chri and I had talked on the phone, and I told her how terrible I felt. I think she called Dr. Rakowski and asked him to check on me. When he called me that night, he may have saved my life.

He asked me how I was feeling, and I told him that I felt all alone. That I had been drinking and that I had tried to slit my wrists. I told him I wanted to kill myself.

He started talking to me. I guess he could have just called the police and told them to go to my house, but he didn't do that. He stayed on the phone with me for hours. He asked me to stop. He told me that my life was important, and that I wouldn't solve anything by killing myself. I believed him. I managed to stop the bleeding in my arm, and I didn't try to kill myself again.

After that, I started seeing him by myself for counseling. I would walk into his office and say, "I don't want you to say one fucking word to me. I just want you to listen." I started talking about my life and about my experiences and about how I felt about my life. I didn't want to be counseled. I just needed someone to listen to me. I knew that I had a problem, but I wasn't prepared to hear solutions yet. I needed to just get all of this stuff out of my body. I needed to confess to someone. He was the only person who would listen to me. Mark wouldn't listen to me, because he basically had the same problem I did. Chri didn't want to listen to me, because I was an abusive husband and I had hurt her too much. My mom didn't listen to me. She just kept telling me to read the Bible and to pray about it. My father didn't listen to me, because his Bible was the local tavern where he hung out.

I was all alone with no one to listen to me.

So I paid $115 an hour to Dr. Rakowski to just listen to me, and it was worth it. I'd want to book his entire day. I'd want to go in at 9 a.m. and stay there until 4 p.m. I wanted to get better, but it was a struggle for me, because I was still out doing crazy things. I think I paid Dr. Rakowski about $18,000 over a six-month period. Basically, I paid his son's four-year college tuition.

I thank God that Dr. Rakowski was there at that time in my life. He didn't cure me of my problem, but he listened to me without judging me, and he got me through a tough part of my life. He believed in me. I think I would have killed myself.

Meanwhile, I was still having affairs, and still trying to get back with Chri. She told me that if I was serious about being with her again, then I should stop seeing other women. But I didn't. I kept going out, and I kept meeting new women. I kept sleeping with other women. Chri and I were separated, and I was miserable. I thought I was a terrible person, but I didn't know how to change.

So I just kept living the way that I had been living. I met a girl named Michelle who was really beautiful and who came to my house a few times. I dated a really pretty girl named Rene who had a gorgeous face and long dark hair. She spent the night at my house a few times, and she even started leaving some of her things there. One day Chri, who still had a key to the house, came over while I wasn't there and saw Rene's clothes. She grabbed Rene's stuff and tossed it out onto the lawn. When Rene and I got back, Chri was gone but a bunch of our neighbors were admiring the collection of clothes on the lawn.

During this time, Chri and I bounced back and forth between trying to get back together and trying to stay apart. Even though we loved each other, and I desperately wanted a second chance, it didn't take much to spark an argument. It didn't take much to get one or both of us to say, "Look. Fuck it! Let's just forget about the whole thing!"

One day Chri called me and asked me to come over to her house, so I did. But when I got there she asked me to leave, and that pissed me off. I didn't want to go. There were a lot of situations like that in which we ended up in the same place, and Chri wanted me to leave her alone, but for one reason or another, I didn't want to leave her alone.

Then I learned that Chri had gotten a restraining order against me. I couldn't believe she had done that. Dr. Rakowski told me that Chri was feeling powerless at this point, and she needed to feel that she had a little power over me. That was why she got the restraining order. He told me that I could get one, too, if it would make me feel better.

I thought about it, and I knew that in her own way, Chri was just as crazy as me. After we separated, she would sit outside my house in her car, and if I pulled up with another girl, she would get out and start fighting with me. She followed me places when I left the house. She came over that one day and threw Rene's clothes onto the lawn. She came to the house on another occasion and we got into a fight. I think it was one of the days that I didn't want to get back together with her (that desire to be together or to break up seemed to change in both of us at least daily and possibly hourly). I was trying to rush Chri out of the house that night, because I had a date. She was leaving, but she was furious. Meanwhile, I was calm, and just laughing about the whole situation. I went upstairs while she was in the driveway and just waved and smiled at her from a window.

She backed out, and yelled "fuck you!" She flipped me off, but I was still laughing. Then she screamed, "I'll run this damned house over!"

I said, "You're not going to do anything to the house. You're just going to tear up your damned car."

Then she hit the gas and the wheels started to squeal as she raced up the driveway and right into the garage door. There was a loud BLAM, and the whole house felt like it was shaking. I thought I was going to fall through the bedroom window. I took off running down the stairs and out into the front yard, but by the time I got there, she was gone. The garage door was destroyed.

Chri had rammed the door with her father's Buick, and when I saw the car a couple of days later, it was really banged up in the front. I don't know what her dad had to say about the damage, but I'm sure that he probably blamed me.

So when Dr. Rakowski suggested that I could get a restraining order, too, I decided to go ahead and do it.

• • • • •

For a while, when Mark was still running his restaurant Scribbles, he lived with me out in Ken Caryl Valley. One night, right after Chri and I had first split up, I went down to his restaurant to hang out. About two or three of Mark's guy friends were there, and Mark had gathered up 10 or 12 girls from a bikini contest to come to my house for a party.

We all cruised over to the 7,000-square-foot mansion that I had built for Chri, and we started to have an orgy. I was the camera man, so I was going around filming everyone having sex. We had a lot of women there and everyone was just screwing everyone. Suddenly, I heard a loud bang upstairs, and I ran up to see what was wrong. I had a large bathtub in the master bedroom and you had to walk up several steps to get into it. There were five or six people in the tub and the damned thing had collapsed. It had fallen two or three feet down to the level of the floor. There were suds everywhere.

I went downstairs to the walk-out basement, and there, lying on the ground sound asleep was Mark. But the crazy thing was that he still had a hard-on and girls were taking turns getting on top of him. He was actually snoring. He never woke up while three different girls had sex with him. I was cracking up laughing. It was the most amazing thing I had ever seen.

The next day, I was really sad. I got up early and went and sat on the back patio. I was really disappointed in myself for having an orgy in Chri's house. Mark came out and sat down beside me after everyone had left.

"I got a fucking problem," he said.

"You ain't lying," I said. "We're both sick. We've got to stop all this shit."

"Yeah, I know," Mark said.

We sat there for a minute looking into the distance.

"But fuck it," Mark said. "We're here now. We're already going to hell, so we might as well forget it."

I was dying inside. I felt like a terrible person, and I wanted to change. I didn't want to continue to live my life the way I was living it. I had just lost Chri, the one person that I really loved. I was sad, but instead of crying or trying to change, I'd had an orgy. I was really upset with myself.

I was feeling so guilty that I called Chri and told her how sorry I was for everything that had happened in our relationship. I told her that I was sorry about all the grief that I had caused. I was sorry about the restraining orders. I was sorry about hurting her emotionally and physically. I said it was all my fault, and that I really wanted to change.

I promised myself that I would change. I would stop doing all of the crazy things that I was doing.

But that night, Mark and I went out and picked up a new batch of girls and had another orgy.

8

The Third Marriage

In 1985, my rookie year, I was having a lot of fun dispatching my new-found wealth. I had loads and loads of money, and I was always buying things for people. One of my purchases was a small ring for Angela. It was a half-carat solitaire that I picked up at Zales for $999. It was on sale. The ring was no big deal to me, I just wanted her to have something special that said she was my girlfriend.

To Angela, that ring represented a special commitment. At times, I regretted getting it for her, because it made our relationship seem more serious than it was. We had only been dating for a couple of months when I gave it to her, and I think I just wanted to impress her. She wore that ring like a trophy.

Angela and I had gone to the Westminster Mall in North Denver to do some shopping. I was buying a little of this. She was buying a little of that. We were having fun spending my money.

One of our stops was in a store called the Merry-Go-Round — it's a women's clothing store. I hung out near the front counter while Angela marched through the store pulling an occasional shirt or pair of pants off the rack and looking at it briefly before returning it to its place. A few minutes later, I heard her all the way in the back of the store bragging to the sales women that she was dating Vance Johnson. She showed them the ring I had gotten her.

That didn't bother me. Angela was very pretty, and I wanted everyone to know that she was mine. It also boosted my ego to hear the note of envy in the other women's voices when they looked at the ring.

But, while Angela was distracted, I was looking at a pretty, blonde sales clerk. Her name tag read: Holly. She stood about 5-feet-9 with a great body and a beautiful smile. I couldn't take my eyes off her. I wanted to ask for her phone number, but I was too shy. She glanced at me a few times, but I wasn't sure if she was interested in me or not. When she walked away, I asked one of her co-workers to give me Holly's phone number. I think her friend thought she was doing Holly a favor by giving her number to a pro football player, so she jotted it down for me.

A couple of weeks later, I called Holly and told her who I was. We talked for a couple of minutes, and I found out that she was 17 years old. I don't know what the laws are about statutory rape, but at the time, her age didn't bother me. I was a very immature 22-year-old, and she was a pretty mature 17, so we were actually about the same age emotionally. I asked her if she'd like to go out some time.

"I'm not going out with you," she said. "Aren't you engaged to that girl Angela who keeps coming into Merry-Go-Round and showing off the ring you bought her? She said she's engaged to Vance Johnson."

"We're not engaged," I said. "We're just seeing each other."

"Well, I'm not going to go out with you, but it was nice meeting you anyway." We got off the phone, and I was disappointed, but I was also intrigued. Her rebuff only made me want to date her even more.

I kept thinking about her all the time, and every once in a while I would call her to ask her out. But every time I called, she would decline my invitation.

I occasionally saw Holly out at nightclubs or at restaurants with a boyfriend, or with some of her girlfriends. She would always be friendly to me, but that was it.

One night — I was married to Angela at the time — I was driving in my Porsche with Mark when I decided that I wanted to see Holly. It was about 7 p.m. When she answered the phone I told her I was cruising on the highway in my Porsche. I said, "I'm coming to pick you up so we can go to dinner."

Holly barely hesitated.

"Vance, I don't know why you keep thinking that I'm going to go out with you, because that's not going to happen."

"Why not?" I said.

"Some of my friends are here right now, and I'm going out with them tonight," she said.

"Tell your friends that Vance Johnson is on the phone," I said. "They'll understand if you want to go to dinner with me instead of going out with them." That was my ever-present arrogance. I thought I was the greatest thing on the planet, and that my name alone was a calling card that opened the doors to whatever I wanted to do.

"Sorry, I'm going out with my friends," she said. "You can call again some other time to say 'hi' if you want to."

After we hung up the phone I looked over at Mark and said, "That damned girl keeps dodging me, but I'm not giving up. I'm telling you, she's going to be worth it.

"Man, you're crazy," Mark said. "You need to just forget about her."

About six months later, Mark and I were at a club called Mardi Gras when I saw Holly across the room. I pointed her out to Mark, and said I was going to talk to her. I walked over to her and asked her to dance. She said, "I can't. I'm here with a date. Besides, where's your wife?"

This was during 1988 when Angela and I were separated, so I told Holly about the problems we were having.

"I'm sorry to hear that," she said. "But you know what? Instead of being here at this club, maybe you should be at home trying to fix your marriage."

I didn't agree with her, but we didn't have time to get into a full-blown discussion about Angela. Holly's date was coming back from the bathroom, so I left.

"Mark, you see Holly over there?"

"Yeah, I saw her reject you and bounce your sorry ass all the way back over here."

"I'm going to marry her someday," I said.

"Yeah, right," he said. "You've been calling that girl forever, and she still won't go out with you."

But I knew there was something special about Holly, and I was determined to find out what it was.

One of the things that I always admired about Holly was that she was so independent. She was a gorgeous woman — still is — and she would come into a club with some of her girlfriends, dance, have a good time and then leave. Except on the rare occasions that she had a date, I
never saw her leaving with a guy. That always made me think that she was her own person. She wasn't the type whose life revolved around some guy. She wasn't the type who was going to let herself be bossed around. And she seemed content to be single.

As a beautiful woman, I always expected some man to scoop her up and protect her from all the other guys out there, but Holly didn't need or want protection. She could take care of herself, and that always impressed me. It increased my desire to be with her.

Holly and I bumped into each other a couple more times at different places, then I asked her to go out with me on New Year's Eve. She said, "I might have other plans." I took that to be a good sign, because she usually just said "no" when I asked her out. This time she said, "I might have other plans," as if she might go out with me if she wasn't already committed. I think she was warming up to the idea of dating me, because she knew that I was getting divorced from Angela.

I said, "Listen, I'll be at Club L.A. on New Year's Eve, why don't you just meet me there." She didn't say "yes," but she didn't say "no" either.

I was at Club L.A. on New Year's Eve, but I had Chri with me. I hadn't planned on taking Chri with me, but when Holly said "no" I wasn't planning on going out by myself, so I called Chri. I didn't have a plan for what I would do if Holly showed up. At the time, I figured that would be Holly's loss. That was how I looked at the world back then. One person's loss was another person's gain. If Holly didn't want to be my date that night, then Chri was the lucky one.

Fortunately for all three of us, Holly never did show up.

The next few times I called Holly, she was a little bit more receptive, because she knew that Angela and I were separated and on the verge of getting a divorce. But she still wasn't interested in getting romantically involved with me, and a big part of that was because she had a boyfriend. We talked on the phone pretty regularly, and I told her about a lot of the problems that Angela and I were having. Of course, I didn't tell her about the many affairs that I'd had during the marriage. I pretty much painted a picture of Angela as just the most evil bitch you could imagine. I don't know if Holly believed all of that, but we became pretty good friends.

But even as friends, Holly wouldn't even go out to dinner with me until my divorce was final.

Meanwhile, Chri and I were going great guns. I met Chri shortly after Angela and I first separated, but I kept that a secret from Holly, too. A few months before my divorce from Angela was final, Chri and I moved into a townhouse together. Another secret from Holly.

After my divorce from Angela, Holly finally agreed to have dinner with me. After that first date, we saw a couple of movies together, but we weren't really romantically involved. A big part of the reason there was no romance was that Holly refused to be one of the "bimbos" (as she put it) that I was always picking up.

One night we went out to dinner and then back to Holly's house to hang out. We were playing cards, and I really wanted to have sex with her. I suggested a game of strip poker. Holly said, "no way."

"Vance, it's very flattering that you want to go to bed with me, but it's not going to happen. We're friends, and that's all," she said. "I'm never going to be with you sexually. I think you're a nice guy when people get to know you, but to most people, you're just crazy as hell."

Holly knew how unhappy I had been with Angela, and she knew how excited I was to be getting divorced. On the day of the actual divorce proceedings, Holly personally delivered a dozen roses and a bottle of wine to my townhouse. I wasn't home, but Chri answered the door. Since Holly didn't really know anything about Chri, I had lied to her and said, "If you ever call my house and a woman answers, don't get pissed, it's just my housekeeper." I didn't know Holly was planning to stop by that day, but when I heard about it from Chri, I hoped that Holly thought it was the housekeeper.

When I got home, Chri was pissed. As far as Chri was concerned, she was my one and only girl, and she wanted to know why the hell some other girl was showing up at "our" house. She went ballistic. She couldn't believe that there was someone else. She was screaming and yelling and saying, "Vance, what's going on?"

I told her that Holly and I were just friends, which was the truth at the time. Eventually, she calmed down and everything returned to normal.

Holly and I continued to see each other every once in a while. I kept trying to get her to go to bed with me, but she wouldn't do it. I was begging, too. I was trying every trick in the book, but Holly wasn't falling for any of it.

Meanwhile, during the summer of 1990, Chri and I got married. I had been lying to Holly forever about my relationship with Chri, so I just kept right on lying to her. Holly didn't know I was married. One night Holly and I were out in one of my Porsches. We'd had a great dinner, and we were having a wonderful time. We'd been flirting with each other a lot throughout the evening. I was certain that this was the night we would have sex.

Being the cocky guy that I was, I started driving toward the Hyatt in the Denver Tech Center. I just knew we were finally going to do it. I figured if I got her to the hotel, I could talk her into going up to one of the rooms, and then things would just happen naturally.

Suddenly, I had an idea that I thought would excite her.

"Holly, have you ever driven a Porsche?" I said.

"No," she said.

"Do you want to drive?" I said pointing to my car. I never let many people drive my cars, so it was a big deal to me to let her drive my Porsche. Plus, Holly is one of the worst drivers I have ever known, so I must have really loved her, if I let her get behind the wheel of my Porsche.

"Sure," she said. "But I feel uncomfortable. What if I wreck it?"

"I'll just buy another one," I said.

I was really excited. I know this sounds kind of crazy, but I thought that letting her drive my Porsche demonstrated my trust in her and my commitment to her. I thought she would later show her trust and commitment to me by having sex with me.

I pulled over to the side of the road and switched seats with Holly. We started cruising around. We were driving all over the Denver Tech Center and my ultimate goal was to get her to the Hyatt. We were getting closer and closer.

Finally, we got to the hotel, and I said, "Why don't we get a room?" To my surprise, Holly said, "okay." I jumped out of the car and went to the front desk to register. By the time I returned to the car, the charade was over.

Holly was holding an envelope in her hand saying, "What the fuck is this?" She completely lost it. She was yelling and screaming, and calling me a liar and a jerk. She couldn't believe that I had lied to her for so long.

The envelope she had discovered was just a regular piece of mail that had been delivered to my house. The addressees were listed as: Vance and Chri Johnson.

Holly had finally learned that I was married.

I had been lying to her all along by first saying that I wasn't married, and then by admitting that Chri and I had gotten married when we were drunk, but had gotten it annulled immediately. Holly believed me.

But then when she saw that envelope, she knew that I had lied to her and that I really was married to Chri. It took a lot of explaining and improvising and flat-out lying on my part that night, but I finally convinced Holly that Chri and I were not married.

When all the talking was done, we ended up going into our room at the Hyatt and having sex together for the first time. It was wonderful.

• • • • •

Convincing Holly to believe me that night at the Hyatt was tough, but it was a pretty typical situation in my life at the time. I constantly told lies, because I was living such a crazy life.

Lying just became another talent I developed. I could make people believe things. I would tell lies, then tell more lies to cover the first lies then tell even more lies to cover the second batch. My entire life was becoming a lie, and it was becoming harder and harder to remember what the real truth even was.

Years later, when I got into counseling, I started to realize that I probably wasn't as talented a liar as I used to think I was. When I was in my prime, I thought I was just a clean, sly, smooth-talking son-of-a-bitch. I thought I could talk anyone into anything, or I could make them believe any story I wanted them to believe.

But through counseling, I began to understand that if people believed my lies, it was because they *wanted* to believe them. Their belief or disbelief, had little to do with my persuasiveness. If someone wanted to believe me, it really didn't matter what I said as long as I had said something. If someone confronted me with an issue and I had an excuse handy, then they had a reason to believe me. If I came into the house covered with water my wife might say, "Vance, you've been in the swimming pool haven't you? You are such a jerk! You promised me you wouldn't go into the pool."

"Honey, calm down. I wasn't in the pool. I just ran into a water buffalo, and he got me all wet."

"Oh. Okay. I didn't realize water buffalos had so much water. Well, here's a towel to dry off with."

Often the lies I told were stupid. They didn't make logical sense, but most of the time it didn't matter. The people who were hearing my stories wanted to believe me so they found a way in their minds to make my lies sound logical.

That's how I was able to convince Holly that I was telling the truth that night at the Hyatt. I told her a story that sounded halfway believable, and she wanted to believe me.

• • • • •

I had spent a lot of years — since 1985 — trying to get Holly to be in a relationship with me, but she had always resisted me. For a long time, I couldn't even talk her into going out on a date with me. Even when we got to the point of being pretty good friends, there didn't seem to be any hope for anything more than that. Holly was just a really strong woman, who knew what she wanted, and I didn't seem to fit into that picture.

I realize now that one of my biggest goals in life has always been to be in love. I wanted to be close to someone. I wanted to have a happy family. I wanted to be a good husband. I wanted to be a good father.

So I spent a lot of time trying to find someone to be in love with. Even when I was living in chaos, I was always searching for love. Of course, I rarely found it in the sexual relationships I entered. And on the few other occasions that I did find love, my lifestyle tended to sabotage the relationship. That's what was happening with Holly. I loved her, but there was no way that she was going to give her heart to someone like me. I was too crazy, too out-of-control, too noncommittal, and too caught up in a world that wasn't real.

When I met Chri, I fell in love with her. She was nice, and she was beautiful, and she was in love with me. She was someone I could be in love with. She was someone I could marry. She was someone I could be happy with. If I could have married Holly back then, I probably would have. But that option was closed at that time, because Holly refused to be in a relationship with me.

So I married Chri in July 1990.

I thought we would have a happy home. I wanted to be a good father and a good husband and a good person. I wanted everything to be perfect in our relationship. I had found love, and I thought everything would be okay.

But, once again, my lifestyle ruined the relationship. I was still driving fast, drinking hard, having affairs and being abusive. I was still living like a fucking lunatic. There was no way that love could survive all of that.

In reality, even though I would like to have married Holly at that time, it probably wouldn't have worked out for us. I was such an emotionally and physically abusive person that I probably would have destroyed her with all of my chaos.

Anyway, after my wedding with Chri, I started lying to Holly about my marriage. Holly knew that Chri existed in my life, but Holly thought I was just dating her. Months after the "Men Who Beat Women" article came out, Chri was in the newspaper, on television and on the radio telling all of Denver that I was not an abusive man. Chri said she and I were getting married, and that was the truth. But when Holly asked me about that, I just lied to her. I told her that the "marriage thing is just something we're saying to get people off my back about those bullshit abuse claims. We're not really getting married."

But somehow, about seven or eight months after Chri and I got married, Holly found out about it. She confronted me again, and I made up another lie. I told her that, yes, Chri and I were married, but we'd gotten it annulled. I said that Chri and I were up in Fort Collins one weekend and we were both drunk. While we were intoxicated, we decided to get married on the spot. So we went to see a judge who was a friend of mine, and he performed the ceremony. I even showed her pictures of Chri and I in which it was plainly clear that we were both drunk. I told Holly that after Chri and I sobered up, we immediately got the marriage annulled. This was an easy lie to tell because everything except the annulment was true.

Holly believed me.

After seven months of marriage — in February 1991 — Chri and I got separated. She decided that she'd had enough of my bullshit, so she moved out of the house.

Later that month, I invited Holly to my house for dinner, and I know it was obvious to her that I lived alone. There was no woman living in my house. There were no woman's clothing lying around. No woman's decorations on the wall. My house looked every bit like the house of a bachelor, so it made my story of drunkenness followed by marriage and concluded by annulment sound even more believable. It was about a month after we had dinner at my house that we ended up outside the Hyatt arguing about a piece of mail that had been delivered to Vance and Chri Johnson.

The thing that pissed off and confused Holly was the fact that Chri and I had the same last name on the envelope. Holly was under the impression that Chri and I had been married for only a couple of days before the annulment. She had that impression, because that's the lie that I had told her. So, she didn't understand how Chri and I could have mail that was addressed to us as a married couple.

I told her that Chri and I had lived together for a while before the wedding — which was true — and after the annulment some people just assumed that we were married because we were living together. I said there were plenty of times that people addressed things to Vance and Chri Johnson just because they didn't know any better. It was no big deal, I said.

I think Holly believed that, too.

Like I said earlier, after the talking was done, we went up to our room at the Hyatt.

• • • • •

Chri moved out of the house in February, but she still had a key to the place. One day she came over when I wasn't there, went through a bunch of things and found a bunch of girls' phone numbers that I had collected. These were all women I had dated before and during our marriage, so she was furious. She started calling the numbers one-by-one just so she could curse out the women who had been sleeping with her husband. One of the phone numbers she had was Holly's. She left some nasty messages for Holly, and I think Holly started to feel sorry for Chri.

Apparently, Holly called Chri back and said, "I didn't know you and Vance were married. Vance and I were just friends, and I never would have even gone to lunch with him if I had known he was married. He was lying to me, just like he was lying to you."

I don't know exactly how it happened, but the two of them decided to set me up to see if they could get the truth out of me. Holly called my house and we started talking about going to Las Vegas together. I told her that I was thinking about her all the time, and I was sexually excited by her, but Holly had called me on three-way, and Chri was listening on the other line. She heard everything I said. She started yelling and calling me a cheating bastard.

I was really pissed off at Holly for setting me up like that, but it was my own fault. I tried to turn it around and make it Holly's fault, but even then I knew I was the one who was wrong.

It was a crazy situation for me, because I was devastated by Chri leaving me. I knew Chri was a good person, and I knew that I had caused most of the problems in our relationship. I was miserable. I needed professional help. I needed a friend. And I desperately wanted Chri back. I wanted her back because I felt like a failure. Marriage is supposed to be forever, and there I was getting another divorce. My self-esteem was in the gutter. I thought I was the most horrible person on the planet. I had ruined another relationship.

I was also afraid of a divorce with Chri for financial reasons. I was living a crazy life and every time I turned around a woman was suing me for ungodly amounts of money. I had lost a lot of money in the divorce with Angela, and I was afraid that I would lose everything again to Chri.

While I was wrestling with this, I think Holly really felt sorry for Chri because of everything Chri had gone through with me. So Holly invited Chri to go out with her and some of her friends. This was probably in April 1991. While they were out that night, they started talking about me. Chri was still in love with me. I guess Holly really was my friend, because she told Chri to give me another chance.

Chri said she would give me one more chance, but she wanted to see me right away. It was about 11 p.m. when Holly agreed to drive Chri to my house.

Meanwhile, I was in my bedroom messing around with the girl named Michelle. When I saw car lights shining in my driveway, I looked out and saw two girls sitting in a car. At the time, my attitude was, "cool. I've got two more girls coming. But what am I going to do with the girl I've got now." That's how warped my mind was. I was always trying to squeeze one more girl into my life. I never thought about the consequences. I just did what I wanted to do.

I told Michelle to hide in my closet, then I ran downstairs.

Chri was at the door, crying, saying that she wanted to talk to me. Holly was standing a few feet behind her with an apologetic look on her face. She said, "Sorry Vance. Chri wanted to come see you."

Then Michelle made a noise upstairs. I got really scared. I was really feeling terrible about everything I had done to Chri, and I really wanted her back. I didn't want to be a failure again. I wanted to try to fix our marriage. I knew I had to change. I thought, "If she hears Michelle banging around upstairs, then I'm fucked. She'll never come back to me."

But Chri was crying so hard that she apparently didn't hear the noise. Holly heard it, though. She said, "Excuse me for a minute" and then walked upstairs. She found Michelle in the closet and said, "You better fucking shut up because his wife is downstairs, and they're not divorced, yet. If she hears you she's going to come upstairs and kick your ass!"

Holly came back downstairs and acted like nothing was wrong. Right then I knew Holly was my true friend. I knew she just wanted things to work out between Chri and I.

But the next day, I forgot those happy thoughts. At the time, my mental attitude ricocheted back and forth between knowing that I had a problem to thinking that everyone else had a problem. Even though I was messing around with another girl in our house when Chri and Holly stopped by, I blamed Holly for the problem.

"Why the fuck did you bring her to my house," I said.

"Because she's your wife, you jerk," Holly said. "She and I started talking and I told her I was just your friend. She asked me to take her to your house, so I did. I didn't know you were going to have a fucking girl hiding upstairs."

But, you know what, that wasn't even the real reason I was pissed. I wasn't just mad at Holly, I was mad at Chri, too. During our conversation the day after that late-night meeting, I asked Holly if Chri had danced with anyone when they were out together.

"Yeah, she danced with a couple of my friends," Holly said.

I was really pissed off and I started screaming and yelling on the phone. I was so hypocritical. Even though I had another girl in my bed that night, I was pissed at Chri for dancing with a couple of Holly's friends.

"It was no big deal, Vance," Holly said. "She just danced with them."

But I would not be mollified. I was really mad at Holly, and she was really mad at me. We didn't talk to each other for several months after that.

Then in May of 1991, I was playing in a celebrity basketball game at a Denver high school, and Holly was there with some of her friends. I think her friends knew someone who was playing on the other team. I was afraid to look at Holly, because I was so angry at her. But I knew that I really loved her.

It was a weird situation, because we'd been friends for so long, but had never really gotten together, but I knew that we both liked each other.

Later that night, I drove my Corvette over to pick up a girl I was dating. We went to a nightclub out in West Denver. I was supposed to meet Mark there, but he never showed up.

I looked across the club and saw Holly again. I decided that I had to stop all of this bullshit. Holly was the woman I really loved. I'd been in love with her since the first day that I met her.

I said to myself, "I'm just going to walk over there, be confident, and tell her how I feel about her."

I excused myself from the girl I was with and walked over to Holly. She was standing there with a smirk on her face watching me approach her.

"Holly, I'm here with someone right now, but I just wanted to tell you that I love you," I said.

She just looked at me, and then started to walk away from me. But she turned back to me and said, "I love you, too. I always have loved you."

I let out a big breath. It was a relief to get that off my chest. I wanted her to know how I felt about her, and I was glad to hear that she cared for me too. I figured nothing else would happen. Here it was 1991 and we'd first met in 1985. During all that time, a relationship had never developed between us, so I figured, "why would that change now?"

Holly closed the little distance that was between us until we were standing almost toe-to-toe. "I would love to spend the rest of my life with you, Vance," she said. "But I don't know if you're going to change."

"I want to change," I said. "I know my life is crazy. I wanted to change for Chri but, I couldn't change for Chri, and I can't change for you or for anyone else. I have to change for me. And now, I want to change for myself. I really want to change."

"Well, if you're going to change, the first thing you need to figure out is what you're going to do with the girl you brought here tonight," she said.

I thought about that for a minute before saying, "I guess she could take a cab home, but her coat is in my car."

"Give me your keys," Holly said.

She went out to my car and got the girl's coat.

Holly delivered the coat to the girl and said, "I think you need to find another ride home." and that was that.

Holly and I have been together every day since then. Even though Chri and I had not yet completed our divorce, I guess Holly was willing to see me because she loved me and she knew my divorce would be completed soon.

I fell completely and absolutely in love with Holly after that.

We were married October 11, 1991.

Our wedding was really beautiful. We held it at our house in Ken Caryl Valley, and Holly planned the whole thing. She did a great job of making a fairly inexpensive wedding look like it cost about $100,000.

About 175 people attended the ceremony, and everyone sat in chairs that had been set up in the front room of the house. I didn't invite any of my teammates — not even Mark Jackson — and at the time I felt bad about that. But I didn't want them to come because I wasn't really close to any of them. Plus, I was trying to change my life, and they represented the life that I wanted to leave behind. I felt like I was already a better person — even though I had a long way to go.

So most of the guests were Holly's friends. That was really cool, because I had a chance to meet a lot of nice families who were going to be part of my new life. I was becoming a family man for real. My nightclubbing days were over, and I needed to start associating with the right kinds of people. I needed to be around people who could teach me what it meant to be a good husband.

Although I was Holly's first husband, and she was my third wife, ours was a first wedding ceremony for both of us. Angela and I had gotten married at a hall in Las Vegas, and Chri and I had exchanged vows in a judges house when we were drunk.

So I had my first — and absolute last — wedding ceremony with Holly.

The ceremony was about 20 minutes, but the reception lasted for about seven or eight hours. It was all really nice and really special. I felt like the ceremony signaled more than just my marriage to Holly. It signified my marriage to a new way of life. During that ceremony, I committed myself to being a good husband and a good father and a good person.

I committed myself to being married to Holly forever.

Holly Speaks
Vance's Third Wife Tells Why She Would Take A Chance With A Guy Like Him

I've been trying to think of a way to explain my feelings for Vance, but it's really hard to put it into words. Love is a feeling. It's not something that can always be analyzed and broken down into neat little components for scientists to examine. Love is a feeling that starts deep inside of you, and usually its roots have spread throughout your body before the words, "I love you" ever blossom from your lips.

There have been other times in my life when I thought I was in love, but they all turned out to be something far less than "true love." What I feel for Vance is completely different from anything I have ever felt before. In the past, I think I fell in love with certain aspects of my boyfriends, such as the way they talked or the way they laughed or the way they carried themselves. There were always certain "things" about my boyfriends that I loved. But I never fell in love with an "entire person," until I met Vance.

With Vance, I didn't fall in love with all of the little things that he did. Instead I fell in love with his unique combination of sensitivity, charisma, vulnerability, courage, shyness and outgoingness. I didn't fall in love with a collection of "actions" or with the way that he combed his hair. I fell in love with Vance "the person." I fell in love with all of the characteristics that make Vance the man that he is. We all do different things from day to day, but the fundamental person deep inside of us never changes. I love the person who is deep inside of Vance, so I know that no *matter what Vance might do on any given day, I will always love him. I've never felt that way with anyone before.*

I'm sure that people who have only read the newspaper or seen television reports about Vance might wonder how I could fall in love with someone who has had so many problems in his past. But the Vance in the media is not the real Vance. That's just a caricature of Vance. Honestly, if I only knew Vance through the newspapers, I probably wouldn't like him, either, but I know Vance the Real Person. I know Vance Edward Johnson, and that person is beautiful both inside and out.

I know the Vance who cares about other people. I know the Vance who is not concerned with impressing other people. I know the Vance who loves children and who loves animals. I know the Vance who wouldn't kill an insect in the kitchen because it's a living creature. I know the Vance who will cry when he is feeling sad. I know the Vance who can be completely honest with his feelings.

I know the Vance who loves me.

The real Vance is a very loveable man. I love him dearly.

• • • • •

When I met Vance in 1985, he was a rookie with the Broncos, and you could see the sensitive side of him if you looked closely. But as his years with the Broncos multiplied, the character "The Vance" became bigger and bigger. It was all you ever heard about in the media, and it was all you ever saw if you watched Vance darting all over the city living the fast life. The character, "The Vance," really started to take over every aspect of Vance's life.

He eventually reached the point where it appeared that "The Vance" had killed the real Vance. But as Vance and and I got to know each other better, I could see that his sensitive side was still inside. As our relationship developed, that side of Vance peeked out more and more all the time, and that was the part of him that I fell in love with. That was the part of Vance that hooked into my heart and kept me waiting in the wings of Vance's life for the six years between the day we first met and the day we got married.

• • • • •

Before I get into my relationship with Vance, I think I should take a little bit of time to explain who I am and where I am from. My life didn't begin with Vance, and the many things that happened to me created the backdrop against which I viewed Vance. When he and I finally did get married we had a lot of his past problems to overcome, but we had a fair share of my problems to deal with as well.

So here's an abbreviated account of my life.

I grew up in Denver, and I had a very large patchwork family. My mother and father had me about two years after they were married. Then when I was 2 years old, they adopted a set of 2-month-old twin boys named Heath and Troy.

   When I was 4 years old my parents divorced. But within a couple of years both of them had remarried. My mother married a man named Gordon, who had three girls and a boy from a previous marriage. My father married a woman named Rosemary, who had two boys and two girls from a previous marriage.

   Suddenly, I had eight new step-siblings, and I loved it. I had a great time getting to know all of the other kids. We all got along really well.

   But the divorce was really tough on me. I was just a little kid, and I didn't understand why my parents didn't want to stay together. I had always been a daddy's girl. I really loved my father, and I loved spending time with him. So it was hard for me to get used to a life in which I didn't have daily contact with him.

   After the divorce, my parents still lived fairly close to each other, so my twin brothers and I would often go visit my father.

   When my mother married Gordon, the twins were still young enough to make the adjustment pretty quickly. They started to bond with Gordon, and they started to think of him as their new father. Gordon eventually adopted both of them. But I was nearly 6 years old when my mother married Gordon, and I was still very attached to my father. I completely rejected the idea of being adopted by Gordon. I wasn't going to let anyone to take the place of my father.

   In the meantime, my mother was going crazy. She got married the first time at age 21, had me when she was 23 and got divorced at 27. Now I realize that she was still a young woman. But back then, I expected my mother to act like the mom from the Brady Bunch, and I was really upset because she wasn't doing that.

   I think my mother was a virgin when she got married, and before then she had led a fairly sheltered life. So after the divorce, she felt newfound freedom, and she wanted to see the world. She wanted to experience new things, and I didn't understand that. She even joined a motorcycle gang and really partied hard for a while. Even after she married Gordon, she continued to be sort of wild and crazy.

   From day one, I blamed my mom for the divorce from my dad, because it upset me that she was having such a great time when she should have been trying to fix her marriage with my dad. Now that I'm an adult, I understand what my mother must have been going through. But as a child, I just had rigid standards for what a mother was supposed to be, and I don't think my standards allowed for her to simply be human. She had to be Super Mom in my eyes.

   But she was struggling with a lot of things. She had been married and divorced at a young age, and then a couple years after she and Gordon married, they divorced, too. So suddenly she was raising three kids — me and the twins — by herself, and it was tough. I realize that now, but at the time, all I saw was a mother who wasn't behaving exactly the way that I thought she should, and it made me very angry.

   Meanwhile, my father was a really accomplished man who had gone to college and who was fairly wealthy. He was a real estate agent and he owned a restaurant and some horse stables. He was a self-made man, and I was really proud of him. He was also taking flying lessons because he wanted to be a pilot.

He had been in pilot school for a long time, and I had just turned 10 when he took his first solo flight. Unfortunately, his first flight by himself ended up being his last flight. They still don't know exactly what happened, but shortly after he took off, his plane just plunged straight down into the ground. It burst into flames and he died.

The day that it happened my mother picked me up from school and drove me up to Red Rocks Park which was not too far from our house, and pretty near my father's house (he lived in Morrison, Colo.). All I talked about in the car on the way up there was how excited I was to see my father that weekend. When we got to Red Rocks my mom told me that he died in a plane crash. Even though I was little kid, I knew what it meant to be dead. I didn't need my mom to explain it to me. As soon as the word "dead" came out of her mouth, I burst into tears and buried my head in her lap. I couldn't believe that my father was gone.

I think my mother took me up to Red Rocks park just so I could be in a peaceful place when I learned of my father's death. We hadn't planned to go there. But now that park is a very special place to me, and I don't think of it as the place where I learned of my father's death. I just have fond memories of my dad whenever I hear someone talk about the park. He used to live right in that area, so the association is really strong for me.

I was really close to my father, and I wanted to be with him. During the days after his death, I was trying to figure out how I could be in heaven with him. I decided that when I grew up, I'd get my pilot's license. Then I'd crash my plane in the same place he died, so I could be with him.

I was a sad little kid.

With my father dead, I blamed my mother even more for the divorce. I thought that if she had tried harder, the marriage would have worked, my father never would have left, he never would have taken flying lessons and he wouldn't have died. It was little kid's logic, but it made sense to me at the time.

My mother and I fought constantly, because I just didn't think she was being the type of mother she should be. And every day, things got worse.

Although my father was very successful in business, there was nothing left to me after his death. In the final accounting, his estate totaled exactly zero. Nothing more, nothing less. So after his death my mother received $800 a month in social security benefits because I was a minor. I assume that every kid, who loses a father, receives social security payments.

But that only caused something else for my mother and me to argue about. I got my first job when I was 12 years old. I delivered newspapers every morning, and I had to use the money from my paper route to buy my own clothes and sometimes to buy food because there was none in the house.

My mother had a job too, so I couldn't understand what was happening with that money. It made me really mad that I had to pay for things out of my own money, when my friends' parents were providing those things for their kids. I wanted my mom to do the same. But I was a kid, and I didn't understand that my mother was a *single parent supporting three children. I didn't understand that she was trying to pay a house note, a car payment, utility bills, grocery bills, PLUS she had to clothe all of us and provide toys, school supplies and whatever else we needed. I didn't understand that she depended on that $800 social security check just to provide our basic needs. I was just 12 years old, and I was sad about my father dying, and I needed someone to blame. My mother became that person, and I blamed her for everything. I fought with her almost every day about that $800-a-month social security check.*

Things really came to a head between my mother and me when I was 14.

About a week or two before my dad died, he picked me up in his arms and carried me into the house. While he was carrying me, he said, "Oh, you're getting so big, but even when you're 14, I'll still be able to carry you."

It was just something he said that was really no big deal at the time, but when he died the next week, it became just about the last thing he ever said to me. It stuck in my mind. Every day and every night I would hear him saying that he was going to carry me in his arms when I was 14. It was a very vivid memory.

So when I turned 14, I had all of this longing and disappointment built up in me. My father was supposed to be there to carry me, and he wasn't because he died in a plane crash. I thought that if my parents hadn't divorced, he wouldn't have died. And in my mind, everything was my mother's fault.

When I turned 14, my arguments with my mother started to become physical.

We wouldn't have knock-down, drag-out brawls, but when she tried to spank me, I would fight back. If she tried to pull me upstairs to talk to me, or make me go to my room, I would fight back.

I had so much pain inside of me, and I was taking everything out on my mother. It was really a tough time for both of us.

• • • • •

After that first paper route, I always had a job. When I was 15, I lied about my age so that I could work at a restaurant in Arvada called Tokyo Bowl. From there, I got a job doing phone soliciting for First American Solar. Then I was hired as a sales clerk at the Merry-Go-Round store. After that, I assisted handicapped and mentally retarded children for Jefferson County Transportation. Then I worked as a workman's comp claims adjuster with Aetna.

I've always had a job, and I think the biggest skill that my mother helped develop in me and the other kids is the ability to be self-sufficient. She always made us work hard for the things that we wanted. Although I didn't really appreciate that when I was growing up, I now realize how valuable that work ethic is. Despite our differences, my mother and I still had our occasional good days. When I wanted to buy a car when I was 16, my mother agreed to give me double whatever amount of money I could save up. So between babysitting and phone soliciting for First

American Solar, I was able to save about $500. My mother gave me $1,000 and I went out and bought a 1965 Baja Bug for $1,200. It was all fixed up. I loved that car. I was really proud of it. And it had been so hard to save up the money to buy it that I really cherished it.

Then my mom and I started arguing again. I was a senior in high school working part time at Merry-Go-Round, and I finally decided that I was moving out of my mother's house. I was 17 at the time, and Mom and I were fighting constantly. We got into a big argument — I can't even remember what we were fighting about — but I said, "Fine. I'm leaving."

A girl named Heather was an assistant manager at Merry-Go-Round, and I knew that she lived by herself. She was a pretty amazing person. She had gone to school in Europe — where her father lived — and had graduated from high school when she was 14 or 15. She had moved to Colorado to stay with friends of her parents — her mother lived in Seattle. At 16, she was the assistant manager at Merry-Go-Round, living in her own apartment, and she was totally self-sufficient. She had once mentioned that she was looking for a roommate, so I went into the store and said, "Do you want a roommate, because I'm moving out."

She said, "sure," and helped me move all of my stuff out of my mother's house. It was that simple. We really didn't even know each other that well. But fortunately, we got along well as roommates.

About a month or two before I decided to move out, my Bug broke down. There was a problem with the shifting, and it would always pop out of gear. One day the shifter just quit working altogether. It was going to cost a lot of money to get it fixed, so we just left it sitting in front of the house. While my car was broken, I drove my mother's Ford Futura to work and to school. She drove her pickup truck.

When I left my mom's house, she wouldn't let me take the Ford with me. I guess she could have if she wanted to, but I think she was trying to dissuade me from moving out of her house. She wanted to make life on my own hard on me, so that I wouldn't leave. But I was determined to leave, so I said, "Fine. Keep the car," and packed up all my stuff. My mother lived at about 104th Avenue and Wadsworth in Arvada. I moved into Heather's apartment at 64th and Wadsworth, and my school was between the two places at about 84th and Wadsworth. Those first few weeks out of the house were tough, but between Heather and my other friends, I was always able to find a ride to and from school and work.

My mother and I didn't speak very often that first month, and when we did talk, we'd get into an argument. She was worried about me and she wanted me to move back home. I was a very angry person, and I simply refused to go back to the house. I just concentrated on working, going to school and trying to survive. About a month after I moved out, my mother called and said that she was going to turn the social security checks over to me. She also offered to sell me the Ford for $500. I agreed, gratefully, and paid for the car by giving her $100 a month from the social security checks.

My mom really wanted me to move back home, but when she realized that I was determined to make in on my own, she gave me the social security because she knew that I really needed the money. At age 17, I thought everything was great, because I felt that the bulk of that money was rightfully mine anyway. Years later, I began to realize how tough it must have been for my mother to surrender that money to me. She had been living with that $800 a month for seven years and to suddenly cut it out of her budget must have been a real sacrifice. She did it because she loved me, but I really didn't appreciate the significance of the sacrifice at the time.

I was 17 years old making some money at Merry-Go-Round and getting $800 a month from social security. I was paying my bills and everything was going great.

During the years after my father's death, I had basically lost contact with all of the kids from my dad's new family. So the people I considered my real siblings were the twins, and Gordon's four children from his previous marriage. Two of Gordon's kids were older than me and neither of them had graduated from high school. So when I moved out of my mom's house, I felt this huge pressure on me to graduate. No one ever said anything to me, but I felt like everyone was watching to see whether I was going to be a failure. Would I have the discipline to continue going to school everyday? I was determined to graduate, and I knew that I could make it if I worked at it. I think my best friend, Ronda, really understood how tough it was for me to be living on my own, because she was always telling me that I had to hang in there and get through school. She told me that a lot of people expected me to just drop out of school, but I couldn't fall into that trap. I had to be strong and disciplined and motivated. Ronda really helped me a lot during that time.

Since I was living on my own, I was able to emancipate myself at school, which meant that I could write my own excuses if I was ever sick or wanted to miss school for any reason. You would think that a kid who had that kind of power would skip class all the time. But the fact that I had that kind of control just made me more responsible. I didn't party or anything. I was determined to succeed at being a young person who was living on her own. I think that's another of the skills my mother passed on to me.

As soon as I turned 18, in December 1985, the social security checks stopped coming, but by then I was making enough money at Merry-Go-Round to pay my bills.

I graduated from Pomona High School in June 1986, and I was really proud of my accomplishment.

· · · · ·

The first time I ever saw Vance was during the summer of 1985 when he came into Merry-Go-Round to do some shopping. He was by himself, and I just noticed that I thought he was cute. I didn't know who he was, because I didn't really pay attention to football.

The second time he came in, it looked like he was by himself again. I still didn't know he was a Denver Bronco. Vance was just another guy to me. But, there was something different about him. He just stood there just giving me googly eyes from afar. Vance is very charismatic, and he has this way of looking at you that just makes you feel weird inside. It makes you want to go hide. It makes you walk stupid. Sometimes it seems like he is looking right through you, or like he can just look at you and read your mind. He didn't talk to me at all that day. Back then, he was a much different person than the one he became in later years. Later in his career, he had a big ego, and a lot of conceit, but back then, he was confident, but he kept to himself. He seemed really quiet, but I guess "proud" is the right word. You could look at him and tell that he felt good about himself, but not in a cocky way.

I remember thinking, "He's kind of cute."

Suddenly this girl came bouncing out of the dressing room literally leaping from rack to rack grabbing different clothes to try on. I said to myself, "Oh, he's with her," and I blew it off. I really didn't think much about it.

He ended up coming into the store again on another day but I wasn't working. He went up to Heather and asked her for my phone number. Heather gave it to him.

When Heather came home she was all excited, telling me that she had given my number to Vance Johnson from the Denver Broncos. I was mad at her because I didn't want her to be giving my phone number to strange men. She really thought she had done me a favor, but I wasn't happy about it.

A couple of weeks later, Vance called me and said, "Hi, this is Vance Johnson. I'm cruising down 285 in my Porsche. I'm talking on my car phone. I'm on my way over to pick you up so we can go out tonight."

I was excited that he'd called, but I had friends over so I said, "Well, I've got like nine girls here and we're all going to go out, so I can't."

"Tell them you're going out with Vance Johnson, they'll understand," he said. I sat there for a second thinking "what a cocky jerk." I couldn't believe how arrogant he was.

"No," I said. "I'm going out with my friends. You can call me again if you want," but he never called back. It was probably a year before we ran into each other again.

The main reason I didn't want to go out with him was that I thought he was engaged. Angela had come into Merry-Go-Round and was showing off the ring that Vance bought her. She said, "We're engaged."

The weird thing is that even back then, when I barely knew Vance, I remember thinking, "I don't want him to get married." I don't even know why I would think that, because I really didn't know him that well. I just knew that I was interested in him.

After that, we bumped into each other every five or six months at different clubs in Denver. He would always ask me to go out with him, and I would always say "no." That's how we became friends. I knew he was going to ask me out, and he knew what my answer was going to be, so whenever we saw each other, we'd just start laughing immediately.

I really began to have strong feelings for Vance because I could see the person that he really was. Through the media, all I ever saw was Vance being wild and crazy, but when I saw him in person, I could see that he was a very sensitive man. I could see there was a nice guy hiding behind that circus he was always performing.

We were in Club LA — sometime during late 1988 I think — when he first told me that he had filed for divorce from Angela. I didn't believe him at first. But he swore up and down that he had done it. Again, he asked me to go out with him. Again, despite my interest in him, I said, "no."

Then he said, "Well, just go out with me on New Year's Eve. I'm going to be here at Club L.A. that night, so why don't you meet me here.

I said, "I might."

I really wanted to meet him there. If he was truly getting divorced from Angela, then I was interested in dating him. I really like Vance a lot, but I was sort of afraid of him, too. He just seemed too wild at times. Although I have a tough exterior, I'm really soft on the inside. I was worried that he would hurt my heart if I dated him.

I had two prospects on New Year's Eve. I could go meet Vance at Club L.A., or I could go to a party being hosted by a guy named Mike. I had just met Mike a few weeks earlier, and he had invited me to his New Year's Eve bash. I told Mike I might show up.

I wasn't sure what I should do.

I decided that I would drive to the club, and if I saw Vance's car in the parking lot, then I would go inside. If I didn't see it, I would go to Mike's party.

I drove through the parking lot at Club L.A., but I didn't see his car, so I went to Mike's and had a great time. I ended up dating Mike for the next two years.

Vance later told me he was at the club that night, but somehow we missed each other. That was just one of the times when Vance and I almost ended up together, but things didn't work out.

● ● ● ● ●

When Vance was married to Angela, I would never go out with him, because I don't believe in that sort of thing. It seemed morally wrong to me to even go to lunch with him if he was married to someone else. But when I learned that he was seriously getting divorced, I thought I should do something to let him know that I was interested in him.

After work one day at Aetna, I went to a nearby flower shop and a liquor store and got a bottle of wine and a bouquet of roses. I was never the type of person who gave gifts to guys, so I was a little nervous about taking this stuff over to his house. But Vance and I had been playing cat-and-mouse for so long that I wanted to let him know that I was ready to be caught if he was interested. I figured I'd better make the first move, to say "Hey, it's okay to ask me out now."

But I was still apprehensive about the whole thing. It was about 5:30 p.m. when

I got to his house, so I thought he would be back from court by then. But he wasn't. Chri answered the door.

"Hi, is Vance here?" I said.

"No, he's not," she said. "Who are you?"

"I'm Holly," I said. "Who are you?"

"I'm his wife," Chri said.

My heart dropped. But right away I knew Chri had to be lying because I knew Vance was in court with his wife at that very moment. Inside I was thinking, "No, you're not his wife," but I didn't say anything. I knew she must be something to him, so I just said, "Okay," and I left.

At that point, I was very naive, and if she had said anything besides, "I'm his wife," then I probably wouldn't have had my feelings hurt so badly. I thought Vance and I we were both interested in developing a relationship, and I was prepared to believe anything. I was in love with him, and I wanted to believe a lot of things. If Chri had said, "I'm his neighbor," or "I'm his sister," or "I'm his fairy godmother," or anything besides "I'm his wife," I probably would have just believed her, and said "Oh, okay. Well, please tell Vance I stopped by." I would have wanted to believe her. But she said, "I'm his wife," and that hurt me. I knew that for her to say that, they must be in some type of relationship. At the very least, they had to be dating.

After that I was really mad at Vance for lying to me. I didn't want to talk to him. I wouldn't take his calls when my roommate said he was on the phone. I didn't want to have anything to do with him. I just wanted to forget about him.

Finally, I talked to him on the phone and he said Chri was an old girlfriend of his who sometimes came over to clean up his townhouse. I believed that she might be his old girlfriend, but I didn't believe she was just there to clean his house, but he said they definitely weren't married. I believed that because I knew he couldn't have gotten married again so soon after divorcing Angela. But I still didn't want to date him.

• • • • •

When the "Men Who Beat Women" article came out, I couldn't believe it.

I was dating Mike at the time, and he and his family knew that I was a casual friend of Vance's. Mike would often jokingly give me a hard time whenever the Broncos' games came on television.

"There's Vaaaaance," he'd say with a smile. I'd just laugh and maybe give him a friendly punch in the arm. But inside, I really did have strong feelings for Vance that I never admitted to anyone.

I was sitting at the kitchen table at Mike's house when his mother brought in the Rocky Mountain News *and said, "Can you believe this article about Vance?"*

I started reading it and my heart just broke. My eyes were watering up and I felt like I was going to cry, but I knew that I couldn't cry in front of Mike's mother. She had no idea what my feelings were for Vance, and if I had started crying, I probably would have shocked her.

I knew that Vance was a really sensitive person and that an article like that would just destroy him inside. I felt really sad for him, but I was oddly non-judgmental about all of the abusive things that were said in the story. I had never seen any violent sides in him. But, of course, I'd never had the opportunity to see the violent side of him because I had never been in an intimate relationship with him.

But I had been in an abusive relationship before.

During my senior year in high school, I dated a guy — whom I will call David — for about a year. He asked me to marry him. When he popped the question, I said, "I'm not sure," and he broke down in tears and started bawling. I tried to console him, but nothing worked. He just kept crying and acting crazy, so I eventually said "Yes, I'll marry you," just to stop him from crying. I figured I could get out of the engagement later.

He stopped crying and got really happy. But soon after that day, he became a very violent person. He had never hit me while we were just dating, but after we got engaged, he became abusive. He was very possessive, and he was very mean.

The first time he was ever abusive, we were driving in his car, and he started yelling and screaming at me. He reached over to me in the passenger seat and started yanking me around. While he was pushing and pulling, he ripped my sweater off of me. It was a really expensive cashmere sweater that a friend had loaned to me, and he just tore one side of it completely down. It was hanging from one shoulder. Then he pulled over to the side of the road, and pushed me out of the car. I didn't have my shoes on, but I took off running across this big field. There were stickers and rocks in the ground that were digging into my feet, but I didn't care. I was desperate to get away from David. I felt like I was running for my life. It was horrible.

When he finally caught up to me in the field he threatened to punch me, but he didn't actually do it. Things eventually calmed down and he carried me back to the car, because my feet were killing me. Somehow he convinced me to stay in the relationship with him after that.

No. I take that back. Somehow I convinced myself to stay in the relationship. I've learned that no one ever convinces anyone of anything. We're all in control of our own decisions, and for some reason, I wanted to stay with David at the time.

The second time he was abusive, he pushed me around in the apartment I was sharing with Heather. He shoved me into a wall, and he kicked me. It got kind of crazy.

David was getting ready to move into a townhouse, but it wasn't going to be ready for another couple of weeks, so he and his two suitcases moved into the apartment with Heather and me.

The third time that he was abusive with me, we were home alone when he dragged me into my bedroom, pushed a desk in front of the door to keep me trapped, and he started punching me with his fists. At one point, David pinned me on my back on the bed and had my arms trapped under his knees. He had one hand on the top of my chest, and the other was cocked in a fist about six inches from my face. He said "I'm going to punch you, so you'd better close your eyes."

I was crying and begging him to stop, and he said, "One. . . two. . . three," and punched the bed about two or three inches from the side of my head. It scared me to death.

At the end of that fight, I had a bloody lip and a black eye. Heather had come home in the middle of everything, but she couldn't get into the room because the desk was blocking the door from the inside. I still don't completely understand why she didn't call the police, but I think she sort of went into shock hearing me crying and screaming in my room.

After it was all over and David left, I found Heather in her room sitting against the window crying. She had completely flipped out.

But after she calmed down, she helped me into the kitchen and got me cleaned up. I went to school the next day. At this point — if no one had ever found out — I think I may have become a chronically battered woman. I started lying to people about how I got the black eye and the busted lip. I lied to my friends and my teachers. And I planned to keep on lying. It was embarrassing to admit that my fiance had beaten me up, so I didn't tell anyone.

But one of my friends — probably Ronda or Heather — made an anonymous tip to our school counselors saying that my fiance had beaten me up.
The counselors called me in and got the true story out of me. Then they called my mother. My mom was really pissed off, which helped me a lot. I wanted to break up with David, but I was afraid. But with my mother and all of my friends standing behind me, it was really easy to take control of the situation. I broke off all contact with David.

But if it hadn't been for my friend — whomever it was — going to the counselors, I probably would have taken David back. I may have ended up married to him and being abused by him for a lifetime.

I know that it was very naive of me, but after David, I always thought that I could detect a violent man because I had been with one. I was young at the time, and it didn't occur to me that not all violent men are the same.

But that's the backdrop against which I viewed Vance. He was nothing like David, so it was hard for me to see him being violent.

So when I read the "Men Who Beat Women" article I was astonished. I probably read it 10 times, and it hurt me a little more every time. I found myself defending Vance. I was reading and thinking, "that can't be true." But I never judged him and thought that he was a bad person. And I didn't judge the women in the article either, because I wasn't there when all of those things were happening, so I didn't know what was real and what wasn't.

A couple of weeks after the article came out, I got a message on my answering machine from a private investigator who said he wanted to meet me to do a personality profile on Vance. I told my mother about the message, and she was really protective of me. She said she wanted to be there when this guy interviewed me, because he could be some psycho or something.

I called the detective and set a date. When he showed up, we all sat down together, and he started asking me questions about Vance. He wanted to know what my relationship was with Vance, and whether Vance had ever been abusive to me. I said that he had never hurt me in any way, but that Vance and I really didn't have an intimate relationship.

"Listen, Vance is in Hawaii right now having a vacation with his fiancee, so you don't have to hold anything back," the detective said.

Hearing that was like getting punched in the stomach. I didn't know Vance had a fiancee. He had just divorced Angela, how could he have a fiancee so fast? I think the detective was trying to hurt my feelings so I would say something bad about Vance, but there was really nothing for me to say. I wasn't in a real relationship with Vance. I had never seen his violent side.

I said, "No, Vance never did anything to me. He was a friend. I think I fell in love with him. I don't know how. He never did anything to me, but we weren't in that type of relationship. If he's really that type of person, I'm not the one to talk to in the first place, because I'm just his friend. People don't usually go around hitting their friends. You have to be in an intimate relationship, and we aren't."

But this detective kept stressing the point that Vance was with another woman at that moment, trying to get me to say something bad about him. He kept hammering it home and throwing it in my face. It really hurt me inside to keep hearing it over and over again, but there was simply nothing bad I could say about Vance, even if I wanted to.

I didn't find out until the end of the interview, but apparently Vance had hired this guy to do some research that would be used in some way to counter the charges that were made in the "Men Who Beat Women" article. Vance had provided a list of the women in his life, and this detective was going around trying to get people to say whether or not Vance had ever been abusive to them.

It was a long drawn-out interview. After he finally left, I broke down in tears and cried on my mother's shoulder. That was the first time that she realized how much I really cared about Vance. I didn't know whom Vance was in Hawaii with, but I assumed that it was the girl who was at the door when I went to his house with wine and roses.

During the next week or two, I kept expecting Vance to call. I was sure he was going to call to say he was getting married. We were friends, and I assumed he would be happy about being engaged and would want to share the news, or I thought he might call to find out what I had said to the detective.

But he never did call. I didn't hear from him for months after that.

When we finally did talk, I said, "I know you're married because you were in Hawaii with your fiancee."

"She wasn't really my fiancee," he said. "Yes, we went to Hawaii. Yes, she had a ring that she was wearing on her ring finger, but we weren't engaged. But, we did end up getting married one night up in Fort Collins when we were both really drunk. But when we sobered up, we got it annulled."

I believed him, and we started talking on the phone more often and occasionally going out and spending time together. We never slept together, because I wasn't ready for that yet. But we were seeing each other.

A few months later, I came home one day and there was an outrageous message on my answering machine. It said, "This message is for Holly. You are a fucking whore and a slut and a bitch and you need to get your own man and stay away from my husband!" It was Chri. The message went on like that for about a minute. I couldn't believe it. It was the most amazing phone message I had ever heard in my life. She just ranted and raved and screamed the entire time.

Then Vance called me, and I told him about the message I'd received from Chri.

"I don't believe it," he said. "Chri is a really sweet girl. She would never do that."

"Well, she did it," I said. He didn't believe me. "Is she your wife or isn't she, Vance?"

He explained again that they were married for a very short time, but they got their marriage annulled. I wanted to believe him, so I did. Plus, a short time before I received that phone message, Vance had invited me to his house and had cooked dinner for me. While I was there, I noticed that there were no women's clothing laying around, and no signs that a woman lived in his house. So when he told me that they had annulled their marriage, it seemed believable to me.

A couple of days after the first nasty message, I received another one just like it. I called Vance but he wasn't home, so I played my answering machine tape onto his answering machine so he could hear all of the things Chri was saying. I guess he listened to the message and then got into a big argument with Chri.

She called my house that night, and she sounded really sweet. Chri said, "Why did you do that? Why did you let him hear my message?"

I said, "Why did you leave a message like that? I should call the police." She hung up. Since I knew they weren't living together, I believed that Vance was telling me the truth about their relationship, so I started seeing him again, but I still wouldn't sleep with him.

He would always say things like, "Let's go check into a motel so we can talk. You have your roommates, and I live too far away. Let's get a motel room, where we can just be alone and watch TV." I would always say "no" because I knew that we wouldn't be watching any TV if we got a motel room.

But one night we went out to dinner and we were hanging out and everything was just wonderful. We were laughing and talking, and Vance was really nice. One of the things I always liked about him was that he was interested in me. Even though he often projected a really cocky image, he was always interested in hearing how my day went. He listened to my stories. He wanted to know about my job and about my family and about how I was feeling. He was very attentive to me, and it was very flattering.

So we were driving around near the Denver Tech Center, and I could tell that something was going to happen that night. I was feeling really close to him emotionally, and I wanted to be closer to him. I was hoping that something would happen that night.

When he asked me if I wanted to drive his Porsche, I thought he was just being nice. I thought he knew that I had never driven a Porsche before, and he wanted to do something nice for me. I said, "sure," and we went flying around town.

He kept telling me where to drive. He said, "Show me where you work," so I drove him to Aetna's building, which happened to be right across the street from the Hyatt. He said, "Show me where you park your car," so I did. To someone reading this, it probably sounds stupid that he wanted to see where I parked my car, but that's just how Vance was. He was always very interested in everything about me. Everyone else in Denver just saw this wild, crazy, bad person, whom they assumed was so self interested he couldn't see past his own nose unless he was looking in a mirror. But, I saw the softer side of Vance. I saw that side of him that cared about other people. I saw the side of him that was very special, and very soft and very innocent. Vance was actually a very shy person who did a lot of crazy things to hide his shyness. I'm sure that Angela and Chri both knew that side of Vance, too.

So we were sitting outside of the Aetna building and Vance pointed over at the Hyatt and said, "Can we go in there and go upstairs?"

I think I shocked him when I said, "Okay."

He went inside to register for the room, and I was sitting in the driver's seat of the car. His car was immaculately clean so there wasn't much to look at. I was just sitting there daydreaming, when I noticed one white envelope in the pocket of the door. I picked it up and glanced at it and put it back down.

After a couple of seconds I said, "What did that say? Chri what?"

I picked it up again, and saw that it said Vance and Chri Johnson. The postdate was definitely after the date that Vance told me the annulment had gone through. I was in shock. I couldn't believe that he was actually married and he had lied to me all that time. But I really wanted to believe that Vance was telling me the truth. I was sitting in the car saying, "Okay, they were married, they got it annulled, but for some reason she kept his name for a little while." I was trying to think up a good reason to explain an envelope that said Vance and Chri Johnson. I really wanted to believe he was telling me the truth.

I just starting crying. When Vance got back into the car, I sped off.

"What's wrong?" he said. Our entire evening had been wonderful, so he really had no idea what I was upset about.

I drove back over to the Aetna parking lot and held out the letter to him. I said, "I thought you weren't married."

"Holly, you already know that we did get married," he said. "Remember, we got married when we were drunk."

He had told me that before, but, I was under the impression that the annulment was already done. If they really did get married then had it annulled immediately, I didn't understand why they would have mail addressed to both of them.

But, Vance half-convinced me that his story was true and I half-convinced myself. Once again, I really wanted to believe him, so I did.

He said they got married, then annulled, but Chri still lived with him for a little while because she didn't have anywhere else to go.

I knew Vance and Chri had been living together in his townhouse before they moved into his new house together, so in my mind even their shared address could be explained. I figured they got married, then decided to get it annulled, but Vance didn't just kick her out on the street. I could understand that, because if I was living with someone, I wouldn't kick them out onto the street, either. I would try to be nice and give them a chance to find a new place to live.

But the biggest factor in the entire thing was that I knew Chri was not living with him at the time. I had been to his house, and I knew a woman was not living there.

So while Vance was talking, I pretty much convinced myself that his story was true. We made up, and picked up right where we left off before I found the envelope. We went into the hotel and made love for the first time.

• • • • •

A few days later, Chri called my house when I wasn't there. My roommate said that Chri sounded really nice and really polite on the phone, and that she would call me back. I decided that if Chri did call back, I would talk to her. I felt sorry for her because of this entire situation, and I felt that she must still be having a lot of pain over the breakup. If she was going to be nice to me, then I thought I should be nice to her.

When Chri called again, she said, "I need to know what's going on between you and Vance."

"Vance and I are good friends," I said.

"Well, what do you think the situation is between me and Vance?" Chri said.

"As I understand it, you guys got married up in Ft. Collins while you were intoxicated, and then when you guys sobered up, you got an annulment. After that, you thought things might work out, but they didn't, and you moved out of the house. Now, you guys aren't married."

"We are married, Holly," Chri said. "Vance calls me every day saying that he wants to get back together."

I said, "Whoa! Tell me your story."

Chri said they got married in July. Yes, they were drunk when it happened, but they did not get an annulment. They lived together for seven months, until Chri moved out.

Chri said, "Are you sleeping with Vance?"

"That's none of your business," I said.

"It is too my business, because I'm his wife!" Chri said.

Vance and I were just starting a relationship, and I was sitting on the phone thinking, "Oh my God! I'm seeing a married man." I was seeing Vance everyday. I didn't understand how this could happen. How could I not know that he was married?

"Vance told me you guys got an annulment," I said again.

"And you believe him?" she said. "How could you be so stupid?"

All of a sudden, I felt really stupid. I believed him because I wanted to believe him.

"Holly, you have to help me," Chri said. "Vance thinks that I'm totally blind to everything that's going on. You've got to help me catch him in one of his lies."

"I don't want to get any more involved in this than I already am," I said. I was ready to just pull out, say goodbye to Vance and forget about this entire thing. I never thought I would be the "other" woman in some man's life, and I didn't want to continue that type of relationship with Vance.

"Please, you have to help me," Chri said. "Please. Just call him on three-way, and I'll listen on the other line. Please. I have to catch him in the act."

I think Chri was a lot like me. There were a lot of situations that came up that made her say, "Vance, what's going on?" But Vance would always have a somewhat believable story to tell her. His lies would have just enough truth in them to knock the sting out of her accusations, even though she knew she was right. Despite Vance's many affairs and despite all of the women's phone numbers that she had found, Vance had never admitted that he had cheated on her. He always had a lie to tell to explain away whatever evidence she came up with.

And apparently, Vance was calling Chri all the time asking her to come back to him. She didn't want to go back, because she knew that Vance was lying to her about a lot of things. But for once, she wanted to have some proof. For once, she wanted to hear the truth from Vance's own mouth.

She begged me to make the three-way call.

Part of me wanted to do this favor for Chri. I had unknowingly been dating her husband, and now that it had been confirmed, I felt terrible about it. I felt that I needed to do something to make it up to her.

Another part of me knew that tricking Vance in that way would really hurt him. He always talked about how women are always hurting him, and I could see that in his life. Everyone took advantage of him every chance they got — mostly for money. When he got divorced from Angela she was awarded some of their joint property plus $3,000 a month child support and $3,000 alimony. All of the other women who got pregnant by him, always got huge child support checks. I never agreed with that, because my mother never did anything like that when I was growing up. I felt like those women were taking advantage of Vance because he had money. I always believed that if a judge ordered him to pay a lot of money in child support, then all of the cash should go to the child. Instead of giving the woman a huge check every month, he should have to pay a reasonable monthly support, and the rest of the money should go into a trust for the child to be used in later years. I think that type of system would have cut down on the number of women who were using pregnancy to take advantage of Vance.

Anyway, I didn't want to make that three-way phone call, because I knew that it would hurt Vance. He had already been hurt enough by people, and I didn't want to be the next one in line. If I made that phone call, Vance would hate me. Plus, I was worried about what might happen to him financially. Vance had once told me that he had gotten the marriage with Chri annulled so that she wouldn't have an opportunity to take him to court to get money. He said if he had divorced her, then she would get a lot of money like Angela did.

So I was worried that my making that phone call might create financial hardship for Vance. I didn't know what to do.

Finally I decided to do it. Chri kept begging me to help her, and I felt a tug of obligation. I also rationalized that if Vance did end up hating me because of this phone call, then it would be that much easier to separate myself from him. I had already decided that the best thing for me to do was just not see Vance anymore.

Also, part of me thought that Chri was lying about everything, and that by making the phone call to Vance, she would be revealed as a phony.

But no matter how much I reasoned it out, I still felt sleazy when I dialed his number. When he answered the phone, I tried to get him to talk about the trip to Las Vegas we were planning to make.

"Are we still going to Vegas," I said.

"Yeah," he said laughing. "We're going to stay at Caesar's. It's really cool. You'll like it. They have these mirrors on the ceilings over the bed."

Then Chri jumped in and started screaming. "Caesar's huh? Isn't that the same place that we stayed!"

They were yelling at each other, and I was just sitting there listening. When Vance started yelling at me, I just hung up.

Vance called me back a couple minutes later and said, "Chri's crazy. Okay. I did lie to you about being married. We were married, but I asked her to move out."

I was too upset to talk to him. I was really mad at him for lying to me. I was mad at him for getting me caught up in all of this stuff. I was mad at myself for being so blind.

Of course, our trip to Vegas was definitely cancelled.

About a week after that three-way phone conversation, Chri called me on a weekend and said, "Have you talked to Vance?"

"No," I said. "And I'm not going to."

"What are you doing right now?" Chri said.

"I'm getting ready to go out with some of my friends," I said.

"Can I go out with you?" Chri said.

"No, I don't think that's a good idea Chri," I said. I was trying to forget about Vance. I wanted to get away from the whole situation, and going out with Chri would just put me right back in the middle of everything. "I just can't get involved in this again."

But Chri persisted. She kept saying "please," and that she needed a friend right now, and that she didn't have anyone to talk to. Finally, I agreed, and she drove over to meet me.

She left her car at my house and rode with me to a bar in Arvada. We were sitting there with a couple of my friends, and I hadn't told my friends that Chri was Vance's wife. I figured that would just be too complicated for everyone, so I just introduced her as my friend Chri.

One of my friends worked at a sports bar downtown called Fat & Mike's, where a lot of the Broncos players hung out. She recognized Chri. She kept looking at Chri saying, "I know you from somewhere, but I can't figure out where. Wait. I know what it is. You look just like Vance Johnson's wife. I mean, you look <u>just</u> like her. Well, I take that back, because I think she's ugly, but you're really pretty."

I was just sitting there not saying anything, because I couldn't believe what my friend had just said. It was so horrible. I felt sorry for both of them. Chri didn't say anything. She just gave a smirky smile. I could tell by the look on my friend's face that she got scared after she said it. It was almost as if she thought that I didn't know that I was sitting next to Vance's wife.

One of my other friends said: "Speaking of Vance, are you still seeing him Holly?"

"No!" I said.

We stayed in that bar for a few hours, and Chri and I both got really drunk. She started talking about Vance again.

"You know he cheats on you, too," Chri said.

"I don't care, because I don't want to have anything to do with him," I said. I just wanted to be done with all of this. I wanted to just pretend that it had never happened. I didn't want to talk about Vance. I didn't want to cry over Vance. I didn't want to even think about Vance. I just wanted to put him completely out of my mind, but Chri kept talking about him.

Then she asked me to take her to his house.

I said, "no," but she kept insisting. She kept asking me over and over again to take her to his house. I knew Vance was very manipulative, and I was learning that Chri was very manipulative, too. I had a lot of guilt about dating her husband, and she was really good at tugging on that guilt to get me to do what she wanted.

Actually, I take that back. I allowed her to use my guilt. I let myself comply.

I was concerned about Chri, and I wanted to help her. Plus, I thought that if she and Vance were really married, then they should try to work things out. I wanted them to be happy together.

Finally, I agreed to drive her to Vance's house.

I stayed in the car while Chri walked to the door. Through a window, I could see Vance racing down the stairs in his underwear. He opened the door and dragged Chri down to his office. I got out of the car and followed them into the house. Vance was really freaking out. I had never seen him like this before. He was nervous and fidgety, and he couldn't stand still. He was in constant motion.

"What the hell are you doing here?" he said to me. "Why did you bring her here?"

"She wanted to come see you," I said. "I'm not here to cause any problems."

He argued with Chri for a little while, then he argued with me, then back to Chri, then back to me. The whole time, we were moving closer and closer to the front door. Chri got fed up and said "forget it," and she raced out the front door and jumped into the passenger side of my car. I followed her, and got behind the wheel. Vance dashed into the laundry room to get a pair of pants, then came charging out the front door. He came down to the car and started talking to us through the window on my side. I say, he was talking to us, but really he and Chri were just screaming at each other. I was sitting between not saying much, but getting hit by the occasional glob of spit.

Every couple of minutes, I would say, "Why don't I go, and you guys can work this out."

At one point, Vance asked Chri to stay in the car for a minute while he talked to me. He opened the door for me, then leaned in and turned up the radio so Chri couldn't hear what he was saying.

"Holly, I am so in love with you, and I want to be with you, but I can't," Vance said. "I lied to you. Chri and I are still married."

"How come she doesn't live here?" I said.

"We've been separated," he said. "Holly, if Chri leaves me, she'll take everything I own, just like Angela did — especially now that she knows about you. I just can't let that happen. I don't know what to do. I'm sorry for everything."

Chri jumped out of the car. "What are you guys talking about? What's he saying to you?" she said to me.

"Nothing," I said.

"I know he's talking about me," she said. "I want to know what he said."

Right then I happened to look up at the house and there in the window was a girl with long brown hair. I couldn't believe it. She was just standing there right in the window watching everything. I knew that if Chri looked up there, she was going to have a fit.

I tried to use hand signals to get Vance's attention when Chri wasn't looking at me. I got him to look up at the window, and his face turned ashen. He was trying to keep Chri's back turned toward the house.

I still felt guilty about being dishonest when I set Vance up on that three-way phone call, so I decided that I would do him and Chri one more favor. "I need to go to the bathroom," I said, walking toward the front door.

Vance was trying to think of something to say to keep me from going into the house. He knew that I had seen the girl upstairs, but he didn't know what I was going to do. He was afraid I might be going to bring the girl outside.

I marched upstairs, and I felt like a parent scolding a child. This girl was sitting on the edge of the hot tub in the master bathroom looking out of the window. Her shoes were on the floor in the middle of the room. I picked up her shoes and threw them at her.

"What do you think you're doing, you stupid idiot?" I said. "That's his wife down there. Are you trying to get busted? Don't you know that he's married."

"Yes, I know he's married," she said. "Everyone knows that."

I couldn't believe it. I grabbed her by the arm and dragged her into the guest bedroom. I pushed her into the closet, closed the door and said, "Don't come out of there until Vance comes to get you."

Then I went back outside and acted like nothing was wrong. I took care of that girl upstairs, because I thought I owed Vance a favor. I figured we were even after that, which was fine, because I didn't want to see him anymore. I told Chri to get into my car, so I could take her back to her own car.

Vance tried to stop us from leaving at first, but I think he realized that I was taking Chri with me to give him a chance to get rid of that other girl.

We drove away, and a few minutes later, he went flying by us in his Porsche taking that other girl home. Chri didn't notice the girl in the car.

Vance called me the next day and we got into a big argument. He was really mad at me for bringing Chri to his house, and I was really angry with him for lying to me about everything. He also got mad because Chri had danced with a couple of my friends when she and I went out that night. He thought I was trying to get back at him by setting Chri up with one of my friends.

Vance seemed completely illogical to me. I didn't understand him at all, and I didn't want to. I just wanted to be left alone.

I didn't talk to Vance for a while after that.

About a month later, some friends asked me if I wanted to go with them to a charity basketball game. At first I said, "no" because I knew that Vance was going to be playing. I had seen a report on TV that said he was being sued for divorce by Chri. So I knew that the two of them had not worked things out, but I still didn't want to see him. Eventually I changed my mind. I figured I was going to be sitting in the stands, and Vance would be on the court. It wouldn't be a big deal.

But as soon as I saw Vance, I felt strange. I still had strong feelings for him.

After the game, Vance disappeared, but I ran into him again at a club called Jubilation out in West Denver. I saw him come in with a date, which was fine, because I didn't want to talk to him. Then we ended up in one of those frequent night club traffic jams, in which the place is so crowded that the only route you can take is one that leads right past the person you're trying to avoid. We passed each other near the bar, and Vance said, "Hey, how are you doing?"

"Fine, thanks," I said in a really snotty way, like I didn't have a care in the world for him. But as I kept walking, I had a twinge inside me. I really wanted to stop and talk to him and hear what he had to say. But I didn't.

Since arriving at the club, a guy with long brown hair had been bugging me to dance with him. Vance had never seen my old boyfriend, Mike, but Vance knew Mike had long brown hair. So the next time this guy — I'll call him Jim — asked me to dance, I said, "Yes." I figured Vance would think I was there with my boyfriend.

Jim and I were dancing together when Vance and his date came out and started dancing right next to us. Vance and I kept glancing at each other out of the corners of our eyes, but for the most part we pretended we didn't notice each other. After a couple of minutes a slow song came on, and we both stayed on the floor with our partners. We were out there dancing figure-8's around each other, trying to make each other jealous.

Finally, I said this is stupid. I left Jim standing on the dance floor and ran to the front door of the club. My heart was broken, and I was going home. But my friend Natalie caught up with me and talked me into staying. We sat down at a table, and I got myself back together. Then Natalie left and I was sitting there by myself.

Then Jim sat down next to me, and asked me if I was okay. I said, "yes," and he stayed there and continued talking. He was being really flirty with me, but I wasn't interested. Vance was all I could think about. I was trying to pay attention to what Jim was saying, but I couldn't. All of a sudden, Vance appeared standing right behind Jim. I looked up at him and he mouthed the words, "I need to talk to you."

"No," I said.

"What?" Jim said leaning closer to me to hear over the noise in the club. Jim didn't know Vance was behind him, so he thought I had said "no" to him.

"Nothing," I said to Jim.

Jim kept on talking and Vance said, "I just need to talk to you for a minute."

"No," I said, again.

"What?" Jim said.

"Nothing," I said.

Vance just stood there and kept calling me, so I finally stood up to talk to him. Jim was in mid-sentence, and he had no idea what was happening. Vance and I were standing right next to Jim

Vance said, "Holly, I'm so in love with you and I'm really sorry for everything that I've done. I've hurt you and Chri and everyone I've ever been with. But I want to change. I know I have to change. And I don't blame you if you don't believe me, because I've lied and bullshitted before, but I really mean it. I want to be with you. I've never felt this way before."

I looked at him and I said, "I love you, too." We're both standing there teary-eyed in this club. It was like a movie. I felt like we were the only two people in there. I couldn't hear the music. I couldn't hear other people. All I could hear was me and Vance.

We sat down at the table. We were toe-to-toe, knee-to-knee, holding hands, and our faces were close together. We were just talking about our feelings for each other, and about how we have always loved each other.

Jim was still sitting at the table, and I don't think he could believe what was happening. He tapped me on the arm and said, "Do you want to dance?"

"No!" I said and turned back to Vance.

Jim eventually stormed away from the table. Vance and I just sat there and talked and talked and talked. Then he said, "Oh my gosh. I brought a girl here and her coat is in my car."

I told him that I would go get her coat. I delivered it to her and said, "I know you don't understand what's happening, and you'll probably never understand. Here's your coat. Vance is going home with me tonight." I felt sorry for her, too, because she was another innocent bystander. She didn't know what was going on.

As I was walking back over to the table, Jim came up behind me and gave it one more chance. "Do you want to dance?" he said.

I said, "No thanks."

Vance stayed with me that night, and we've been together ever since.

My younger sister Tammy and me. I'm 6 years old. She's 5.

Age 11, I'm showing off my pitching arm in the front yard. I wanted to be a pitcher, but I always ended up in the outfield because I could run fast.

The name of the team is the Lions. I'm number 33 standing next to my dad who was the coach. We went 0-10 that year.

I broke my arm when I was 9 and returned from the hospital before the end of the game. All of the cheerleaders crowded around to sign my cast.

Here I am at age 12 with my German Shepherd, Sam.

Me and Tammy again. I'm 8 and she's 7. This was about the time she passed me in height. It took me a few years to catch back up to her. I hated being shorter than my little sister.

Despite my desire to be a wide receiver, I was a running back during my
tenure at the University of Arizona.

Here I am winning a 100-meter dash.

At the end of a leap like this, I hit the pit nearly 27 feet away from the take-off board. It was the longest jump of my life, and it won me the NCAA National Long Jump Championship in 1983.

My hair has come a long way since
the untamed days of my rookie year.

The media and Broncos' offensive coordinator
Mike Shanahan greeted me at the airport when
I first came to Denver in 1985.

I wore number 11 during the preseason of my rookie year. Fellow wide receiver Gary Rolle celebrates with me.

Turning upfield after a reception against the Buffalo Bills.

These are three of the women that I sketched and hung on the walls of my house during the chaotic years. I was so distrustful of women over the years, that I used to talk to these drawings. I considered them the only women who would never hurt me.

Two more sketches that hung on the walls of
my home. I used to have names for all of
these women, but now I can't recall them.

Hard at work on one of my sketches during the Broncos training camp at the University of Northern Colorado.

I created the two women on the wall behind me. During that period of my life, my work looked a lot like that of Patrick Nagel. In fact, the pieces were so similar that the people in charge of Nagel's art, contacted me and wanted me to stop painting. But finally they decided there was no conflict because I wasn't trying to sell my work.

I performed with the Colorado Ballet during 1990, and this was a poster that was created to promote the event. It looks like I'm standing on my toes, but I'm actually in the air. I had to jump up more than 300 times before we got the perfect shot. I was exhausted, but I think the poster turned out great.

These ballerinas are so tiny, they make me look like a linebacker.

This is my dad and my
white Porsche 911
Turbo slant-nose.

This is the front of my 7,000-square-foot mansion. The backside of the house is
virtually all windows. Parked in the driveway is my red 1972 Corvette convertible and a blue 1993 BMW 325. In the appendix, I've listed every car I've ever
owned, but — wouldn't you know it — I left these two off the list. I'm sure I've
probably forgotten others as well. There were just too many cars over the years.

My blue, 1966 Corvette
was my pride and joy. I
kept it in storage in
Arizona for three years,
and rarely ever drove it.
But, alas, I had to sell it.

During this drag-racing competition, I was matched up against a professional driver, and beat him — twice. Then he complained that my car was faster than his. So we switched vehicles, and I beat him again. One thing I do know how to do is drive FAST.

The way I used to fly around town, I'm surprised I didn't die on this motorcycle.

We sold 150,000 of these posters in less than three months during the 1987–88 season. Since Mark was perceived as a nice guy, and I was perceived as a hell raiser, and Ricky was so ugly, we thought about naming this poster: *The Good, The Bad, And The Ugly.* Ricky wouldn't go for it.

The Three Amigos in uniform. I'm running, Mark Jackson is No. 80 and Ricky Nattiel is No. 84.

Mark Jackson and I talking to some of the fans during a Broncos road trip.

Despite all of the crazy events that were happening in my life, I always had time to give autographs for Broncos fans.

Me, Holly, her mom Jeanne and a random guy who happened to be in the picture.

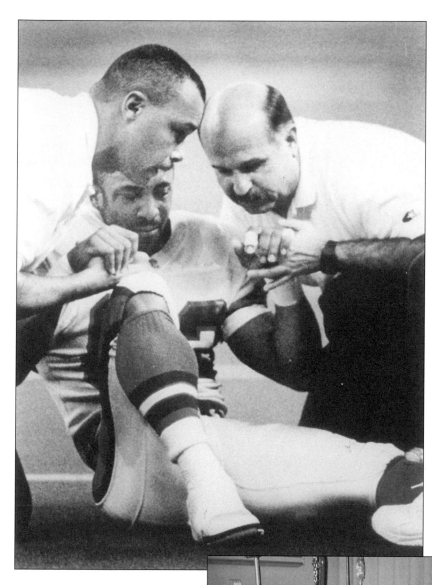

When I broke my ankle in Seattle in 1993, I thought my career was over. I was sitting on the ground with my knee pointed toward the ceiling, while my left foot was rotated outward laying flat on the ground. I didn't think I'd ever play again. But the doctors patched me up, and now I'm good as new.

Rat Taylor's the tough hombre in the white coat.
I'm the cocky quick-draw they call Vance the
Varmint. Sidled up next to me is a lady called
Holly the Hat. On the end there is Pa. We ain't
looking for no trouble, but if trouble's what you're
packin' then I guess we're 'bout ready.

Holly with our red 1989 Porsche 911 Cabriolet.

Holly with our red 1992 Jaguar. We traded it in on a $14,000
1993 Volkswagon Cabriolet.

My first wife, Angela, my mother, my niece, Katherine and my sister, Tammy.

Lisa and Vance Jr. at his first birthday party. Unfortunately, I haven't seen my son since that day.

This is my daughter Paris, my son Vincent, and my son Vaughn.
This was the day that Paris first met her two brothers. We had a
slumber party.

Left to right is Vaughn, me, Vincent, my father, Paris (in the
stroller), my daughter Nicole, and my wife Holly. We're on
our way into Westminster Mall to do some toy shopping.

This was our beautiful wedding ceremony. Above is me with my parents.
To the right is Holly and I. Below is
me with Tom and Kathleen Byington,
two very good friends.

Above is Nicole with her Cabbage Patch twin. Left, is Nicole and Vance Jr. Below is Paris and her Cabbage Patch twin.

Nicole and her mother Ana at
Nicole's first communion.

Paris and Holly.

Me and Nicole.

Some modeling photos Holly
posed for while working for
Maximum Talent Agency

Holly and me

This is my slicked back haircut.
Notice the pony tail in the smaller
picture. For a while, I had a
weaved pony tail that extended
down to my waist. I thought it
looked cool, but I hated it on the
football field. Defenders would
always grab me by the hair to
tackle me. Every week I cut a few
inches off the end of it until it was
gone.

These two images probably accurately portray the way people saw me in Denver. When I got traded to the Vikings in 1993, some people (like the cartoon suggests) were glad to see me go. But when I returned to the Broncos roster two weeks later, some fans were happy to see me back.

Whether I was on the field playing or on the sidelines with an injury, I always found a reason to celebrate.

The top picture shows what Holly used to call my George Washington haircut. I'd put rollers into my head, and when it was finished it looked like one of those old 18th century wigs. Below, I'm just waiting to play a little football.

Drew Litton of the *Rocky Mountain News* offered this commentary after two more paternity suits were filed against me in 1991.

This came after I appeared naked on HBO's *Inside the NFL* show during 1992.

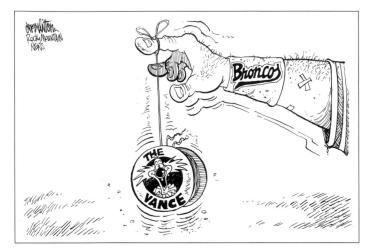

During my crazy years, I was basically a clown or a yo-yo or a clown in a yo-yo. However you choose to look at it, I was way out of control.

During the 1991 training camp, I did resistance sprint work with a parachute. This cartoon's accuracy lies in the fact that there were plenty of times when I was totally out of touch with reality.

This one speaks for itself.

Special thanks to Drew Litton for allowing me to use his cartoons in my book.

I Played A Little Football, Too

always got along well with Dan Reeves, who was the Broncos head coach during my first eight years with the team. Despite all of the crazy things that I was doing on the field, Dan always stood behind me and was willing to let me make my own decisions in life. Maybe it would have been better if he had cracked the whip on me and forced me to shape up, but I can't complain about any of that. I was a grown man who was making his own decisions. It was not Dan's responsibility to babysit me. In fact, I'm glad that he didn't, because I might never have come to the realization that I was killing myself. If I was changing my life because my boss forced me, I probably would have jumped right back into the chaos the minute he turned his back. I had to reach the point at which I wanted to change for myself, and I was the only person who could make that decision.

By living through all of the crazy and sometimes stupid things that I did, I finally was able to get some perspective and realize that I was going to die if I didn't change my life. I really feel like I owe Dan Reeves a lot, because he allowed me to mature as a person and as a man at my own pace.

But that doesn't mean that I wasn't scared to death at times. There were days when I was sure that I had stepped too far over the line and the hammer was about to drop on me.

I arrived in Denver as a rookie making trouble, so when the phone rang at about 7:30 a.m. one morning midway through the 1985 season, I was scared. It was Dan Reeves secretary.

"Vance, Dan would like to see you right away," she said.

I was sitting at home panicking. What the hell is going on? Who have I screwed? Who's pregnant? What have I done wrong? And that wasn't even the real question, because I had done plenty of things wrong. The real question was: What have I done wrong that Dan might know about?

I jumped in my car and flew down to the office. I was so nervous I sweating to death. Dan told me to come in, close the door and sit down. I was damned near about to pee on myself. I was prepared to apologize for whatever I had done. I was ready to change my life and live the way I was supposed to be living. I was ready to give myself a more normal haircut. I was ready to do anything.

I was a 22-year-old rookie. It was only the sixth or seventh week of the season. We were scheduled to play San Francisco that weekend, and I was sitting in the head coach's office about to get reprimanded for something.

"I've made a big decision, Vance," Dan said.

My eyes were probably twice as big as normal, because I was so scared of what his decision might be.

"I've decided that you're going to be one of my starters at receiver," he said. "We have a lot of faith in you and your ability. You're going to be the future for the Broncos at the wide receiver position. It's going to be tough on some of the veterans. We're going to have to demote Butch Johnson, but you're the man we're going to go with."

I was stunned. I couldn't think of anything good to say, so I just said, "Thank you."

I walked out of that office with a big smile on my face. I was really excited about being a starter, but I was also a little scared. I had confidence in my ability to perform in the position, but I was afraid of some of the veteran players. How were they going to feel about having a rookie come in and replace one of their buddies? Not only did I bump Butch Johnson out, but I had leap-frogged veterans Clint Sampson and Ray Alexander, too.

Today, I'm a seasoned veteran in the NFL, and I understand that the young replacing the old is just part of the game. While those veterans might not have liked my promotion, they probably didn't blame me for it, because I was a pawn in the system just like them. If anything, they were probably pissed off at the coaches for making the decision. I understand that now, but back then, I was scared of what they might try to do to me.

Of course, no one said or did anything to me. I went out and had a great game against San Francisco that weekend. Being a starter just enhanced my celebrity in Denver, which was cool with me. In my mind, the more people who knew me, the better off I was.

As the season progressed, I caught more and more passes and scored a few touchdowns. But John Elway was getting a little pissed at me because I always fell down after I caught his passes. He, and pretty much everyone else, thought I was afraid to get hit after I made the catch, but that wasn't true. I was never afraid to get hit.

There were a couple of reasons that I often fell down or dove when I was catching a pass from Elway. To understand the first reason, you have to realize how hard John throws passes at times. He has a really strong arm, and sometimes, especially when he was younger, he would really fire the ball to you. I dislocated my left pinkie in 1985 while catching one of his passes. Throughout the rest of my career, I constantly had some type of dislocation or bruise from catching his balls. If a receiver was a little off-balance while making a catch — like one foot off the ground or leaning in a certain direction — the force of the ball would often just push him right off his feet.

But, while John's ball was sometimes tough to catch, that was one of his greatest strengths, too. He could get the ball to you so fast, that a lot of times defense backs didn't have time to react to try to break up the play. Gary Kubiak, who was the Broncos back-up quarterback for many years, threw much softer passes. You had a better chance of catching Kubiak's ball, but you were also more likely to get blasted by a defensive back right when the ball arrived.

So I really began to respect Elway's ability, and appreciate the speed with which he delivered the ball. But that velocity forced me to concentrate as hard as I could on just catching everything he threw. There are a lot of guys who simply can't catch John's ball. During a game, you might see a guy drop a ball that hits him right in the hands. It could be because he misjudged it, or he just didn't do a good job looking it all the way in. But some of those drops are caused by the fact that John's passes are not always easy to catch. So during my years with Denver, I knew that as long as I could catch John's passes, I would have a place on the Broncos team.

That was one of the reasons I often fell down after making a catch. Every once in a while a pass might knock me over, but usually I fell down because I was concentrating solely on making the reception. I didn't care about getting more yards after the catch. I just made sure that I snatched the ball out of the air. To me, that was the important thing.

The second reason I often fell down or dove is kind of a silly one. But it didn't seem silly to me at the time. I used to look in the newspaper and see the action photos on the sports page. They always showed receivers who were high up in the air making catches. They showed guys who were stretched out parallel to the ground making catches. Those are the exciting pictures. Those are the type that photographers are going to put in the newspaper.

Being the media monger that I was, I wanted to get my picture into the paper as often as possible. I dove for balls even when I didn't have to, because I wanted to look good for the photographers. They never take your picture when you're running down the sideline. They always print the shots of you turned upside down in the air or diving over a pile to make a catch.

Elway hated the way I always dove. He wanted me to catch the ball and run for a touchdown. "They brought you here, and gave you all that damned money, so catch the ball and turn upfield with it," he would say.

I'd work on it during practice. I'd make the catch and then turn upfield and show off a couple of moves.

"You've got all the damned moves in the world when you're working against air, Vance," John would say. "Let's see you do that during the games, against defensive backs."

But for many years, I never did become the guy who caught the ball and got a lot of yards afterward. As a result, people generally thought that I was afraid of being hit.

Regardless what people thought about my courage, and despite the crazy things I was doing, I continued to flourish as a Broncos' receiver.

When I sat down to write this book, I purposely did not intend to mention many of my on-the-field accomplishments. This book is about my problems, it's not intended to be a resume of my football career.

But I've decided to list some of my statistics here briefly, so that you can see that I was still a solid performer on the field despite my chaotic personal life.

During the 1985 season, I made the transition from running back to wide receiver and caught 51 passes, which was a new Broncos record for a rookie receiver. I also set the rookie record for passing yardage (721), and scored three touchdowns. My performance that year boosted my ego, because it taught me that I could compete in the NFL. It also swelled my head, because even more people recognized me in the clubs and bars.

In 1986, I injured a knee and had to have arthroscopic surgery. I missed four games but came back to make 31 receptions for 363 yards and score two touchdowns. We went to the Super Bowl that year, and I led all Broncos' receivers with 12 playoff receptions, including five in the championship game.

In 1987 — despite missing five games because of the players' strike and two games because of a dislocated shoulder — I had 42 catches for 684 yards and scored seven touchdowns.

In 1988, I was the Broncos' leading receiver with 68 receptions for 896 yards. I scored five touchdowns.

In 1989, I hit a career high 76 catches for 1,095 yards and seven touchdowns. I thought I was going to the Pro Bowl that year because I was one of the top receivers in the American Football Conference (AFC), but I didn't get voted in. I was really disappointed.

In 1990, I finished second on the team with 54 receptions for 747 yards and three touchdowns.

In 1991, despite spending the beginning of the year in jail — I'll talk about jail a little later -— and then in rehab for a preseason knee injury, I made 21 catches for 208 yards and three touchdowns.

In 1992, I missed five games due to injury and had 24 receptions for 294 yards and two touchdowns.

• • • • •

The 1991 and 1992 seasons were very different for me than previous years had been because my life had settled down a great deal. Holly and I were married and going to counseling regularly, and I wasn't out running around in the streets.

I felt more in control of myself at all times. Even though I had been a good performer for the Broncos for many years, I always felt a little crazy on the field. There was always something going on that might take my attention away from the game. My life was so chaotic off the field that I sometimes worried whether my teammates would trust me on Sundays.

During the chaotic years, I wasn't getting much sleep at night. I wasn't spending a lot of time studying my playbook or watching film at night. I wasn't staying home and leading a quiet life. I was everywhere. I was out until the wee hours of the morning, and sometimes, I look back and I don't know how I did it. How could I go play football effectively when all of this other stuff was going on in my life.

Plus there was all of the hate mail I was creating. I was running all over Denver sleeping with single women, married women and any woman in between, and I was pissing a lot of people off — especially men. I got hate mail from men who would say, "My wife is in love with you. You've ruined our marriage. I hope you die. If I see you, I'm going to kill you." At autograph sessions men would come up to me and tell me how much they hated me.

After the 1988–89 Super Bowl game, I got an anonymous letter that read, "I hate the way you show off after a touchdown, and if you do it again, I'm going to kill you."

On another occasion I was doing an autograph session at a hair salon in Colorado Springs. There were hundreds of people standing in line when suddenly the police came in and escorted me out. I didn't know what was going on. I later learned that someone had called the salon and said "Vance Johnson will be shot tonight." The guy called twice.

Well, the police told Chri, who was with me, and they asked her if she wanted me to stay. She said, "No, get him out of there, now." So they came and got me. No one told me what was going on, they just kept saying, "Come with us. Come with us." I was looking around trying to figure out what was going on. I figured it might have been a bomb threat or something, but I didn't understand why everyone else in the mall wasn't being evacuated.

When we got to the police car, they put me in the back seat and told me that I could duck down if I wanted to. Even though I really didn't believe that someone would try to kill me, I laid down on the back seat just in case. Everything turned out okay.

I got letters from a couple of guys who said that they were going to shoot me at the stadium when I was going up for a pass, or that they were going to shoot me right after I scored a touchdown.

There are some flat-ass crazy people in the world, and I knew that someone could easily walk into the stadium with a gun. So I went through a period where I really toned down my act. I wasn't as flamboyant, and I didn't try so hard to get attention, because I was afraid that someone might really try to kill me.

At times it was nerve-racking to be on the field playing football, and to always know in the back of my mind that one of those crazy people might be serious about shooting me. Every time I went up for a pass I worried. Every time I scored a touchdown I worried.

· · · · ·

During the spring of 1992, head coach, Dan Reeves was entering the last year of his contract with the Broncos, and everyone expected him and owner, Pat Bowlen to sit down and work out a contract extension. Dan had been coaching the team for 11 years at the time, and everyone assumed that he would continue to coach the team.

But when no contract extension was negotiated before the start of the 1992 season, the media started speculating that Dan wasn't going to be rehired. It was a strange year, because every week you would read stories about the team followed by an update on the likely status of Dan's future in town. If the team won a game, the press would say, "Bowlen should renew Reeves' contract." If the team lost a game, the press would say, "Dan Reeves' future in Denver is questionable." It really began to turn into a circus. The press even started making a lot of predictions about who would be the coach in 1993.

I noticed a lot of things during my many years in the league because Mark Jackson and I used to always sit up at the front of the bus whenever the team was on road trips. We rode buses from the airport to the hotel, and back again. During the beginning of my career, Dan and Broncos owner Pat Bowlen seemed to be best friends. They'd sit next to each other at the front of the bus laughing and talking and damn near holding hands. They appeared to have a great working relationship.

But toward the end, you could tell that they weren't such good friends anymore. They rarely sat next to each other, and when they did, they didn't joke and talk together. They really didn't seem to communicate as much as they used to. And sometimes, Pat wouldn't ride the bus with us.

The last game of the 1992 season, we played Kansas City at Arrowhead Stadium. If we had won that game we would have gone to the playoffs as a wildcard team. But we lost and finished the regular season 8-8. I felt bad after the game because everyone knew that it was probably Dan's last game as the head coach of the Broncos.

I was sitting on the bus and I could see Pat Bowlen, and Broncos general manager John Beake standing out in front of the bus talking. I don't know what they were talking about, but I had the impression that they were planning to do something about Dan.

Dan came out of the locker room, walked right past them and got onto the bus. Pat and John got into a limousine together for the ride to the airport. The tension between the three of them was palpable.

One of the head coach's jobs at the end of every season is to sit down for a minute or two with every player and tell him what kind of year the player had and what the team expects from him in the future. This is a ritual that happens on the Monday morning immediately following the last game of the year. Guys sign up on a sheet in the coach's waiting area and then sit around until it's their turn to spend two or three minutes with the head man.

When it was my turn to meet with Dan, I went into his office and he looked really sad. He didn't speak the way he usually did, either. He's normally really positive. He usually just talks about whatever good things you did that year, and he talks real optimistically about the future. But that day he just said that it had been an honor working with me.

"Unfortunately, some guys think they're the reason that we've gone to three Super Bowls," Dan said. "But believe me, it's people like you and other guys on the team who should receive the real credit for getting us to those Super Bowls. Whatever happens, it's really been a pleasure working with you, and I hope it won't be the last time."

"I'm going to miss you if something happens," I said. "But I want you to promise one thing. If you end up leaving Denver, please take me with you."

Dan laughed and said that he hopes he has the opportunity.

We got up and shook hands and I asked if I could give him a hug. I said, "I really love you. I think you're one of the greatest coaches I've ever played for."

Later that day, Dan Reeves was fired as head coach of the Denver Broncos.

• • • • •

A few weeks later, Dan was hired as the new head coach of the New York Giants.

I wanted Dan to make a trade so that he could get me out to New York with him. I still had one more year left on my contract with the Broncos, so the only way he could get me was by trading someone. But he didn't make any moves in that direction. A few weeks after he took over, Dan signed Mark Jackson to a three-year, $4.5 million contract. I couldn't believe it. I really envied Mark because he got to go with Dan. I wished that it was me. I wished there was some way that I could be in New York making all of that money.

I decided that I would just have to work really hard and make sure that I had a great season with the Broncos in 1993 so that I could demand a lot of money when my contract ended the next year.

The 1992 off-season was the first time that I actually showed up for the off-season workout program everyday. I've always been blessed with a great deal of God-given athletic ability, and I never really had to work out a whole lot in order to be ready to play.

So usually during the off-season, I wouldn't work out. Instead I would spend my time partying, dealing with my emotional problems, trying to get out of debt, trying to clear up my tax problems (which I'll discuss in the chapter titled "Where did all my money go?"), going through divorces and taking care of a number of other extracurricular activities in my life.

The off-seasons were always really tough for me, there was always something crazy going on.

But during the 1992 off-season it was easy for me to work out, because my life had settled down so much. My home life was very stable. I wasn't running around in the streets every night. I was just being a good husband and a father. So I was the first one to arrive at workouts every morning and the last one to leave. I was just excited about playing football again.

Plus, I had begun to realize that I can't play football forever. I used to think that I was so good that I would play until I died. But by 1993, I had seen enough good players leave the league because of injuries, because of younger players, because of salaries and because of a lot of other factors, and I knew that I could not play forever. I knew that my career could be over at any time.

I decided that I would work hard and try to get in three or four more years before I retire. When training camp started that year, I was in great shape and ready to do battle.

Then I Got Fired

When I woke up on Monday, Aug. 23, 1993, I had a really bad feeling about my future with the Broncos. Although I'd had a decent training camp, I wasn't sure where I stood with the team. The coaches hadn't played me very much during the preseason games, which can be good or bad. Sometimes if you're a proven veteran, the coaches won't play you during the preseason, because they want to save you for the season. They don't want to risk getting you injured.

But, sometimes if the coaches don't play you during the preseason, it means that you're not going to make the team. It means that they'd rather give playing time to other guys who are going to be needed during the regular season.

During most of the 1993 training camp, I thought I was one of the guys who might be let go. Although I knew that I was the best receiver in training camp that year, I didn't feel that I was part of the Broncos' plans.

When I woke up that morning — Aug. 23 — I could feel that something was wrong. I know it sounds crazy, like I'm psychic or something, but I'm not. I just had a feeling something was going to happen that day.

I went to the Broncos' facility early, like I often did, and did some work in the weight room. I was excited about football. I was excited about the season, but something was burning in the back of my mind.

I decided to go talk to head coach Wade Phillips. During my eight years with the Broncos, I had only gone up to the head coach's office on nine occasions. Once each year when we were required to visit with the coach at the end of the year. And once during my rookie year when Dan Reeves called me up there to tell me that I was going to be a starter on offense. Since then, I had been causing so much chaos off the field that I was afraid to go visit the head coach. I was afraid that he would see me, remember that he didn't like all my off-the-field shenanigans and fire me on the spot.

But that morning, I put aside my fear of the head coach, and marched upstairs.

Wade's secretary sent me into his office after only a brief delay. I was really nervous as I walked in and sat down. Final cut day was exactly one week away.

Throughout that training camp Wade had told all of us that if we ever wanted to know where we stood with the team, all we had to do was ask. The coaches might not tell us what we want to hear, but they will be honest with us. So as I sat across from Wade that morning, I was hoping that he would be honest with me as he told me exactly what I wanted to hear.

"I just wanted to find out what my position is with the team," I said.

Wade said, "Vance, you're a Bronco. I want you here and right now you're the starter."

I was very relieved to hear that.

"But there is a 10 percent chance that something could happen with a trade," he continued. "We need players and teams want you, so we have to leave that door open. But it's 90 percent that you are here and you're one of our starters. There's only a 10 percent chance that you would be traded."

I walked out of that room with the biggest smile on my face. I was so happy that I was going to be a starter for the Broncos again this year. I was so happy that I could put all of the anxiety I was feeling behind me. I was so happy that Wade had expressed so much confidence in me.

I bounded down the stairs thinking, this is going to be a great year for me. My marriage is going great. I'm being a good father. I'm meeting with the men's group and I'm becoming a better person. Now I'm going to have a great football season. This is going to be the new beginning of my life.

A couple of hours later, me and my teammates were divided — as usual — into our position groups and were meeting with our coaches about the upcoming game. The running backs were together in one room, the defensive backs were in another, the quarterbacks were off by themselves, and the linebackers had their own room.

All of the receivers were sitting in the Broncos big team meeting room watching film. Suddenly the door opened at the top of the room. This meeting area is just a big cavern built to accommodate the entire team and coaching staff whenever that is necessary. From front to back the room is probably about thirty or forty yards long, and it is designed like a college lecture hall — with the back of the room being higher than the front.

When the door opened, the room was dark because we were watching film. All of the receivers were sitting in the front row, and everyone turned to look back. At first all you could see was a silhouette, but as the figure moved down the steps, we could see that it was Wade. It looked like he was walking down those steps in slow motion, and with every step he took, my heart sank deeper into my stomach.

"Vance, can I see you for a second," Wade said when he'd come most of the way down the steps.

Right then I knew that I was no longer a Bronco. After eight years, my days in orange and blue were over. He turned toward the door, and I fell in beside him. We were in complete silence as we walked out of the meeting room, down the hall and into the trainer's office.

Once we were inside, Wade said, "Remember that 10 percent chance I told you about? Well, it's 100 percent now." He told me that I had been traded to the Minnesota Vikings.

I was so shaken up inside that I went completely numb. I didn't know how to react. I shook his hand, and I thanked him for being honest with me. "I think you're a great coach," I said.

I walked through the locker room, and saw a few guys standing in there. I said, "Hey, it was nice playing with you guys. I'm out of here. I just got traded to the Vikings."

No one believed me. They all thought I was joking. I was shaking hands with guys and hugging guys, saying goodbye. I felt completely disoriented. I felt like someone had punched me in the stomach. All of a sudden my life was changing. After eight years as a Bronco, I was suddenly going to pack up and move to Minnesota.

I was on the verge of crying.

I walked into the defensive backs' meeting room and asked coach Charlie Waters to turn off the projector for a minute so I could say goodbye. I was supposed to fly to Minnesota that evening. I went to the quarterbacks' room and told John Elway that it had been great playing with him and that I thought he was a great quarterback. I had never told John that to his face before, but it seemed important to me to tell him that before I left.

I went back to the receivers' meeting room to say goodbye to them, and there was a vast range of emotional responses. I could tell they all felt sorry for me, and that they were disappointed to see me go. I could also see the relief and the joy in their eyes, because suddenly the main veteran in camp, the guy who had a starting position locked up, was leaving. Now that I was leaving, there was another slot open for one of the young guys to make the team.

Arthur Marshall stood up and gave me a hug and said, "Thanks for everything V.J. I've really learned a lot from you." That was when tears really did come to my eyes, because I knew I was going to miss being a Denver Bronco. The Broncos' name had been a part of my personality for so long, that I wasn't sure how I was going to survive without it.

I walked upstairs to the coaches' offices and talked to Bob Ferguson, director of Football Operations/Player Personnel. He told me that the Vikings needed a receiver, and they were really excited about getting me. He said it was a wonderful situation for me. He said I would be at least their number three receiver, and I would probably be a starter before the end of the year.

I went back downstairs and started cleaning out my locker. I threw away a lot of stuff, and packed everything I wanted into a big plastic garbage bag. Most of the guys were in the locker room getting ready for practice, and I was loading up my shit, because I'd been kicked out.

It was really humiliating. Despite what Bob Ferguson said about the Vikings really wanting me and needing me, I still felt like the biggest factor in the trade was that the Broncos didn't want or need me. I'm sure a lot of teams would want and need John Elway, but the Broncos wouldn't trade him away, because he's too important. When they traded me, I felt rejected. I felt unimportant, and I was embarrassed.

I walked out to my car and got in. I sat there for a minute thinking that this was the last time that I would ever pull away from the Broncos' facility. I looked in my rear-view mirror, and I could see all of my old teammates on the field practicing. Again, I almost started crying.

I called my wife, Holly, on my car phone and told her what had happened. She was devastated. When I got home, we sat and talked for a little while, and I started panicking. I didn't want to go to Minnesota. There was only a week left before final cuts. How were the Vikings going to get a look at me in four days of practice. There's no way I can make the team in four days. I was afraid to go to Minnesota.

But, then I tried to be logical, and reasoned it out. I figured that if they were bringing me there with only four days left before final cuts, then they must plan to have me as part of their team. They must think I'm good enough to make it without trying out. Buoyed by that kind of thought, I decided that maybe I shouldn't go to Minnesota right away. Maybe I should hold out for more money, but I decided against it.

I arrived in Minnesota Monday night and reported to the facility Tuesday morning. When I got there, I met a couple of players and a couple of coaches, but I didn't meet the head coach, Dennis Green. I know from past experience with the Broncos that when a new player arrives, the first place they take him is to the head coach's office, but that didn't happen in Minnesota. I didn't get introduced to him. I thought that was odd, but I tried not to let it bother me too much.

In Denver, all new players are introduced to the entire team during the first team meeting of their first day. Wade would stand up there and say, "I want to introduce a new player to you guys. Joe Blow, from Wherever, if you'd please stand up." The guy would stand up and everyone would look and him and say, "What's up?" or something.

I was prepared for that during the Vikings first team meeting on Wednesday. But no one ever introduced me. I was sitting in a room with 60 strangers, and no one introduced me. That's when I started to get worried.

I reported to the receivers' meeting room with the rest of the wide outs, but no one really talked to me. After that meeting, I went to the office of the receivers' coach. He gave me a playbook and told me to learn four or five plays for practice that day.

The locker they gave me was in a corner near the front door. Despite it being late August, I got a blast of cold air every time that door opened.

I was getting the shaft in every possible way.

I put on my uniform, donned a baseball cap and carried my helmet out to the practice field. I sat on my helmet and watched all the guys practice. I ran exactly two plays that day. Beyond that, the coaches didn't even look in my direction. I couldn't figure out why the hell they had brought me here.

After practice, I went back to the hotel and called Holly. I told her how depressed I was, and that there was no way in hell that I should be in Minnesota. They had traded for me and had flown me up there, but that was it. Beyond that, I may as well have been a fly on the wall that no one noticed.

I think part of the reason that no one was excited to see me, was that everyone was so disappointed about losing offensive lineman Gary Zimmerman, who ended up in Denver. Zimmerman, was a 10- or 11-year veteran, who had been a contract holdout throughout the 1993 training camp. He had made it clear that he had no intention of signing the contract that the Vikings wanted him to sign. He was living on his farm somewhere out in Oregon or Washington state and he told the Vikings that he was prepared to just retire rather than sign their contract.

Zimmerman's departure in the trade really eclipsed my arrival. Everyone was so disappointed about him leaving, that they didn't even see me come in.

The Vikings were going to play their final preseason game that Thursday, so their Wednesday practice was just a walk-through of their plays. I went out that day, and caught a couple of passes from the quarterbacks, but I never ran a one-on-one route. I never had an opportunity to show the coaches what I could do.

On Thursday night, we played the Pittsburgh Steelers in Minnesota, but I sat on my helmet and watched most of that game, too. I just sat there staring out into the distance not even knowing what was going on. I was just a spectator who happened to have a pretty good seat. The coaches put me into the game during the last two minutes when all the fourth-string players went in. Those were all the guys who were going to get cut in a couple of days, and they had me out there at that time. I already knew that I wasn't in their plans, but if I'd had any doubts, that would have confirmed it for me.

The Vikings' fourth-string quarterback only threw one ball to me, and that one hit a lineman's helmet and then skipped off the ground and into my arms. That was my one almost-reception as a Minnesota Viking. There were still a few older veterans on the field for the Steelers, and a couple of them came up to me between plays and said, "What the hell are you doing here, Vance?" I couldn't answer the question because I had no idea.

After the game, I showered and dressed and Steeler's quarterback Mike Tomczak walked up to me and said, "Why didn't they play you?"

"I don't know, man," I said. I was dejected.

"You're a great receiver," he said. "Just hang in there, I'm sure you must be on the team."

I said thanks, and that I hoped I was on the team. But in my heart I knew that I was not on the team. The way I had been treated since the minute I arrived indicated that I was not going to make the Vikings' roster.

It was a couple of days before final cuts, and I was wondering what was going on with my life. I was really sad. I wasn't a Bronco anymore. My roots had been ripped out from under me. I went from being the best receiver in the Broncos' training camp to being a fourth-string receiver in the Vikings' camp.

I went to the Mall of America that night just so I could say that I had seen it.

Saturday morning I went golfing with some of the Vikings' players — Anthony Carter, Vencie Glenn and Chris Carter. I didn't have my golf clubs with me, so I rented some. I had a good time. In fact, that was the only good time that I had during my week in Minnesota.

Sunday morning we all reported to the facility to watch the film of the game. I had sat through the entire game at the stadium, so I just sat through it again in the meeting room. Afterward, I went back to my hotel room and watched television. There was an Applebee's restaurant across the street from the hotel, so I decided to go there for dinner.

It was really strange to be in that restaurant, because I was completely anonymous. I am so well-known in Denver that whenever I go out in public people always recognize me and want to get my autograph. When I was living it up as The Vance, I used to crave that type of attention because it really fed my ego. During the past couple of years, I've started to understand that people ask for my autograph because they think I'm a good football player, or because they see that I am changing my life, or there is something about me that that person admires. I used to think that I was a God, and that people asked for my autograph because I was a God. But now I am very flattered when people ask for my autograph, because I know they don't have to do it. They make me feel special when they do it.

But there I was, standing near the bar in the middle of a crowded restaurant , and not one person recognized me. It had been eight years since that had happened, and it was sobering. I was standing there thinking, "This is horrible. What a horrible feeling. God, is this what I'm supposed to be learning from this situation? Is this what you wanted me to see?"

I figured God must be trying to humble me. I had been in counseling. I was trying to take responsibility for my life. I was trying to understand that I wasn't better than other people. But in one quick trip up to Minnesota, God put me in my place. He showed me what it would be like to not be famous again. He showed me how special it is to have people who admire you and who respect you enough to ask for your autograph. He showed me that I should never take that type of adoration for granted.

In Denver, I could walk into any restaurant in town and get seated before everyone else who was waiting. In Minnesota, I had to wait 45 minutes for a table. I ate my food, and was sitting there nursing a coke and just hanging out. In Denver, if I hung out at a restaurant, the manager came over to thank me for my patronage. In Minnesota, the restaurant was crowded, and a waitress came over to ask me to surrender my table to other diners.

I said, "Okay," and went back to my hotel room.

I felt completely alone, and I was absolutely humbled. I started crying like a baby. I just sat there on my bed in my hotel room and cried for about half an hour. I couldn't believe how much my life had changed in just five days. I called Holly and told her how much I loved her. She was very supportive throughout this process, and I don't think I have ever appreciated her more than I did during that week. I asked her to fly up to be with me. She flew in Monday morning — final cut day.

As always, I reported to work early. I got to the facility at about 6:30 a.m., even though meetings didn't start until 9 a.m. I was in my locker studying my playbook when I looked up and saw the wide receiver coach staring at me from the trainer's office. We looked at each other, then he looked away. He made no move to approach me, so I got up and walked over to him.

"I'm being released, aren't I," I said without preamble. I'd known it since the minute I arrived in Minnesota, but I needed to hear if from someone official.

He said, "Yeah. You need to go up and meet with Coach Green."

Oh, so now, after being in Minnesota for a week, I was going to meet the head coach. I was really disappointed and my feelings were hurt, but I went up to see Dennis Green.

He said there was a possibility that they might re-sign me after I cleared waivers, but I knew that was a crock of shit. I wanted to ask him why I didn't get a fair tryout, but I didn't have the guts. I just sat there listening to him, and when he finished I said, "Thanks. You're a great coach. Good luck with the rest of the season."

I walked out of there. I left my playbook and my uniform in my locker. I went to the hotel, got my wife and caught a cab to the airport. I didn't check out of the hotel. I didn't return the rental car the team had rented for me. I didn't even ask the Vikings to send me home or anything. I paid for my own plane ticket, because I just wanted to get the hell out of Minnesota.

When we got back to Denver, I sat in the living room of our 7,000-square-foot house, and it began to sink in that I was unemployed. I'd put my house on the market nearly a year and a half earlier, but it had not yet sold. Our failure to find a buyer didn't bother me too much as long as I was playing football. But sitting there after just being released, and not knowing if I was ever going to play football again, I was worried. I wondered how I was going to pay the $3,800-a-month mortgage? I had two acres of grass, and a waterfall in the back yard. How was I going to pay the $500-a-month water bill?

I've mentioned this house several times in the book, but let me describe it for you. It wasn't just a house. It was my dream house. It was my pride and joy. I loved that house.

I had seen this house design while visiting a friend who lived in the Piney Creek subdivision in Englewood, Colo. It was just a beautiful house. So when I bought a plot out in Ken Caryl Valley just outside of Denver, I wanted to have that house built. It's pretty much the same house as the one I saw, with a few minor changes.

For starters it was a big, clean white house with grey brick mixed in. When you walk into the front door there is a huge entry way — the ceiling was 35 feet high. All of the walls inside the house were white-washed, and the design was really bright and open.

There were 96 windows on the first floor alone.

During the three years that I lived there (December 1990 until September 1993), there was never even one stitch of a curtain on any window in the house.

The fireplace was really tall and long, and the kitchen featured whitewashed wood cabinets with a big island in the middle of the room. The house was furnished all in white leather pieces. Out in back was an 880-square-foot red cedar balcony that overlooked the bulk of my two acres of land.

To get to the second floor you walked up a glass staircase with a glass banister.

The master bedroom was a monster. It was more than 600-square-feet by itself. There was a big fireplace and you could walk down into a sitting area. If you looked out one window you could see the city of Denver. If you looked out of practically any other window in the house, you'd see the mountains.

There were four guest bedrooms upstairs. An intercom system was wired through the entire house, and surround sound stereo boomed into every room of the house — even the bathrooms.

Downstairs from the main floor was a fully finished walk-out basement. There was a glass staircase leading there, too. The basement featured a marble fireplace and a marble bar big enough to accommodate 10 bar stools.

Also in the basement was a 10 person indoor jacuzzi and lots of windows.

My property included 16,000 square-feet of sod and more than 100 tons of rock that was spread all around the house. More than 60 trees of various types had been planted in the backyard. It looked like a damned forest.

There was also a three-tiered waterfall that fed a pond that had goldfish in it.

There was a 500-square-foot red rock patio that had a stream running through the middle of it, and a small bridge over the water.

I easily spent more than $70,000 on landscaping alone.

The oversized three-car garage was easily large enough to accommodate five cars, and I generally kept it full.

With all of these extras in the house, my mortgage was $3,800 a month, but my actual cost to maintain the house was about $5,000 a month. Suddenly I was going to have to find that money when I didn't have a job. I desperately needed to sell the house, but it had been on the market for 18 months without a buyer.

Would you believe that two days after I got cut by the Vikings, we found a buyer? After a year and a half of nothing, a buyer magically appeared. We were asking $429,000 for the house, and this guy came out from California, took one look at the house and gave us our asking price. He didn't haggle, he didn't take a day to think about it. He just said, "I'll take it."

I couldn't believe it, but I was so happy that God had relieved me of that burden. If I hadn't sold the house, I may have had to file for bankruptcy after a few months. There was no way that I could afford to keep making those payments.

God had put me through a lot of emotional challenges during that week, but I felt really good about myself, because I had handled them in a very mature way. I was not The Vance of old. I was a new person. I was a responsible person. And I was a guy who was going to survive no matter what. I felt that God got me into counseling in 1991, so that I would be emotionally prepared to handle all of these changes in 1993.

So I was sitting at home feeling comfortable because the house had been sold — although the closing wouldn't happen for a couple of months — but I was worried about my future in the NFL. Is my career over? Is this how it ends for me? Over the years, I'd seen so many veteran players leave the game for a variety of reasons, and people always ask, "Whatever happened to old what's-his-name?" I wondered if people in Denver were going to be asking that question about me.

But I was confident that some team would call me. I talked to Dan Reeves in New York, and he said he was interested in me, but they had just spent $10 million on two receivers, and he couldn't do anything. Dan told me to stay in shape and be patient because someone would call me. Someone was going to need me that year.

So I sat around waiting by the phone. Meanwhile, I was reading all of the newspaper articles that had been written since I was traded. There was a lot of talk about the Broncos youth at the receiver position (the team's top four receivers had four years of NFL experience between them). I thought there was still a place for me with the Broncos, but when my agent called the team, they made it clear that they were not interested in me. When I read the things that wide receiver Derek Russell had said about me, it really hurt my feelings.

Derek said, "Vance hasn't played a game this year. And in the two years I've been here, he hasn't played much, either. So they can't really say he's been doing a whole lot or that he's been productive because he hasn't. It was time for a change, definitely. The Three Amigos are gone. It's time for some new guys to come in and show what they can do, and I think Arthur (Marshall) and Cedric (Tillman) can do a good job, just as good as Vance would have done."

That cut me to the bone. I was already an emotional wreck after being traded by my team of eight years, after being ignored and then cut in Minnesota, and after thinking that my NFL career might be over. Reading that just devastated me, because I thought Derek and I were friends.

I felt like a has-been. I was the forgotten man. I knew that I was still a good player. I knew that I could still be the best receiver on the Broncos' team. But instead, I was reading quotes from guys on the team saying that I wasn't good enough.

I watched the Broncos play their first regular season game against the New York Jets, and I nearly had a heart attack. I saw rookie Tony Kimbrough wearing No. 82 — my old number. I couldn't believe it. Just that quickly I had been moved out and already someone else was wearing my number. It may seem stupid to someone who has never played sports, but you really get attached to a number. You sign that number every time you sign your name for an autograph seeker. You say that number every time someone asks you what jersey you wear. You put on that number every day during practice and during every game. In a lot of ways you become synonymous with your number. There are thousands of people who watch football games who may never have even a remote clue what your face looks like, but they know your number.

So when I saw Kimbrough in a Broncos' uniform with my number on his back, I felt violated. I felt like I had walked into my house one evening to discover that someone had stolen my television. The loss of the appliance didn't bother me as much as the thought that some stranger had been in my home. That was my number. I was No. 82 for the Broncos for nine years. No. 82 for the Broncos was supposed to have the name V. Johnson stitched over it — not Kimbrough.

Seeing him wearing my number just added to the emotional load that I was carrying at that time. I was a wreck. I wanted to turn off the television and turn my back on the Broncos in the same way that they had turned their's on me.

But I didn't. I continued to watch the game, because I wanted to see how the team did without me. I wanted them to fail without me. I wanted them to flounder. I wanted the coaches to say, "We'd be much better if only we had Vance back."

The Broncos won.

I found solace in the fact that the receiving corps was not very productive that day. There were a lot of talented young guys playing receiver for the Broncos, but none of them had any experience. That gave me hope that I might have a chance to return to the Broncos. No one had more experience working with John Elway than I did. There had to be some value in that to the Broncos.

Meanwhile, my agent was calling every team in the league. But everyone had the same response: "We just finished final cuts. Our rosters are set for the year. We don't have room for Vance."

He called the Broncos, but Bob Ferguson, director of player personnel said, "We're not interested."

This period was really tough on Holly, too. She was worried about me emotionally, and she was worried about my future. I was a hard person to be around. I was really irritable, and I didn't want to talk to anyone. I didn't eat and I didn't sleep.

I called my agent every day, sometimes two or three times a day, to find out if he had heard anything. It was the longest 10 days of my life. That was when I started making tapes for this book. I was sitting up at 2 a.m. and 3 a.m. every night talking into a tape recorder telling the story of every crazy and stupid and irresponsible thing that I had done in my life.

My agent called the Broncos frequently for a week and a half. He could never get any response. He asked to talk to Wade, but was denied. Finally, he got through to Wade, and said, "Vance would love to be a Bronco again."

Wade said, "Vance wants to come back? Well, I want Vance back."

Although I was scheduled to make $750,000 in 1993, the Broncos said, "We'll give you a $275,000 base salary and a $25,000 bonus if you play in four games. That's our offer. Don't ask for anything more."

I had no choice. My only request: I wanted my jersey number back. The Broncos said, "of course." I signed the contract.

When I walked back into the locker room the next day, I was really humiliated and embarrassed. I had gone from being the number one receiver in camp to being a guy who was desperate to sign a contract. I felt like I had been duped. I couldn't understand why the Broncos had put me through all of that. I thought I was their seasoned veteran. I thought I was the guy they wanted to be a leader for the other receivers. I had been working really hard at changing my life, and I had become a good person. Well, this time the good guy lost. I was miserable. I didn't talk to anyone. I just went to work, got my playbook and started learning my job.

I was really pissed off at Derek, too, because of all the things that he said about me. I wanted to get in a fight with him so bad, if for no other reason than to vent my anger on someone. But I didn't speak to him. I just held my tongue and tried to do my job.

I wasn't a starter anymore, either, and that was very tough. I had to sit on the sidelines during practice and watch the rookies play my position. I just had to sit and watch, and listen and be humble. I was so pissed off, because I had so much ability. I knew that no one on our team was going to catch the ball better than I could or get open better than I could or know Elway better than I did, but I wasn't getting the opportunity.

About the only thing that really made me happy during all of this happened when I went walked out onto the field at Mile High Stadium during my first game back with the Broncos. I went out during pre-game warmups, and I could hear people in the stands calling my name. I looked up and saw that two banners had been hung in my honor. They both read: "WELCOME BACK, VANCE."

I waved to the crowd and a whole section of people waved back and cheered for me. I've always loved the great fans in Denver, and it made me feel good to know that some of them still loved me and were glad that I had come back.

I just had to be patient and quiet and wait. The best receivers in the league play 60 or 70 plays during each of the 16 regular season games, and they catch five or six passes a game. To catch 100 passes in a season — which is a lot of receptions — you need to catch 6.25 per game. Well, in my first game back, I only played five plays, but I caught two passes. The next game I only played six or eight plays, but I caught three passes. By the fourth game of the season, I had earned the starting position back. I went ballistic. I wanted to prove to everyone that I was not over the hill. That I was not unproductive. That I should never had been traded from the Broncos or cut by the Vikings. I caught everything in sight. I caught every ball in practice. I ran extra wind sprints after practice. I got back into a groove.

Still, it wasn't the same. I didn't feel like a Bronco anymore. I didn't feel like I was an integral part of the organization. The team had already shown me that I could be dismissed at a moment's notice, and that was a constant fear in my mind.

But I was playing football, and I love the game. I was going to play hard during 1993, so that I could get a good contract when I became a free agent in 1994. I was going to show everyone what I was worth. Whenever John Elway looked my way, I was there. Whenever he threw me the ball, I caught it. In seven games, I had 36 catches and not a single dropped pass. Every catchable ball that came my way was caught.

I was scoring touchdowns when we needed them. It got to the point that Jim Fassel, the Broncos offensive coordinator, was designing plays that would put the ball into my hands. Everything was going great for me. After going through that tough week with the trade, the cut, the sale of the house and the new half-price contract with the Broncos, I felt everything was working out. Things were going to turn out okay in the end.

Then disaster struck.

We were playing the Seattle Seahawks in the King Dome. I was lined up wide on the left side — right in front of the Broncos bench. At the snap I exploded out of my stance and started to run my route. At a glance I could see that the two safeties were dropping back into a cover two look. In cover two, the safeties are each responsible for half of the field in the deep passing zone (beginning about 15 yards from the line of scrimmage). The corner backs in cover two roll up to about five yards to play the flats. At the snap, the cornerback who was over me started to drop back, but I guess he realized his mistake after a second or two, and started to come back down into the flat. I was running straight at him, and I didn't expect him to stop and come at me.

I tried to avoid him to the outside, and he shoved my upper body back right when I planted my left foot. My body fell backward, but my foot stayed planted firmly in the Astroturf.

I screamed out in shock as I heard and felt my leg pop. I looked up at the Broncos sideline, and I saw all of my teammates saying, "Oh my God!" and turning and walking away from me. They were actually putting their hands up to their eyes to shield their view of me. I looked down at my foot and nearly passed out because it looked so gross. My knee was pointed at the ceiling of the dome, but my foot was rotated outward laying flat on the ground.

Is this how it ends for me? I wondered. After everything that I'd gone through I wondered if this was how my career was going to end. My leg looked totally mangled. I was sure that my career was going to end with that injury. It looked like a really bad injury. It felt like a really bad injury. The trainers rushed out to me, and one of them grabbed my foot and popped my ankle back into place. The pain was incredible, but my mind was flip-flopping through the future. My career was over.

At the hospital, the diagnosis was the I had dislocated my ankle joint, torn a ligament and broken my fibula. It was not nearly as serious an injury as everyone first believed. There was a good chance that I would recover fully and play football again.

This injury reconfirmed my long-held hatred of artificial turf. I probably would not have been hurt if the same situation had happened on a grass field. On the turf, when the defender pushed me, my turf shoes gripped the ground firmly, and there was no give. Since a certain amount of force was created by the combination of my forward velocity and the defender's push, something had to absorb that force. My ankle joint and fibula ended up being the weak links in the chain, so they broke.

If we had been playing on a grass field, I would have been wearing long, seven-spike, grass cleats. When the defender pushed me, my cleats would have been planted in the ground, but as the force increased, my cleats probably would have dug themselves out of the ground at an angle creating a divot, just like in golf. In that situation, the ground would have been the weakest link in the chain, so some grass and dirt would have broken to absorb the force that was created.

Since divots cannot be created on turf fields, a lot of players suffer injuries when their shoes grip the ground and force their bodies to absorb the bulk of the impact. It would be like playing golf on concrete instead of grass. Instead of carving up a soft piece of grass and dirt with every shot, your club would clank against the ground and send painful vibrations back into your arms and shoulders. Something has to give.

• • • • •

I wasn't sure if I would ever play football again. I had been playing my ass off during the 1993 season, because I knew that if I had a good year, I could demand a big salary when I became a free agent. Then the injury hit and ruined all of my plans.

It hurt a lot, and when I was going through rehab, I was really discouraged. I was hoping that my leg would heal fast and I'd get back to full speed in a hurry, but everything seemed to plod along slowly.

But I was determined. I reported to the Broncos' facility diligently and put in the required hours of treatment and exercise to try to rehabilitate my leg. While that was happening I was so stressed out about my future, that I couldn't sleep at home. I'd stay up damned near all night every night just fretting over what was going to happen to me.

I wasn't eating much, either, and my weight plummeted dramatically during the first two weeks of my injury.

At the time I got hurt I was about 190 pounds. Less than two weeks later, I weighed only 172 pounds. I stayed at that weight for many months after that, and a lot of my teammates gave me a hard time about being skinny. They'd see me in the training room and say, "Damn V.J. What are you doing, smoking crack? You're ass is skinnier than a mother fucker."

I'd just laugh and say, "Yeah, I know," but inside I was hurting.

I wasn't just losing weight — I was losing everything.

• • • • •

When the season ended, my contract with the Broncos was completed. I was an unrestricted free agent, which meant that I was free to negotiate with any team in the NFL. I was determined to come back and play football, and I wanted to do it in a Broncos' uniform.

My agent asked me what kind of contract I wanted, and I told him to tell the Broncos that I wanted a two-year $2.4 million deal. I told him I wasn't willing to negotiate.

He presented my offer, and about a week later, he called to tell me that the Broncos hadn't responded in any way. I was really disappointed because, I wanted to be a Bronco, and I felt that I was worth that type of money. When the Broncos ignored that offer, I took it off the table. I knew I was a good receiver, and I knew that if I just kept working out, and kept rehabbing my leg, another team would call. My agent was calling every team in the league trying to arrange visits and tryouts for me.

But there wasn't much interest. Apparently everyone was scared off by my injury. During the latter part of the season, the Broncos had said a lot of things about my injury in the media. They had compared my injury to Steve Sewell's career-ending ankle break, but my injury was not nearly as severe as his. They said they didn't know if I would ever play football again, but based on my rehabilitation both myself and the trainers knew that I would come back.

I think their statements to the media were designed to scare off other teams. I think the Broncos wanted to sign me, but they were going to play it smart from a business standpoint. Why pay me $2.4 million over two years, when they can scare off the competition, wait until I'm desperate and then sign me for less than $1 million for two years.

Meanwhile, the Broncos launched an effort to get wide receiver Tim Brown from the Los Angeles Raiders. They considered him to be the best available talent, so they put together an $11 million, four-year offer sheet to him. Brown was listed as a transitional player for the Raiders — meaning that he is a free agent who can sign with any team, but the Raiders have the right to keep him by matching any offer he gets — so the Broncos weren't sure if they could get Brown. But they made a high offer and sat back to see what would happen.

For the fans, this was all exciting stuff to watch on television and read about in the newspaper, but I was sitting at home thinking that I was screwed. If the Broncos are trying to get Tim Brown to sign, then they didn't want me. There's no way that they could afford both of us. There was no way that I could have a future in Denver. I loved Denver. I loved living in the city, and I loved playing in the city. Since 1985, I had been an integral part of the Broncos' organization, but suddenly everything had changed. I had already been traded away to the Minnesota Vikings by the Broncos, so I had no illusions about whether or not I was important to them going into the 1994 season. I knew that I was not a priority.

After the Broncos made their offer to Tim Brown, the Raiders had seven days to decide what they would do. I was relieved when the Raiders matched the offer, and retained the services of Brown.

I thought there might be hope for me getting my deal done with the Broncos.

That hope was short lived. Just a couple of weeks after the Brown deal fell through, the Broncos tendered a four-year $10.5 million deal to Anthony Miller of the San Diego Chargers.

I was devastated again. Why didn't the Broncos try to sign me? I was as good as Brown or Miller. Why were the Broncos trying to find someone else when they already had me. It was another tense week for me waiting to see what would happen with the Miller offer.

Then in the middle of the week, the Chargers called and said they wanted to fly me out to San Diego for a physical. They had reserved a seat for me on a plane the following day, and wanted to know if I was interested in talking about a contract.

I said, "Of course."

My agent then called Bob Ferguson at the Broncos and said that he wanted to give the Broncos an opportunity to make an offer because another team was really interested in me right now. I think Ferguson thought we were bluffing. I don't think he believed that any other team would be interested in me. He thought it was just a negotiating ploy.

When my agent called me and told me this, I told him not to work to hard with the Broncos, because I didn't feel like part of the team there anyway. I wasn't interested in getting into a long contract negotiation that might land me back on the Broncos' squad with the type of contract that I wanted. I wanted to go somewhere where I would be appreciated and where both I and the team would feel good about the deal that we signed.

I didn't think that could ever happen for me with the Broncos.

When I got to San Diego the next morning, I couldn't believe the way they were treating me. Everyone was really excited to see me and everyone was making a big fuss over me. They treated me like I was a star and like it was important to them to sign me. That was a really good feeling for me, especially after sitting for so many months wondering if any NFL teams were ever going to call me. I knew that I was still a good football player, and I knew that I could contribute to some team.

The way the Chargers' organization treated me really confirmed those thoughts for me.

When I got there the Chargers' management sat down and talked to me and said, "If we can reach an agreement, would you be willing pull the rug out from under the Broncos?" I said, "Yes, I would." After that we talked about numbers in a really general sense. They didn't tell me what they were offering, and I didn't tell them what I was asking for, but I think they got an idea of the ball park that I was looking at.

Next, they sent me to a medical office in San Diego where I was examined by several doctors. They checked every part of my body, especially my hurt leg. When they checked my leg, they were pleased, excited and even surprised to see how much range of motion I had in my ankle. I think they expected it to be stiff, sore and immobile, but I had nearly full range of motion. They ruled that my rehabilitation was ahead of schedule and that I should be back to full speed within a few months.

I was taken back to the Chargers' front office, and they led me to an empty room so that I could use the phone. I called Holly and told her how well the physical had gone and asked her how she felt about the possibility of me signing with the Chargers.

She said she knew how sad I was after the Broncos traded me to Minnesota, and she knew that I had never felt like a part of the Broncos team after that. She said she was behind me in whatever decision I made. That was important to me, because Holly is a big part of my life. I didn't want to just go back to Denver and say, "Hey, I signed with San Diego, start packing." I wanted both of us to be involved in this decision. I wanted her to be happy with it. Her family lives in Colorado, and I wanted to make sure that she felt comfortable with moving to Southern California. I was really happy when she said she wanted me to sign with San Diego.

The situation for the Chargers looked like this. They had two days before the deadline to sign or release Miller. They were trying to find someone who could come in and take his place. If they could find that receiver, then they'd let Miller go. If they couldn't find a suitable replacement, then they were going to match the offer and keep Miller.

The Chargers told me that they wanted to sign me and let Miller go.

I was very excited.

I was still sitting in the room by myself with the telephone. My agent was in Chicago talking on the phone to Chargers' General Manager Bobby Bethard, who was in Florida at the time. While I waited, I called my parents, and I called my friend Tom Byington in Fort Collins, Colo. and I called Holly again. I was really praying that everything would work out well.

Finally, one of the Chargers' staff people came into the room with a piece of paper. They said my agent had asked them to present these contract numbers to me. The person who delivered the paper left the room, and then someone transferred my agent to that phone. The Chargers' initial offer to me was a two-year $2.2 million deal. It included a $650,000 signing bonus, a $750,000 base salary for 1994 and an $800,000 base salary for 1995.

I was amazed at how close the Chargers were to the $2.4 million contract that I was looking for. In all my years of contract with the Broncos, we were always about $500,000 apart when we started negotiating.

My agent asked me how I felt about their offer, and I told him that I thought it was really good, but I really wasn't willing to negotiate. I didn't want to change my mind. I didn't want to settle. I felt like I was worth what I was asking for, and I was going to hold out for that amount of money. I wasn't going to be making as much money as Anthony Miller was making, and I knew that I was as good as him.

My agent went back into negotiations with Bethard and when everything was said and done, I had a two-year $2.4 million deal. The final agreement included a $850,000 signing bonus, a $650,000 base salary in 1994 and a $900,000 salary in 1995.

I'm really excited about my new contract, but I'm more excited about the 1994 season. Everyone in San Diego has a lot of confidence in me, and I can't wait to show them that they made the right decision.

12

Where Did All My Money Go?

During my NFL career, I made a lot of cash, and I spent a lot of cash. I blew money on everything from cars to houses to good times to bad times. I never really worried when I spent a lot of money, because I always knew there was more money coming in. My attitude was that I was going to enjoy my wealth by giving myself the things that I wanted. If I wanted a $20,000 watch, I bought one. If I wanted a $90,000 Porsche, I bought one. I never worried about running out of money because it didn't seem like that big a deal to me. For most of my life, I didn't have very much money. If I ended up going back to that type of life then that's cool. I was born poor and I didn't care if I died poor.

During my nine years with the Broncos, I made about $4 million dollars in salary, and that doesn't include any of the money that I made doing different sideline ventures. Four million dollars, that's a lot of bank. If you were working a good job making $50,000 a year, it would take you 80 years to make $4 million. If you had a great job making $100,000 a year it would still take you 40 years to earn $4 million.

I made that much in just nine years, and I basically blew it all. I wish I had been more frugal with my money. I wish I had been smarter about investments and about the types of things that I purchased. If I had planned a little better, I could have put myself into a position where I would never have to work again in my life.

I plan to do a much better job of planning for the future with the money that I'm earning with the Chargers.

• • • • •

Ever since my first day in the NFL, I was a spending fool.

My first major purchase was the Porsche 944 that my agent helped me get right after the 1985 draft. The draft was in April, and I was still about three months away from signing a contract and getting some cash, but that didn't stop me from getting the car of my dreams. My agent took care of all the details with the dealer and with a local bank, and I drove away with the car that day.

After I signed my contract, my agent called and said we needed to send $25,000 to the bank that financed my Porsche 944. No big deal, I said. I had plenty of money. I happily paid the bank.

Probably the biggest mistake I ever made was placing too much trust in my agent. I think most agents are pretty honest people who are legitimately concerned about taking care of their clients, but there is a small percentage of agents who will do whatever they can to milk money off their players.

Unfortunately, I ended up with one of the latter guys. I'll call him Kevin. He was a real scumball.

During my senior year in college, I received about 60 letters from different agents all over the country who wanted to represent me. Probably about 10 or 11 of those invested money flying to Tucson to meet me in person. Out of all the agents I met, Kevin was the most impressive to me.

From the time that I first met Kevin, I really liked him. He was a very charismatic guy who won me over with his sense of humor, his compassion, his intelligence and his concern for me.

One of my most vivid memories of him is one of the nights that he flew to Tucson and took me to dinner. At first we engaged in the usual small talk about this and that. Then we got started talking about the NFL. Like every agent, he told me I would probably be a first-round pick. He told me I would make a lot of money and my standard of living would change dramatically. I was only half-listening at that point, because I had heard it all before.

A whole lot of agents sell themselves by convincing players that they will be very successful in the NFL. A player is much more likely to sign with the agent who says, "Yeah, you're going to be a first-rounder and you'll probably get a $1.5 million first-year salary," than he is with the agent who says, "You'll probably be a seventh- or eighth-round pick, and you'll make about $150,000 your first year." Since most players already think of themselves as studs, they're more likely to sign with the agent who strokes their egos.

I had heard that song and dance many times before, so I wasn't as impressed with Kevin's account of my future as I initially was when agents told me what was going to happen. By that time I already believed all of the hype, and I didn't need an agent to confirm it for me.

But all of that was just a prelude to the stuff that would eventually lead me to sign with Kevin. During that dinner we started talking about our personal lives. Kevin told me about his wife and kids and his home in California. He told me how his kids were doing in school, and how he hoped his family would grow in the years to come. He told me about his background, his current business and his personal goals. He really seemed to open up to me as a friend, and it made me feel good to be trusted by him.

He asked me a lot of questions about myself. He wanted to know about Nicole, my first child. He wanted to hear my plans for the future. He listened intently to a brief account of my life. He wanted to know what my mother was like. He wanted to know what my father was like. He wanted to know about my sister and my cousins, aunts and uncles. He wanted to know everything about me, and I think I got a little drunk on the attention he was giving me. It's very flattering to have someone sit across the table from you and just listen to you talk about yourself. It makes you feel good about yourself and good about that person.

I was prepared to sign with him that night.

It wasn't until a year or two later that I realized that his real motive for talking to me that night was to pump me for information that he could use to win over my parents and my sister. And I learned much later, that his minor in college was psychology — a field of study that he put to very good use in trying to woo me.

He went to my parents' house once when I wasn't there, and he spent the better part of the day visiting with my mother. I had told him how religious my mother was. So he showed up at the house wearing really casual clothes — jeans, a T-shirt and some regular tennis shoes. From the first moment he sat down, he talked to her about how much he loved the Lord, and how he loved to attend church with his family every Sunday morning.

By the time I got home, my mom's face was full of teeth. She was just smiling away saying, "This is the one, baby. This is the one."

None of the other agents had tried to manipulate my mother at all, and I think Kevin had figured out early that winning over my mother was the way to get me to sign.

That night he and I went to dinner, and he was a completely different person. To me he portrayed a real cool character who was wise to the ways of the world. I told him I was into nice cars and having money and having a good time. He said he was into that, too. In fact, if I was interested, he would fly me out to his condo in Palm Springs. He said there were a whole bunch of pools out there and a whole bunch of women. He also had a shitload of cars, so I ought to fly out and hang with him.

That sounded like a great plan to me. I was looking forward to getting a taste of the fast life out in Palm Springs.

When I got home my mother said, "The Lord told me this is the one, Vance."

I said, "Yeah Mom, he told me, too."

We were both happy because we were both getting what we wanted in an agent.

The other agents had come to the house and talked to us and told us about financial planning and tax preparation and telling me that I needed to try to save money. I didn't want to hear that shit. I felt like I was going to be in the NFL forever. I wanted to have a good time.

Of course, during the day that he spent with my mother, Kevin talked that whole song and dance with her. He told my mother that the Lord wants young men to work hard and save their money and invest right and raise their families up. He never talked about saving money to me. We may have brushed over it once or twice really quick, but there was never a full-blown discussion about it. Kevin was smart enough to know that I wasn't interested in talking about that.

I guess I should have known that Kevin was a little bit sneaky when he was doing all of this. The guy was like a damned chameleon constantly changing his personality to fit in with whomever he was talking to, but it didn't bother me too much at the time. I thought he was just a good businessman who was making good use of the information that was available to him. And that's what I wanted in an agent — a good businessman.

I began to look up to him. I liked him a lot, and I trusted him. When he flew me out to Palm Springs, I played games in his backyard with his kids. I slept in his house. I felt like I was part of the family and that he would look out for my interests in the same way he would look out for his kids' interests.

Plus, he was giving me a sweetheart deal. Most agents charge 4, 5 or 6 percent as a negotiating fee. The way that works is: Whatever the gross dollar value of your contract is, you pay your agent a percentage of that. For example an agent who charged 4 percent and negotiated a $300,000 one-year contract for his client would earn $12,000 in fees. If you want your agent to manage your money, pay your bills, do you taxes or anything else like that, those services involve extra charges.

But Kevin gave me a rate of 2.5 percent, which included negotiating my contract, managing my money, paying my bills and doing my taxes. He would do it all for 2.5 percent. It seemed like a hell of a deal to me. I couldn't argue with it, so I hired him as my agent.

My first contract with the Broncos was a four-year deal worth $960,000. Based on this contract, an agent making 5 percent would have earned $12,000 a year for four years for a total of $48,000. That agent could make additional money from his client by providing additional services.

But Kevin didn't want any money for extra services. He was making only $6,000 a year — or $24,000 total — on my deal, and he was providing all of the other services for free. Plus, he spent money on me when I flew out to his house in California a couple of times.

When I look back, I can see that at only 2.5 percent commission, I would not be a very lucrative client for Kevin. I should have known that he wasn't representing me out of the goodness of his heart. I should have known that he would make additional money based on the clauses that were written in invisible ink at the bottom of the contract. But I didn't really think about it or worry about it. I just thought about all of the exciting things that lay ahead of me. All of the fun I would have, parties I would attend, and money I would spend.

Right before camp started in 1985, Kevin showed up with a stack of papers for me to sign. Since he was going to be negotiating my contracts, managing my money, doing my taxes and even paying some of my bills, he needed to have a bunch of documents signed. It seemed like he put 1,000 different pieces of paper in front of me. I just kept signing my name over and over again wherever he told me to sign. I didn't read any of the forms because I trusted him. And plus, I didn't really care what they said. I just wanted to get it over with.

Well, I found out years later that one of those pieces of paper was a power of attorney that gave Kevin the right to do whatever he wanted with my money. To tell you the truth, he could have sat across from me that day and said, "Vance I want you to sign this power of attorney," and I probably would have. For one, I don't think I really understood what the words "power of attorney" meant. And two, I trusted him so much that even if he explained everything to me, I still would have given him the right to hold my money.

But things were sailing along nicely through my rookie year. I wasn't very good at paying bills, so Kevin agreed to do that for me. I think his intentions were good in this regard, but he simply didn't have time to monitor all of my monthly bills and make sure they were paid on time. A lot of them were paid late, and although I wasn't aware of it, my credit was going to shit.

Meanwhile, I was living in La-La Land being the big stud Broncos' player who was making a ton of money, and I wasn't worried about a thing. But, I first started to think that Kevin might be stealing from me, when I noticed some discrepancies in my account statements during my second year in the league. But honestly, I wasn't even sure if money was missing. The way Angela and I were spending money, we could easily have spent $50,000 more than we thought we had. But over a period of months, I began to realize that there was a steady leak in my accounts that was not caused by Angela or myself. Someone else was withdrawing money.

I wanted to ask Kevin what was going on, but I was afraid to. I knew that he had control over my money, so I didn't want to alert him to my suspicions. I was afraid he would take more money out of my account and stash it somewhere before I could fire him and regain control. So I played the role of the little dumb black kid and tried to gather as much information as I could.

For the first three years of my career, he used and abused my money in any way he saw fit. I was spending so much money my first few years, that I think he was quietly slipping cash out of my accounts and into his pockets thinking that I would never notice.

During my rookie year he took $200,000 out of my account and invested it in some apartment complex in Michigan. But he didn't tell me about it. When I asked him about the missing money, he told me about this great investment that he couldn't pass up. He said that he had tried to get in touch with me, but couldn't reach me. He didn't want me to miss out on the opportunity, so he invested the money.

He told me that he and his wife had invested in the apartment complex, too, so we were all in it together. That sounded good to me so I said, "cool" and didn't worry about it.

During the next few years, every time I asked him how our investment was going, he would say, "Oh, it's going great, Vance. It's value is getting better every day. We just need to hold onto it for a couple more years, then we'll be able to sell it and we'll all make a killing."

Years later with the help of a CPA and a lawyer, I learned that what Kevin really did was sell me his and his wife's interest in the apartment complex. They had been invested there for years, but the complex was failing and they wanted to get out. So they used my cash to finance their exit and strapped me with the struggling apartment complex.

Meanwhile, Kevin was still the general partner, but he stopped taking care of the complex because none of his money was involved. But he kept giving me rosy reports about how the complex was doing.

His holding this huge chunk of my money only reinforced my fear of letting him go. I thought that I would lose all of the money that I invested in the complex if he found out that I knew about his schemes. So I just kept working with him and kept worrying.

But along the way, I was meeting people who were as powerful as my agent, but who also cared about me and my well-being. Tom Byington a banker, a lawyer named Michael Burg, my public relations people and others like them who continually told me that I didn't have to worry about Kevin and that I shouldn't let him control me, told me that I had to be in control of myself, and that they could help me in different ways. But they said they didn't need or want to be in control of my money.

These people became very influential in my life and they really helped me a lot. But they didn't try to control me. They basically just told me that I needed to grow up. Plus, Holly let me know every day of my life that I was making a mistake by letting Kevin continue to represent me and take advantage of me and rip me off. If you hear something everyday, you start to believe it. So with Holly buzzing in my ear everyday, I started to open my eyes and see the full truth about the things that I had turned my back on for a lot of years. I'd known for a long time that Kevin was stealing from me, but I guess part of me didn't want to admit it. Part of me turned a blind eye to all of the things that were happening. Part of me was content to just sit back and let him continue to rip me off rather than trying to confront him and end the relationship. For most of my career, I had been going out and partying and not even thinking about what was happening with my money.

But finally, I was looking at the situation, and I knew something had to be done.

Then Holly came up with a great idea that changed everything. She had a Dictaphone from her old job. She told me to use her recorder to tape everything that Kevin said to me. Fortunately, the very next time I talked to him, I taped the conversation without his knowledge and he sat there and lied about us still owning the complex. The reality was that it were gone. It had been sold from our portfolio almost three years before then.

I asked him if we still owned the apartments.

He said, "Well don't you have the K-1s in front of you?" (A K-1 is a financial statement filed with the IRS. It's a reporting device issued by a real estate investment trust).

I said, "Yeah."

He said, "Well, don't you know how to read them. You can see we still have the apartments."

The truth was that I had no idea of how to read the K-1s. It was all just a bunch of numbers to me. But I'd had my CPA read them and he told me that they indicate that I didn't own part of the property anymore. My entire investment had been lost.

So I had Kevin on tape telling me that the apartments were still part of my portfolio. I hung up the phone and looked at Holly and she was smiling because she had heard the whole conversation. We knew then that we had him by the balls.

In 1992, I finally sued Kevin. My suit alleged that he had abused me as a client, taken advantage of my ignorance about financial matters and taken liberties with money that I had entrusted to his care. I didn't ask for a specific monetary award in the suit, because my attorney and I had no idea what I might be able to reasonably recover from Kevin. Instead, we decided to leave the award to the discretion of a jury.

When we went to the deposition, I told the truth about how Kevin had treated me and how he had used and abused my money. My attorney told me that the picture any jury would see was of a powerful, rich white man taking advantage of a young black man who didn't have any knowledge about investments. Plus, I had the tape of him flat-out lying to me on the telephone. A jury would rip his ass apart. I guess that's how Kevin saw it, too, because we reached a settlement the day of the deposition.

According to the settlement agreement, I'm not allowed to disclose his name or the amount of money that we settled for. But I thought it was important for me to tell the truth about what happened to me, because other young players may be able to learn from my mistake.

Most agents are fundamentally good people, and they want to do what is best for you, but there are a handful of agents out there who will take you for everything you're worth if you let them. You have to be really careful about whom you sign with, and you have to try to educate yourself about financial matters so that someone can't take advantage of you. You can't just meet a guy, dump all of your money into his lap and say, "I trust him." You've got to make him account for every dollar in that pile, and if you ever suspect that someone is ripping you off, don't be afraid to break off the relationship.

• • • • •

The Porsche 944 I bought a few days after the draft turned out to the the first in long progression of cars that I would own during my career. And that Porsche got ruined less than four months after I bought it when I loaned it to my roommate, Larry Willis. Larry was one of the top rated wide receivers in college during the 1984 season, but he ended up not being drafted because he was very small and there were questions about his ability to catch over the middle. Apparently teams were concerned about whether he could withstand the punishment in the NFL.

I watched Larry play throughout that first camp, and I thought he was pretty good. He ran great routes, he always got open and he had good hands. During camp I learned that he was the second or third leading receiver in the nation the year before. I couldn't figure out why no team had drafted him. He simply didn't get any respect from the league.

Larry was really jealous of me because of the way the Broncos treated me. He was right. It wasn't fair. I was a second-round draft pick, and he was a free agent. When the coaches looked at me, there was always that gleam in their eyes, because I was one of the guys they had hand-picked. They were going to do everything they could to make sure I was successful. They were going to give me every opportunity to prove myself. If I did good, then they looked good for having picked me.

On the other hand, Larry was a free agent. He wasn't getting the same opportunities that I was getting. He was being treated really unfairly as a receiver, and he and I both knew it.

Another factor in the equation was that I was a running back throughout college, and I was converted to a wide receiver when I got into the pros. It was a great switch for me, because I had always wanted to be a receiver, but it was tough, too. I had never really run deep routes before. I wasn't good at reading coverages. I wasn't really sure of myself lined up as a wide receiver. My strong points were that I was fast as hell, and I could catch pretty decent.

But I think Larry resented the fact that most of the time I didn't know what the hell I was doing, and the coaches were still fawning over me. Meanwhile, he was a premier receiver in college, and he can't even get them to glance in his direction.

All of this resentment was boiling just under the surface throughout camp, and Larry and I were just trying to get along. Two things happened near the end of training camp. The first thing was that Larry borrowed my Porsche. The second thing was that Larry got cut from the roster. The details about that time are a little blurry to me, but I think both of those events happened on the same day. One of the dynamics of training camp is that except for the designated cut days, getting released from the team is not a real public event for the player involved. Guys would go to the cafeteria for breakfast or lunch and they would get pulled to the side by a front office person and given the word about their halted futures with the team. There was never an announcement to the team, you just wouldn't see that player anymore. The next day you might see a small note in the paper saying that so-and-so got released.

Throughout camp, I had given Larry frequent use of my Porsche, because I liked him and I wanted him to like me. I was always giving him the keys. And like I said much earlier, even during training camp I was usually out at night trying to pick up women. So Larry and I didn't see each other a whole lot, because I was never in the room. We had a better chance of running into each other in the lobby or in the cafeteria than we did of meeting up in the room.

So when I gave him the keys to my car, it was usually two or three days before I got the keys back.

On the day that I found out he was cut, he already had the keys to my car. After he got released, he took off to Denver in my Porsche to visit a girl that he'd been dating. Later that night he called me — it was one of the rare nights that I stayed in the dorm — and said that he had my car.

I told him that I wanted him to bring it back that night. He said he wanted to wait until the next day. I demanded that he bring my car back, and deliver the keys to me before curfew.

He hung up on me. But apparently he decided to try to make it back that night. He was flying down the highway back to Greeley when the motor in my Porsche blew up. He didn't even care what happened to my car. He just left it sitting on the side of the road, and later called and told me that I needed to go pick up my car on the side of highway 85.

I never saw Larry again.

I called a towing company and said, "look for a maroon Porsche 944 on the side of the highway. I don't know exactly where it is, but it should be on the northbound shoulder somewhere between Denver and Greeley." The tow truck guys just rode down the highway until they found the car. I can't remember exactly, but I think it cost me between $10,000 and $15,000 to have a new motor shipped over from Germany and put into my car.

While my car was in the shop, Angela came to Greeley to visit me. We jumped in her car to go get something to eat. Angela had this raggedy, beat-up, gray car and I had to sit on the floor because the passenger seat was missing. Since I was Mr. Money Man, I bought her a used car that ran pretty well, just so I would have a place to sit when she drove.

A couple of weeks after my Porsche 944 got out of the shop, I traded it in for a brand new Porsche 911.

I still don't know why I bought so many cars over the years. Since joining the NFL I have owned 40 cars, six motorcycles and three boats. I would often buy a new car, and then get tired of it after a few months, a few weeks or a few days, so I'd trade it in for another new car. I estimate that during the past nine years, I have spent more than $200,000 on automobile down payments. That doesn't include monthly loan payments, or annual license fees or maintenance or anything else. That's just the amount of money that I paid in cash in order to drive the cars off the lot. (Listed in the appendix are all of the cars I've owned during my career).

The three main reasons that I spent so much money on cars are: 1) I wanted to impress women, 2) I wanted people in general to think that I was rich and successful, and 3) I was very insecure, so I always had to have a nicer car than all of my peers. If one of the other players showed up at work one day with a really nice car, then I'd end up buying something better than his.

Plus I would sometimes do crazy things like constantly upgrade to the next nicest car of a particular type as they became available. My first Porsche 911 was a Carrera, which is just the base model 911 coupe. Then I traded that in for a Porsche 911 Targa, which has a panel in the top that pops out. After that I traded for a Porsche 911 cabriolet which is a convertible. Next was a Porsche 911 Carrera turbo, which is a much faster car than the regular 911 and about $30,000 more expensive. I later bought a slant-nose Porsche 911 carerra turbo. My next acquisition was a Porsche 911 turbo cabriolet.

It just never stopped. I just kept buying and buying, and I did the same sort of thing with Corvettes. I bought different color Corvettes, different years and different styles.

I've always loved old cars, too, because they are so distinctive. I always thought it looked really cool to see a guy get out of a nice older car. I used to see commercials with guys driving old cars or with a guy standing next to an old car on the side of the road. Even with smoke billowing out from under the hood the car looked really cool to me. I was always very fascinated by older cars, and when I was driving a perfectly restored old Corvette or Mercedes, people were always really impressed. They would whistle at the car or scream, "Nice Car!" as they were going past.

Of all the old cars that I have ever owned, if I could only have two of them back, I would want my 1962 Corvette 327 with a fuel-injected 360 horse-power engine and a hardtop convertible design. The second car I would want back would be my 1959 Mercedes 190SL hardtop convertible.

Unfortunately, I had to sell the Corvette so I could afford to get an attorney to pay for my divorce from Angela. In fact, most of my older cars got sold whenever I needed money to survive during the off-seasons or whenever I got sued. Any time I needed to raise money in a hurry, I would hawk one of my cars.

The Mercedes was one of the few vehicles that I sold when I wasn't desperate for cash. I made about $5,000 on the sale of that car.

I have always loved Porsches because they are the ultimate car, but after I got into the NFL I fell in love with Corvettes, too, because they're sleek, low to the ground, really fast, and come with a convertible option. And I had this really silly theory about my sports cars. I'm really embarrassed to admit this now, but here goes. I believed that if I drove around in a Porsche girls would think I was rich. And I thought that if I drove around in a Corvette, girls would think I was available. I know, it's stupid, but that's the way my mind worked at the time.

I don't know if the girls actually thought these things about me, but in my mind, I felt rich in a Porsche, and I felt available in a Corvette. Now that I think about it, during the crazy years, I know I probably looked available no matter what I was driving.

And this little quirk of the mind was costing me a fortune. Let me give you a quick run-down of just how fast your money can disappear when you're buying expensive cars.

When you buy a $90,000 Porsche you're paying a lot of padding to the dealership. A dealer may pay $14,000 for a Honda Accord and then list the sticker price at $17,000 in order to make a profit. If a dealer pays $26,000 for a BMW, he may set the sticker price at $34,000. So you can see that the bigger the price tag, the bigger the markup. When you talk about a $90,000 sticker price on a Porsche, the dealer's cost is probably only about $70,000. But it doesn't matter how much they mark it up. People who buy cars in that price range aren't paying for simple transportation. They're buying ego gratification. And since it's your ego you're catering to, you don't even want to haggle on the price of the car. You want the salespeople to think that you are made of money, and to be impressed by how coolly you purchase a $90,000 car.

So I'd go into the dealership to purchase a $90,000 Porsche, and the bank would demand a $20,000 down payment on the car. I'd write the check. The minute I drove the car off the lot, it depreciated to $70,000. Now the car is worth exactly the amount of the original loan. My $20,000 down payment is irretrievable. I'd drive the car around for a few months before I got tired of it, then I'd take it in and trade it for another $90,000 Porsche.

By the time I trade it in, the dealer will only give me $50,000 for the car. So I have to write a check for $20,000 to pay off the bank, then another check for $20,000 as a down payment for the new car I'm getting.

So you can see that in less than three months, I paid $60,000 in down payments and depreciation losses. But I didn't care about any of that at the time. I just wanted my cars, and I was willing to pay for them at whatever cost.

I really didn't like used cars — unless they were vintage automobiles. I could have saved a lot of money on my Porsches, my Ferraris and my Corvettes if I had bought them when they were a year old. But I never wanted to have a car that someone else's ass had been sitting in for any length of time. I wanted a fresh seat.

Plus, I didn't think there was any way I could ever go permanently broke, so I didn't worry about how much I paid for cars.

I'd walk into dealerships, and the salesmen were always glad to see me. They'd be damned near tripping over themselves trying to be the first one to get to me. I'd test drive the car I liked, and then I wouldn't even negotiate on the price.

In my mind the only argument someone could use when negotiating was, "I can't afford it." I couldn't say that. I knew damned well I could afford it and so did they. In fact, most of the time when I did try to haggle on the price the salesman would play up to my ego by saying, "Come on Vance, you've got plenty of money. Why are you worried about a couple thousand bucks?"

That made sense to me, so I'd just pay the sticker price on the car.

Sometimes they'd even talk me into throwing Broncos tickets into the deal. Yes, that's right. I'd pay the inflated sticker price of the car, plus I would sign a contract that forced me to give them between 4 and 8 tickets for every Broncos home game. And I felt comfortable with that, because I thought all these guys were doing me a favor.

A couple of months later when I went to trade in the car, I'd lose even more money. I really had no concept of depreciation. I couldn't truly understand how much money I had lost on the transaction. I didn't really comprehend the reality that I was sometimes spending $40,000 for the right to drive a car for two or three months. The value of a dollar was completely lost on me.

Now that I look back, I can see that every car dealer I ever came in contact with took advantage of me. I can't say it's really their fault. I was very uneducated about things like that, and they saw an opportunity to make some money. I guess it's the American way.

I had relationships with a bunch of them, and they were always really nice to me — until it was time for me to cough up the cash. And salesmen always had smiles on their faces when I drove away. They knew I'd be back shortly to give them another chunk of money.

When I was buying vintage cars, I look for ads in the paper and then call to make an appointment. When people found out who I was, they were always really excited. They'd invite me over to dinner, and be really nice to me. I made a lot of friends that way. After I bought the car, I would still be friends with the previous owner. I didn't get too many deals in that arena either, because I didn't feel like I had a whole lot of negotiating leverage. They knew I was rich, so I couldn't claim poverty. I'd just pay their asking price and drive away.

The best deal I ever got on a car came from a car dealer who lived in my neighborhood and wanted to do something nice for me. There was a man who had a 1962 fuel-injected Corvette. He gave the car to his son on the kid's 16th birthday, but the kid didn't like the car. He traded it in so that he could buy a big four-by-four truck. The dealer gave him $1,500 in trade-in value for the car.

The car was worth at least $15,000.

I had been studying old Corvettes, and my neighbor knew that I would be interested in this car. So he called me up and sold it to me for $3,500. It was a steal.

I spent another $5,000 getting it painted and getting a few other minor problems fixed, and the thing was good as new. It was a beautiful, beautiful car, and I was determined to keep it forever.

Then the first divorce arrived. I'll talk about the actual dollar figures of the divorces a little bit later, but just believe me when I tell you I gave up a shitload of money.

Well, my spending patterns created fluctuations in which I went from having a lot of money to not having a penny. The divorce came at a time when my funds were very low. I had to sell a lot of things in order to make all of the payments that were ordered by the judge.

One of the things I had to sell was my Corvette.

It killed me to have to do it, but I knew I had to. Of course, when I went to the dealer to sell the car, I made the mistake of telling him that I needed the money because I was going through a divorce. That was all he needed to hear. He was prepared to rape me on the sale of this car. With all of the work that I had done to the car, it could easily be sold for about $30,000.

The dealer offered me $15,000. I haggled with him, but I was desperate for cash, and I needed the money right away. I started thinking that $15,000 would really help pay for some attorneys fees. It would help with alimony and child support. It would pay for a lot of things.

I took the money.

I planned to keep checking on the car though, because I was hoping that there would be some way for me to buy it back. I loved that car, and I really did want to keep it forever.

A day after I sold it, it was sitting on the lot with a sign in the window. The price tag: $35,000.

The car sold in three days.

Once again, I had gotten out-foxed by a car dealer.

But after that deal, I never again lost a penny on an old car. I always did my research, and I always knew the value of the car. I'd buy cars that were in pretty good condition, make them perfect and sell them for their book value. I became very good at it.

• • • • •

Usually when the money ran out during the off-season I would have to sell one or two of my cars to get some money to live on. One of my biggest regrets is that I had some really valuable old cars that I had to sell during the off-season. I had spent myself into poverty. Sometimes I needed money to simply survive, and sometimes I needed to round up money to pay divorce settlements and child support.

The list of 40 cars in the appendix does not even include all of the cars that I bought for women over the years. Those are just cars that I personally owned. I know I bought a Mazda Miata for one girl when those cars were popular, and I bought Chri a Mazda RX7 one year. I bought my first wife, Angela, a whole bunch of cars. I bought her that first used car during training camp my rookie year, and as we continued to date, I kept buying her cars. If her car broke down, I wouldn't mess around with getting it fixed. I would just buy her a better used car. I kept buying her better and better used cars, until we got married, then I got her a new car. I think I bought her four or five different cars while we were dating. And as was the case with all of my other girlfriends and wives, they always kept the cars when we broke up. I think Angela passed on the cars to other people in her family every time I bought her a new one.

Unfortunately, I never spent much money on cars for my family. I always wanted to wait until I could afford to buy my parents a home. I thought a car wouldn't be enough for them. But I was spending so much money all the time, that I never put aside enough to buy a nice house for them.

Meanwhile, I still wasn't doing a very good job of paying my bills. It wasn't all that important to me. So I had three or four cars that were repossessed over the years (including the Chevy Blazer and the Porsche Cabriolet I mentioned earlier).

My credit was completely jacked up. No one in their right mind would trust me enough to lend me a dime. It wasn't that I didn't have the dime to repay them, it was just that repaying that money wasn't high on my list of priorities because I was very irresponsible. Plus, I flat didn't care what my credit report looked like. I was making so much money that credit seemed irrelevant to me. But the companies of the world didn't stop worrying about my credit rating.

To give you an idea of how bad things got, during 1991 I was earning more than $600,000 in base salary. I went to a furniture store and picked out a living room set for my mother. I wanted to get financing for the $4,000 loveseat, couch and chair arrangement, but I was rejected. The store checked my credit, and despite my enormous income, they refused to let me finance a $4,000 purchase!

My bad credit began to affect my car purchases as well. Since my payment history was so shitty, and since I'd had several cars repossessed, banks wouldn't finance cars for me unless I coughed up 50 percent of the car's value as a down payment. The same thing happened when I bought that $500,000, 7,000-square-foot house in Ken Caryl Valley. The going interest rate near the end of 1990 was about 8.75 percent, but I was having a hell of a time finding a mortgage company who would trust me with their money. When I finally did find a company, I had to make a 25 percent down payment and finance the remainder at 13.5 percent interest.

And I always lost a lot of money to women. There just didn't seem to be any way to get around it. As I mentioned earlier, the first woman to get money out of me was Ana, the mother of my first child. She received $20,000 cash plus $750 a month in child support. Then Lisa, the mother of my second child, got $5,000 or $10,000 cash, plus $980 a month in child support.

Bettina, another girlfriend from college, received a $10,000 settlement from me for mental anguish. The "Men Who Beat Women" article reported that I had kicked down the door to Bettina's apartment, and she sued me for $100,000. That's only partly true. I did not kick down her door, but she did sue me.

Angela and I were in Arizona for a visit, and I decided that I would go visit Bettina to see how she was doing. When I got to her apartment, she invited me inside. We were sitting on the couch talking when her boyfriend arrived. Apparently, he looked in the window and saw me — her apartment was on the first floor — and got pissed off. So he went to the front door and kicked it in. He didn't knock, didn't ring the door bell, didn't do anything normal. He just raised his foot and kicked the damned door in.

By the time he barged into the living room, I was on my feet and prepared to defend myself, if necessary. But he calmed down pretty quickly and ended up leaving after a few minutes.

I left shortly after him.

The next day, I went out to run an errand, and when I returned home, I discovered that Angela was gone. She had left me a note indicating that she had talked to Bettina on the phone, and she knew that I had gone to see Bettina the previous day.

Angela was pissed off at me because I had talked to Bettina. I figured that Angela had gone to Bettina's apartment, so I raced over there.

When I got there, I saw Bettina through a window, but when I knocked on the door, she didn't answer.

The door was completely busted. The dead bolt had been engaged when her boyfriend kicked it in, so the entire door was destroyed. A huge chunk of the door frame — where the bolt would have slid — was missing, and the door itself was warped and cracked. Everything was going to have to be replaced.

Given the condition of the door, it wasn't locked. So when Bettina didn't answer, I just pushed the door open and walked in.

I just knew Angela was there, and I was pissed at her for coming to see Bettina. I walked into the apartment with a golf club in my hand, because I didn't know if Bettina's boyfriend was there or not. I didn't want to get into a fight with him, and I thought that club might dissuade him from trying to start anything with me.

I was screaming at Bettina and demanding to know where Angela was. In my rage I was flapping my hands around, and waving that golf club threateningly. Bettina kept insisting that Angela wasn't there, and eventually I became satisfied that she was telling the truth.

I apologized for yelling at her and I left.

About a week later, I learned that Bettina had filed suit against me for mental anguish. I didn't fight the charge against me, because I felt I was wrong. Plus, I didn't want to go to court. I had already been to court too many times, and I was tired of going. Court was horrible, especially when you're the one being sued. And especially when you generally lost the decisions like I did. I didn't want to go through all of that again, so I settled with Bettina and gave her $10,000.

I honestly don't think that Bettina even wanted to sue me, but an attorney talked her into it. That was another of the things that I had to deal with whenever I got involved with women. When the relationship ended, there were always aggressive vulture-type attorneys who would convince the women that everything I owned should be theirs.

I'm sure most of the women would have sued me anyway, but some of them might not have sued. And a lot of them would not have sued me for as much money as they did if they hadn't been driven to that by attorneys.

When Angela and I divorced in 1989, we were living in a townhouse that I purchased for $109,000. That became Angela's property. We owned a truck on which $12,000 or $13,000 was still due. The judge ordered me to pay off the vehicle and give it to Angela. All in all, the judge ordered me to resolve about $250,000 in debt that Angela and I had created. Plus, I had to pay her $3,000 a month in "rehabilitative maintenance" for five years — so that she could attend college and eventually get a job — and $3,000 a month child support. I also had to give her two or three months worth of back pay, pay $4,100 in fees to her attorneys and give her lump sum payments of $15,000 in March 1990 and $15,000 in March 1991.

At that time, I was so cash poor it wasn't funny. Angela and I had been spending money with reckless abandon so when the judge ordered me to pay her all of this money, I was in shock. I simply didn't have any money. I didn't know how I was going to pay for all of the things she got in the settlement and pay for my living expenses. I was broke, and I was praying that I would make the team again that year.

When I finally did make the team, most of my first check went to pay off the settlement damages with Angela.

When Chri and I got divorced, I didn't even want to go haggle in court. I knew that I had done a lot of wrong things in our relationship, and I just wanted everything to be over, and I wanted to treat Chri fairly.

But I think she took advantage of me, too.

Because I was feeling badly about everything, I was pretty much willing to give her whatever she wanted. I knew that if we went to court, the judge might not give her very much because we hadn't been married for very long — we married July 16, 1990 and separated Feb. 3, 1991. We didn't have any children together, and Chri didn't own much when she entered the relationship. So a judge probably would not have awarded her a whole lot.

But I wanted to be fair, so I offered her $2,000 a month for one year. She agreed to that, but as time passed leading up to the actual divorce proceedings, she kept calling to ask for different things. She called once and wanted a TV. I said okay. She called and wanted a stereo for her car. I said okay. She called to ask for the furniture downstairs. I said okay. She called to ask for $5,000 so that she could go back to school. I gave her the money, but as far as I know, she never went back to school. A couple of months later, she called to ask for another $5,000. This time she didn't make up any lies about the intended use of the money. She said, "I want $5,000 more because you put me through fucking hell." I gave her the money.

But after that, I said "No More. I'm not giving you a single other fucking thing." I was so pissed off, because she just kept hitting me for more and more. It seemed that every woman I was ever with just wanted more and more from me when the relationships ended. Everything always seemed to boil down to money, and I was sick of it.

When we finally went to court, the judge ordered me to give Chri an Eagle Talon that I owned, in addition to everything else I had given her. I couldn't believe it. I was trying to be generous with Chri. I had given her everything that she asked for. Now the judge was ordering me to pay off one of my cars and give it to her. I didn't have the cash for that. I had spent everything, and there was no way I could afford all of that. I was so pissed off I couldn't stand it. I was sitting in court sulking like a little kid. Once again the American Judicial System had given Vance Johnson the shaft.

The divorce was nearly final. But right before the judge announced that we had irreconcilable differences and our marriage was dissolved, he asked if there was anything else that either of us wanted to say.

I was pissed off and there were plenty of things that I wanted to say, but I didn't want to get put in jail for contempt of court.

There was a brief moment of silence, and then Chri leaned over and whispered to her attorney, and he stood up and asked for one more little thing from me. I can't even remember exactly what Chri wanted, but it tore me apart. It was something simple like the remote control for the television or something like that.

The judge ordered me to give it to her.

Everyone was always taking things from me, and the courts were always giving away my money to different people. It was driving me crazy. I could never win in these situations.

And now at the very last minute when the judge gives us an opportunity to say anything that we want to, Chri took the opportunity — like everyone else — to ask for one more thing.

Did I mention that the judge also ordered me to pay Chri's attorney's fees? Ours was a mutual consent divorce that took only a few months to complete, and I got stuck paying between $8,000 and $10,000 in legal fees for her. How could anyone rack up that much in legal fees in just a few months? Why did I have to pay for that shit?

Every time I turned around some judge was ordering me to pay more money to whoever in the fuck asked for it. "Oh, you know someone who knows someone who used to know Vance Johnson? And you'd like to go spend a week at Disney Land? Well, since Vance has a lot of money, why don't I just order him to give you some of it . . . hmm . . . let's see . . . how does, say, $20,000 sound? Would that be enough? Great. Vance, you are hereby ordered to pay $20,000 to what's his name because he showed a little initiative in bringing this matter to court."

That's how it always worked out for me. Whenever someone sued me they always won. And they always won big, because judges loved to be generous with my cash.

By the time I got home from court after the divorce proceedings with Chri, I was so pissed off I couldn't stand it. I couldn't believe that I had been raped by the courts again.

I was so pissed off that I walked into my garage, looked at the Eagle Talon that was about to become Chri's property, and it made me sick. I grabbed a 9-iron out of one of my golf bags and started wailing away on the car. I hit the front hood and the side of the car, and banged it up pretty good.

My white Mercedes was in the garage, too. It was parked about two or three feet away, but I wasn't worried about accidentally hitting it, because I had dead aim on that Talon. I wasn't swinging like a mad man. I was aiming carefully. I hit the car seven or eight times with some really good shots. I would aim, swing and then listen contentedly to the resounding THUMP! As the club connected with the fiberglass body. Aim. Swing. THUMP! Aim. Swing. THUMP! Aim. Swing. THUMP!

I was just really mad that the judge made me give up so much. I took out my frustrations on the car. It felt great at the time, but I felt like a complete idiot afterward, because I was obligated to get the car repaired for Chri.

It cost me $2,300 in body work.

Oh well.

One thing that really bothered me about that situation was that after I gave the car to Chri, a Denver television station went to her parents' house to get some footage of the damage to the car. They did a report about me hitting the car, and they made the whole thing sound worse than it was.

I beat up the car at my house, inside my garage, late at night when I was home by myself. My house sat on two-acres of land, so my neighbors couldn't hear anything. No one knew I beat up the car until I told them. And no one was in any danger at any point.

The TV report made it sound like Chri and her parents were sitting on their front porch sipping lemonade when a crazed maniac in a Porsche slammed on the brakes in front of their house. He jumped out with a golf club and started beating the shit out of the Eagle Talon that was parked in the driveway. Then he jumped back into his sports car and burned rubber heading down the street.

That's not how it happened at all.

• • • • •

The crazy aspect of my life during my NFL career is that I was often broke. I was making hundreds of thousands of dollars every year from the Broncos, but I was broke all the time. My entire salary with the Broncos was paid in equal installments over the 16-week regular season. The problem was that during the season, I would live paycheck to paycheck, which means I lived high on the hog during the season, and I generally ran out of money during the off-season. Basically, every time I got a check during the season, I would go buy a car. Every check simply represented another down payment to me.

· · · · ·

Another part of my problem with money and life in general was that I was hanging out with a very low class of people. And by low class, I mean people who really didn't have an interest in doing anything in the future; people who partied all night and slept all day; people who were irresponsible, and who couldn't hold down jobs; people who didn't try to make a positive difference in their lives or in the lives of anyone else; people who got drunk on a regular basis; people who wouldn't think twice about joining an orgy and having sex with a big group of complete strangers; people who judged their worth by how many people they'd had sex with; people who constantly had bill collectors chasing after them; people who wouldn't hesitate to take advantage of you if the opportunity arose, and people who wouldn't hesitate to steal from you if you turned your back for a minute.

These were the people that I was hanging out with. These were the people I was calling my friends. These were the people I was becoming more like with every passing day.

It was a quick transformation.

I had grown up in a somewhat chaotic environment, so a lot of the things that my so-called friends were doing seemed normal to me. Those were the type of people I gravitated toward.

I hung out with a few guys who were Broncos' players, but most of my friends were people that I met in nightclubs. At that time in my life, I thought a nightclub was the only place to meet new people. Whether I was looking for a friend or a girl to date, a club seemed like the only source of new people to me.

I'd run into different people at night who would always try to impress me by saying where they worked or what kind of car they drove or what type of business they were planning to start. Even people who sold drugs would approach me and tell me that I could make even more money than my Broncos' salary if I was interested in entering their profession. I never responded to the drug scene at all. I was just not into that whole world. I was afraid of it. I knew it was trouble, and I didn't want to go to jail.

But plenty of other people would approach me and say, "How are you doing, Vance Johnson? My name is so-and-so. You know, you need to have one of these bars, because you see how popular you are here. If you had your own place, people would come, and it would be jam-packed and you could make a lot of money. I've been in the business myself, and I could run it for you."

At that time, I was always very interested in these pitches, because I thought these people were really looking out for my interests. I thought they wanted to help me be successful after my football career ended, but really they were just looking out for their own interests. Many times I was tempted to open up my own nightclub. In fact, Mark Jackson and I always talked about opening a club together. We would have called it Club 8280 (my jersey number was 82 and Mark's was 80). But we never got around to it. I was spending so much money on cars, attorneys' fees, divorces, child support and whatever else came up, that I never had enough capital to start that type of investment.

I met with people and talked to them all the time about getting a club up-and-running, but despite my interest, I could never pull together enough money to get the deal off the ground. In retrospect, I think it's really fortunate that I didn't have the money, because I just would have been giving a different group of people a chance to rip me off.

But hanging out in the world I was living in, put me in contact with a lot of bad people. One year, during the 1989 off-season, I was so broke that I desperately needed money just to survive. After I had sold everything that I could easily sell — like my cars and jewelry — I ended up meeting some people who specialized in loaning money to people who had good income potential, but who were currently in need of a quick buck. They were damned near gangster-type people, whom I met based on a recommendation from some of the scum-of-the-earth people I was running with. I was going around telling people, "I'm in a situation. I need to make a buck. You know anyone who can lend me some money?"

I was so cash-poor that I began looking for change underneath my beds and inside my sofas just to get a dollar or two for gas or to get something to eat. If I could find 70 or 80 cents, I'd go through the drive-thru at Taco Bell in a Porsche with hardly any gas and buy one taco.

At the time Angela and I were separated, I had moved into the townhouse Chri shared with her sister. And there I found a bounty that helped tide me over. Chri's sister had a huge jar full of change. It was a mammoth jar. She had probably about $200 in pennies, nickels, dimes and quarters. I was so desperate that I would steal change out of that jar to put gas in my car or to buy a meal. She never knew I was taking that money from her, and if she ever suspected that her change supply was diminishing, she probably would have blamed Chri. She surely wouldn't have thought to point the finger at the guy who was driving a Porsche, making $400,000 or $500,000 a year and basically living fast.

But eventually I had to get some real money because stolen quarters weren't going to make my car, mortgage or insurance payments.

The people I hung around with knew different guys who gave loans to people like me. I was in the category of someone who needed to borrow a $1 today, but who could afford to pay back $1.50 tomorrow.

This particular off-season, I was talking to a friend of mine who was involved in the crazy world that I was living in. I told this person that I was desperate for some money, and this person told me about a group of people in Denver that I could go meet.

When I walked into their office, I noticed that there were some chairs and desks in the place and nothing else. No pictures on the walls. No file cabinets. No coffee machine. Nothing extra. A secretary was up front, and several offices in the back of the suite housed different men. When I got there, I could hear a couple of guys in the back discussing ways that they could get repayment on a delinquent loan. I could hear them say that they could either steal something or add more money to the amount the guy owed.

They pretty much ignored me for a few minutes while they worked through their plan. A couple of minutes later, a guy — I'll call him Nick — came walking in and he was all beaten up. From the fragments of the story that I heard, I gathered that Nick had beaten up a guy who had failed to repay a loan. Then the borrower's family had caught up with Nick and had beaten the shit out of him in retribution.

Even after seeing all of this and knowing what kind of people I was dealing with, I still asked them for a loan. I was desperate. I borrowed $5,000, in March or April 1989, and I promised to pay $7,500 to them in July when training camp started. But a couple of things happened between the day I borrowed that money and the day I reported to camp. I can't remember how I spent that $5,000 loan, but I didn't use it to make my two car payments that were long overdue.

In fact, I fell so far behind on all my payments during the 1989 off-season that my 1988 Porsche Cabriolet and my 1987 Chevy Blazer were repossessed by the General Motors Acceptance Corp. The company was suing me for the balance — plus interest — on both of the loans. For the Blazer they wanted $16,470.54 and for the Porsche they wanted $72,746.93.

Plus, during that off-season, a huge tax lien was levied against me by the IRS. With the Tax Reform of 1986, the tax laws were changing a lot, but I was oblivious to them. All I thought about was how much money I could put into my pocket today. I usually always filled out my W-4 the right way, but if I started to run low on money, I would go into the Broncos' front office, and change my form so that the Broncos withheld less of my check. I never really worried about the consequences of that action. I just did it. Also, my second year in the league, my agent told me that I should file tax exempt — for whatever reason. That sounded good to me, because it meant I would have more money to spend, so that's what I did. It all came back to haunt me in 1989.

I was scheduled to receive a $205,000 reporting bonus in 1989, but my tax liability was such that the IRS took nearly half of that money. Then I had to spend the other half getting my two cars out of repossession. So I simply didn't have any money left over to make a $7,500 payment to those loan sharks.

They called me a couple of times to remind me that I owed them money and to tell me that they expected repayment immediately. I would always say, "Okay. I'm going to get it to you as soon as possible."

I was really worried about what these guys might do.

Angela and I were separated at the time, so I thought she would be safe. And I was up in Greeley living in the dorm during training camp, so I figured they wouldn't come after me up there. But when I returned to Denver after training camp the garage door and the back door of my house were standing wide open. When I walked inside, I saw that everything of value was missing. Most of the furniture, televisions, appliances, art work, a pool table and a lot of other stuff were missing. It was a terrifying feeling to know that someone had been inside my house and had cleaned me out. My first thought was that the loan sharks had come to collect their debt, and since I wasn't home they took my stuff. I never filed a police report, because I was afraid of those gangsters, and I didn't want them to come after me.

I never heard from them again about the money I owed them, so I assumed that they were the ones who had robbed me. I never borrowed money from anyone like that again, because I was scared to death.

I later learned that Angela had taken some of the stuff with her when she moved out, but there was no way that she could have taken everything that was missing from my house. I know she had the microwave, and she had one or two paintings at her house, but there was just too much stuff gone for her to have taken it all. The house was completely cleaned out.

• • • • •

A huge money-making scheme that unfortunately didn't pan out really well was the Three Amigos' campaign. Mark Jackson, Ricky Nattiel and myself became famous as the Three Amigos during the summer of 1987.

I was drafted by the Broncos in the second round in 1985. Mark was acquired in the sixth round in 1986. Ricky was selected in the first round in 1987.

So during Ricky's rookie training camp the three of us were working together, and we all had pretty much the same build. All of us were under 6-feet-tall, weighed about 180 pounds, got open pretty well, ran pretty fast, and caught the ball well. When we watched films of practice, it was sometimes really hard to tell who was who, because we looked so much alike in uniform.

It was really a fluke for the Broncos to have three receivers who were that size, because at that time in the NFL most receivers were tall guys with average speed. The trend toward having smaller receivers with more speed was just beginning.

One day at football practice, John Elway jokingly called us The Three Midgets. Everyone laughed about it.

That night, Mark and I went to a bar. We were sitting there talking, when suddenly I had an idea. I said, "We should tell the press that John called us the Three Amigos, like the guys in the movie."

"No, that's not what he said," Mark said. "He called us The Three Midgets."

"I know that," I said. "But we should tell everyone he called us the Three Amigos.

It sounds cool and you know that if John said it, everyone will think it's cool."

"Yeah, that's cool," Mark said.

So the next day, I told everyone in the media that John had called us the Three Amigos, and the name took off all over the country. The media loved it.

Every news report about the Broncos referred to us as the Three Amigos. Kids called us the Three Amigos. Everyone thought of the Three Amigos when they thought of the Broncos' receiving corp.

Shortly after this all started, several members of the media asked John why he called us the Three Amigos. John said, "I never called them that." But the media either didn't believe him, or they didn't care whether he said it or not. They liked the name and they were going to use it.

The Three Amigos were born. And it didn't take us long to realize that it could be a huge money-making venture for us.

But there were problems with the Three Amigos. I guess the biggest of the problems was that we hated each other. No, I take that back. Mark was my best friend, and I loved him like a brother. Mark and Ricky weren't good friends, but they got along. But Ricky and I flat-out hated each other. We didn't keep it a secret. I couldn't stand his ass, and he couldn't stand mine.

The root of the problem lay in the fact that I was a second-round draft pick, Mark was a sixth-rounder and Ricky was a first-rounder. I always hated Ricky because he was so arrogant about being a first rounder. I know it sounds crazy for The Vance to be calling someone arrogant, but at the time, I thought he was even more arrogant than I was.

In the NFL, first-round draft picks seem to be in a class all their own. No matter how many years they've been in the league, the fact that they originally came in as first-round picks is always in the back of your mind. It means that they were good enough coming out of college that a team was willing to spend it's very first pick that year on that player. First-rounders get huge up-front money when they sign, and they get mammoth multi-year contracts. They get more media attention than anyone else, and they generally get more respect from other players.

It's a very big deal.

So in 1987, when Ricky came strutting into the Broncos' locker room as a first-round selection, I disliked him on the spot. But Mark and I were the two starting receivers, and I figured this young rookie would have to be pretty damned good to displace one of us. Then, because I was having some problems in my personal life that were affecting my performance on the field, Coach Dan Reeves moved Ricky into my starting position and made me a backup.

Suddenly, my dislike for Ricky turned into hate.

Then I started to get my act back together and my play improved. I earned my starting position back. But Ricky didn't become a backup. Instead, he was moved into Mark's position, and Mark became second string. Mark was my best friend in the world, so I hated Ricky even more for bumping him out of a spot.

The reality was that there were three receivers, but only two starting positions. For us to truly be the Three Amigos, one of us had to be content to be a backup, and none of us were willing to do that. We each wanted to be a starter, so even from the outset, the notion of us being the Three Amigos was a farce.

There were a lot of bad feelings floating around.

But we weren't stupid. We knew there was a lot of money to be made by milking this Three Amigos' idea, so when the cameras came on we'd be damned near holding hands, smiling and basically acting like we loved each other.

Shortly after the name got launched, I spent $5,000 of my own money to get 150,000 posters made. The photo shows from left to right Mark, me and Ricky standing with our hands on our hips wearing football pants, shoulder pads on bare upper bodies and sombreros hanging off the backs of our heads. The background is a desert scene and at our feet is a cow skull and a football. At the bottom it reads: ADIOS AMIGOS.

One of the other ideas we had for the poster was to write The Good, The Bad and The Ugly at the bottom. Mark, who was on the left, was always viewed by the media and by the fans as a nice guy, so he was The Good. Everyone thought of me as a wild and crazy guy. I was The Bad. And Ricky was damned sure Ugly, so this idea seemed to make logical sense. Me and Mark both wanted to go with that idea, but Ricky said "Hell no!" He didn't want to be The Ugly on the poster.

I said, "Hell, you're ugly in real life, why not in the poster, too?"

It didn't fly.

When the season started, the three of us started doing autograph sessions all over the state to further promote the name and the posters. We'd sell posters for $6 to $9 a piece. For an additional $5, you could get your picture taken with one or all three of us.

We sold every single one of those posters in less than three months. We were raking in the dough.

One time we were scheduled to sign at a mall opening in Colorado Springs and when we go there, more than 5,000 people were already waiting in line. Almost every one of those people bought a poster or two, plus a picture.

We rode in limousines to every event, and of course, after every show, we'd have a stable of women scheduled to meet us at various nightclubs and bars.

But things didn't always go smoothly.

The second major problem with the Three Amigos was that all three of us were very irresponsible, and all three of us had some major problems in our personal lives. I was constantly fighting with my wives and my many girlfriends. Mark was constantly fighting with his wife and his many girlfriends. And Ricky was constantly fighting with his main girlfriend, and his many other girlfriends.

There was always something crazy going on that would stop one or two or occasionally, all three of us from getting to an appearance.

One time we were scheduled to appear at a mall in Denver, and Mark and I got drunk in the limo on the way over there. Ricky couldn't make it for some reason or another. When we got to the mall, there were more than 2,500 people waiting for us. We got behind the table that had been set up and started signing posters.

Everyone had to pay between $6 and $9 for the posters — depending on what we decided the price would be that day — and this price included the opportunity to have the poster signed by all three Amigos.

So when one of us didn't show up, people were always a little upset, because they wanted to get autographs from all of us.

People kept asking, "Where's the third Amigo?"

We'd say, "Oh, he couldn't make it."

Then one of us would either sign Ricky's name or we'd take a big black marker and X-out his face. We didn't ask people if they wanted us to do this to the posters they had paid cash for. We didn't offer them a partial refund since Ricky wasn't there. We just signed his name or marked him out, because we thought we were cool, and we could do whatever we wanted. Fortunately, I think most of the people liked it when we did that. They would always laugh and say, "That's cool."

Since we really didn't like Ricky that much, we crossed out his face a lot more often than we signed his name that day.

But there were plenty of other times when myself or Mark couldn't make it, too. We really abused the power that we had. Sometimes we'd be hours late for different appearances, and we wouldn't care. We didn't care if we made people wait for us or if we messed up someone's schedule or if we caused someone to lose money because of us. We just did whatever we wanted to do without having any consideration for others.

One time we had an appearance at a mall in Greeley, Colo., but Ricky and Mark didn't show up. I got out of the limousine and was led in through a back door at the mall. I peeked out to the front and saw thousands of people waiting. It looked like everyone in the city was waiting at the mall.

I got a little scared, because I knew all of those people were going to be upset when they found out that only one of the Three Amigos was present. I stood back there getting myself psyched up to deal with the crowd, and I started to feel more confident.

I was thinking, "Hell, I'm better than Mark and Ricky, anyway." I figured I would go out and entertain the crowd and make them forget about the two other guys.

There was a stage set up in front of the crowd, so I ran out onto it, grabbed a microphone and started the show. The place erupted in applause.Everyone was screaming and hollering and whistling. I just stood there and enjoyed it for a few minutes. I always loved it when a crowd went crazy.

When they quieted down, I started telling the kids to stay away from drugs. I told them to stay in school and to be good citizens. I thanked everyone for supporting the Broncos, and I told them a lot of funny stories about Mark, Ricky and myself.

Then I started playing a little trivia game. I gave free posters to people who could answer certain questions, such as, "In which games did Mark, Ricky and I all score touchdowns?" After a while people were going crazy trying to win free posters, and I felt like I had made up for the absence of Mark and Ricky.

I was happy, and everyone else seemed happy. I signed posters for a couple of hours, got a $4,500 check from our promoter, jumped into the limousine and took off.

The money was rolling in from the sale of posters and pictures, but the real cash was coming from licensing deals that we were getting. The NFL recognized the Three Amigos as a marketable name, so they bought the rights to make T-shirts, hats and other apparel with our names and likenesses. Everywhere we looked we saw more Amigos' products.

Then Taco Bell approached us about doing some commercials for them.

But even with a big money deal with Taco Bell looming, we were pretty irresponsible.

One day we were supposed to shoot a television commercial at a Taco Bell restaurant in Denver. I think we were supposed to start taping at about 11 a.m., but we were delayed because Ricky wasn't there. Mark and I were there waiting. The Taco Bell people had flown in from wherever their front offices were; the restaurant manager had pretty much closed the place down in order to shoot this commercial; the camera crew was in place. Everything was ready, but Ricky wasn't there.

Mark and I had talked to him a couple of minutes after 11 a.m. He was still at home, but he said he was on his way. Then we got disconnected. When we tried to call him back, we got his answering machine, so everyone figured he was on his way.

The restaurant wasn't that far from his house, so when he hadn't shown up 45 minutes later, we tried to call him again. There was no answer, so we left a message. We tried to call him on his car phone, but there was no answer there either.

Meanwhile, everyone was just sitting there waiting for Ricky to show up. That commercial was a big deal to the Taco Bell people, and they needed to get it shot as soon as possible. That was really the only time that the commercial could be shot. After that day, the Taco Bell people were going back to their front office. The camera crew was being paid for that day, and setting a new appointment would cost more money. It was during football season, and Tuesday was the Broncos only day off. And the manager of the store couldn't afford to close up his shop and turn away paying customers for another day. So if we didn't tape that day, then we wouldn't be able to do it again until the next week, and I think we Amigos already had an autograph session scheduled for the next Tuesday. Everything was in place, and if it didn't get done that day, it was going to be really tough to try to reschedule. So everyone just sat there and waited and waited and waited. First Ricky was one hour late, then two hours, then three hours, then four hours. We were all still just waiting. There was nothing else we could do.

Eventually people started gathering outside the store, because they wanted to come in and buy some food. I think the manager wanted to open for a little while and sell some tacos, but Mark and I asked him not to open the place because we didn't want to be bombarded by people asking for autographs. So he left the door locked.

Everyone was getting more and more anxious with each passing hour, and I was feeling pretty embarrassed. Mark and I were trying to keep everyone cool by entertaining them. We really had a lot of charisma together and great timing. We were a good team, and when we started telling stories about the Broncos or about things that had happened during football games, we could keep people entertained.

Ricky finally showed up at about 4 p.m — 5 hours late!

He told everyone he said he was sorry he was late, but he'd had car trouble. He said his car broke down, and he had to walk a long way to get to a phone so that he could get another ride.

Mark and I busted out laughing, but everyone else was sitting there with a straight face like they were afraid to say that they doubted his story.

I said, "We tried to call you on your car phone."

"Yeah, my battery went dead," Ricky said.

We started laughing again, and even Ricky was smirking a little bit.

That was standard fare for all three of us. We didn't have any respect for anyone else's time. We did what we wanted when we wanted, without regard for anyone else. Ricky was late that time, but on other occasions it was Mark or me.

We did a couple of commercials with Taco Bell, but the big money was waiting for us after the Broncos won the Super Bowl. If the team had won, we would have signed a high-dollar endorsement with them. They might have made us their corporate sponsors.

The potential of that opportunity loomed large during Super Bowl week. I was trying to do everything that I could to show Taco Bell that I could be a good and willing spokesman for them.

Mark, Ricky and I had each received from Taco Bell these big black sombreros that the company had ordered. These weren't cheap hats. They were the real deal from Mexico. They were made of a really high quality material, and they had a big Taco Bell logo stitched on the front.

They told us that during Super Bowl week they would give us $50,000 every time we wore one of those hats during a national interview. Mark and Ricky laughed when they saw the hats, and said they probably wouldn't wear them because they didn't want to look stupid on national television.

But for $50,000 I'd be willing to wear anything. I couldn't wait for an opportunity to collect that money.

Then came my invitation to do an interview on the *Nightline* show with Ted Koppel. He was going to interview Washington Redskins player Dexter Manley and myself about the game, and I was planning to wear my hat the entire time.

When I walked into the studio, one of the production people asked me what I was doing with the hat. I told him that Taco Bell had asked me to wear it, so I was planning to have it on my head during the interview.

"Vance we really can't allow that because we can't give them free promotion," he said. "The only way we can make money as a show is to sell our advertising time, and so if Taco Bell wanted to get some advertising on this show, they'd have to pay for it."

I said okay, and I just sat the hat underneath the table in front of me during the interview. Dexter and I were on the air for about 15 minutes. The interview was going great, but I couldn't get that $50,000 off my mind. It was easy money and I was determined to earn it.

When Ted said, "We're going to take a commercial break and come back to finish up with Vance Johnson and Dexter Manley," I knew that was my opportunity. It was a live show, and I knew there was nothing they could do to stop me if I just reached down and put the hat on my head.

During the break, I put my hands under the table, scooted my chair back a hair and basically got into position to quickly slam the hat onto my head when we went back on the air. The camera guy was counting down, with his fingers . . . five . . . four . . . three . . . two . . . one. During his countdown, I could see in the television monitor off to the right, that the camera was focused on me. When he got to two in his countdown, I pulled the hat up and put it on my head.

The show resumed and there I was with my big Taco Bell Sombrero, looking like a fool, but feeling pretty good. The camera stayed on me for about four or five seconds before they flipped to Manley. That four or five seconds earned me a $50,000 check from Taco Bell.

After the interview ended, no one on the *Nightline* crew said anything to me, but I got some funny looks from people, and I could tell that they were pissed off at me. But I didn't care. I had just made $50,000. I bet every single one of them would have done the same thing if there was $50,000 riding on it.

Unfortunately, during Super Bowl week, that was the only opportunity I had to wear the sombrero during a national interview.

But we were still doing commercials with Taco Bell.

And I was so committed to the further growth of the Three Amigos that I was also risking injury for them when we shot our video.

Yes, I said video — as in music video.

Near the end of the 1987-1988 season we played the Houston Oilers in a playoff game. During that contest, I got kneed in the groin by one of the Houston defenders, and that blow tore a branch of my femoral artery. I had to spend a few days in the hospital because my leg was hemorrhaging, and I was losing a lot of blood.

I was worried for a while because I thought there was a danger that it might be a life-threatening injury. After I got over that fear, I was afraid it might be career ending. But the doctors did a great job, and they alleviated that concern, too.

After that, I was just trying to figure out how I was going to get up onto a horse for the Three Amigos video we were scheduled to shoot. Although I caught a little bit of flack from the media and from my team doctors for getting onto a horse so soon after my discharge from the hospital, everything went okay. The video turned out great.

Mark, Ricky and I had been talking about making our own video for a while, and we finally got together with a production crew to create a song called *Three Amigos, Touchdown Banditos* and an accompanying video.

.   It started out with the Three Amigos astride horses that were walking slowly through the snow. As we entered a place called San Diego (where the 1988 Super Bowl was being held) we learned that there were problems in the town. Mark Jackson pointed toward the city and we could see a few jerseys hanging in front of us. There was a Cleveland Brown's jersey, a Seattle Seahawk's jersey and a Houston Oiler's jersey — they were the teams the Broncos defeated enroute to the Super Bowl.

There was havoc in the saloon, so we walked in there and basically scared everyone to death. The video showed highlights of the Three Amigos making big catches and scoring touchdowns.

It was really cool.

It aired on a bunch of the Denver television stations and I think MTV even showed it once. It was just another fun thing for us to do together.

• • • • •

The Three Amigos were huge during the 1988 Super Bowl, and if we had won that game, we would have moved on to bigger and better things.

But the Broncos didn't win. The Washington Redskins thumped us 42-10, and the Three Amigos played terrible. That was our audition for superstardom and we flopped.

After that, the Three Amigos were never the big name that they used to be. Of course, everyone still referred to us as the Three Amigos, but we could never again generate the hype that we created during the 1987-88 season.

In 1992, Ricky Nattiel got released by the Broncos, so there were only two Amigos left. Mark and I were sitting around one day trying to decide on a poster that the two of us could make and we thought up the idea, *Partners in Crime*. But that was too negative, and probably too close to the reality of our off-the-field lives. We never did it.

After the 1992 season, Mark Jackson signed a three-year $4.5 million contract with the New York Giants (former Broncos' head coach Dan Reeves recruited him away from Denver). So I was the lone Amigo.

After the departure of those two guys, Holly told me that I should do another poster and title it, *And Then There Was One*. I thought it was a pretty cool idea, but I never got around to doing it. Then, as I mentioned earlier, I got traded to the Vikings just before the start of the 1993 season. But I came back to Denver after 10 days and played out the 1993 season with the Broncos. After the season, I signed a contract with the San Diego Chargers.

All of the Amigos had run to the border.

• • • • •

Although a lot of money was being generated by the Three Amigos, we personally weren't collecting the cash. We had a promotions manager who handled all of that for us. He was supposed to collect the money from the poster sales, from the Joslins, from the May D&Fs, from the Foleys, from the Taco Bells and from the NFL. He apparently didn't do a very good job of staying on top of everything, or he was simply not passing the riches on to Mark, Ricky and me.

Hundreds of thousands of dollars changed hands during the 1987–88 season, but I only received $16,000. Mark received $16,000. And Ricky received about $30,000. We have no idea what happened with the rest of that money. And don't ask me why Ricky made more than Mark and I because we still haven't figured that out. At one point, Mark and I each got a check for $4,500, then a month or so later, we each got another check for $11,500. To my knowledge Ricky didn't receive anything on those occasions. But later, he got a check for $30,000.

Go figure.

So a lot of money disappeared, but at the time, we didn't really care. We were making so much money on the football field that none of that really mattered to us. We were pocketing between $20,000 and $50,000 each every two weeks from our Broncos' checks, plus we were getting extra money for being in the playoffs. Money from the Three Amigos merchandising was just icing on the cake and we'd worry about that later.

It wasn't until 1993 that I decided to file suit. I called Mark and Ricky and asked them if they wanted to join me in the suit, and they did. We figured our promotions manager owed us about $500,000 from all of the commercials and merchandising that we created during the big Three Amigos hype.

The suit was settled out of court, and we didn't get anywhere near $500,000. Mark dropped out of the suit fairly early because he owed a lot of money to the promotions manager, and he didn't want to pay the debt. As soon as our suit was filed, our promotions manager filed a counter suit against Mark. Mark dropped out of our suit, and he and the promotions manager called it even.

In 1992, Ricky was released by the Broncos and picked up by the Tampa Bay Buccaneers. But he was later released by them as well. So he wasn't playing football in 1993, and when our promotions manager gave him a low settlement offer, he jumped at it. I think he probably needed the money.

So then I was the only one left, and we eventually hammered out a settlement. I did better than Ricky, but we're still not talking about huge money. The Three Amigos earned a lot more than the amount we recovered.

• • • • •

Besides losing a lot of money through the Amigos mismanagement, I also squandered a lot gambling. I loved to gamble. It was one of my many vices. Mark was an avid gambler, too, and he and I would visit Las Vegas and any other gambling venue as often as we could. One year — I think it was 1987 or 1988 — he and I were flying to Vegas once a week to try our luck at the tables. During the season, the team played on Sundays, watched film on Mondays and had Tuesdays off. So Mark and I would leave Denver Monday evenings, spend the night and the entire next day gambling and then fly back to Denver on Tuesday nights so we could rest up for practice on Wednesdays.

I was losing tens of thousands of dollars in Las Vegas, but I didn't really care. I had a lot of money coming in, so I always spent what I had in my pockets. I didn't think anyone would or could ever turn off the free-flowing money spigot.

I became such a regular in Vegas, that the casinos would usually issue me a line of credit after I lost all my cash. I think my largest line was for $10,000 and I lost every penny of it. That was one of the first times that I ever got pissed off about losing money in a casino. Usually, whether I won or lost, I was in the same mood because it was just Monopoly money to me anyway. But for some reason — I still don't know exactly why — I was pissed off about losing that extra $10,000 they had loaned to me. I flew back to Denver, and decided that I wasn't going to repay the debt.

The casino kept pressing me for the money, and finally they just called the Broncos' office and said, "Vance owes us money, and if we don't get paid we're going to the press and tell them that a couple of Denver Broncos' players are in Vegas every week losing tens of thousands of dollars."

At first the team just passed these messages on to me, and didn't give them much thought. But when the casino kept calling, I think the team started to weigh the public relations impact of having someone in Las Vegas tell the media that one of the Broncos' star players had a gambling problem.

I guess the Broncos' front office people decided they didn't want the team to look bad, so they wrote a check directly to the casino to cover the debt. One of the Broncos' front office people mentioned this check to me once. After that I never heard another thing about it, and no money was ever taken out of my wages.

But that pretty much cured me of getting lines of credit in Vegas, too. I knew that I wouldn't always want to pay back the money, and that was no big deal to me. I wasn't making payments on a lot of my loans, because I was very irresponsible. But if I became delinquent and the Broncos were going to foot the bill, then I was jeopardizing my job. The team would reach a point at which the management decided that it would be easier to cut the player rather than continue to cut checks to cover his debts. So I never took out another line of credit in Las Vegas. And to tell you the truth — I hadn't thought about this until just now — I might not have been able to borrow money in Vegas anymore. That one delinquent episode may have ruined my credit with all the casinos.

Only now have I started to realize the value of money. At the end of the 1993 season — in which I earned $300,000 in base salary — I had more money saved from that season alone than I'd saved during the other eight years combined. And during those eight years, I made about $3.7 million. I thank God that he gave me another chance to be smart with the $2.4 million contract I signed with San Diego.

• • • • •

Remember the story I told earlier about the medical staffer who hid me from the cops because my blood-alcohol level was too high? Well that night, a friend — I'll call him Jimmy — was in the car with me when I was hit from behind.

He was a guy I met at a bar. He was a really good pool player, so we would travel all over town hustling people on the pool table. He was a legitimate pool shark, and I would back him with money. We'd place bets against people, and we'd usually win. A couple of times we lost pretty big, too. But Jimmy was good, and most of the time we won.

After the accident, Jimmy sued me.

Why does everybody want to sue me all the time? I think I must look exactly like an ATM to most people. They think they can just push some buttons and make money spit out of me. The worst part is that most of the times, that's how it works. Jimmy sued me because the guy who hit us didn't have insurance. He won the lawsuit simply because he was in my car. I ended up paying him $5,000 or $10,000, plus his attorney's fees.

After he filed against me, I learned that Jimmy had a pretty extensive criminal record. He had been to jail many times. He had several aliases. During all the time that I was traveling around town with him putting up money for pool games, I never knew all these things about him.

When I look back now, and I realize the number of sketchy people I was hanging with, it amazes me that I'm still alive. It wasn't like I just went to a nightclub every once in a while. I was around these people all the time. I was in daily contact. I was always carrying a fat wad of cash and driving a fancy car, and always naively flaunting my wealth. I lived the way they lived. I acted the way they acted. I can't believe that I didn't get into more trouble with the law. And sometimes, I can't believe I'm alive.

• • • • •

During my NFL career, I have spent so much time in court that I think I'm nearly qualified to be a lawyer. For a while, it seemed that every time I turned around, someone new was suing me. I was tired of the suits. I was tired of lawyers. I was tired of judges. I was tired of hearing people say, "Vance Johnson did this to me, and I want some cash."

I felt that I had been used, abused, accused, persecuted and raped by the criminal justice system. I'll admit that I've done a lot of fucked up things in my life, but every time I made a mistake it seemed to cost me $50,000. Every time someone said anything about Vance Johnson, the judge would say, "You know what? You deserve some of his money."

So I became very leery of courts.

But in 1992, I found myself in court again, only this time I was standing on the other side of the court room.

You see, after the Broncos AFC playoff game against the Houston Oilers on January 4, 1992, I got my most prominent national exposure ever. People saw more of me than they did when I was on *The Tonight Show* with Joan Rivers, more than when I did *Nightline* with Ted Koppel, and more than when I was a guest VJ (that's "Video Jockey" not "Vance Johnson") on MTV. In fact, the exposure I got was more significant than all of those shows combined.

This time I was buck-ass naked.

In the locker room, a camera man from NFL Films Inc. was shooting footage of the post-game celebration and of Broncos' head coach Dan Reeves handing out game balls. From what I understand, NFL Films shoots post-game footage in the locker room and then turns the tapes over to different networks who purchase and edit the cassettes.

This particular tape went to Home Box Office for use in its *Inside the NFL* show.

Someone forgot to edit the tape. Someone didn't notice that I was standing in the background with nary a stitch of clothing on. In fact, the show aired twice with me naked before someone realized the mistake and deleted that part of the tape.

But by then, it was too late. By then, the entire world had gotten a full-frontal view of all my secrets.

I didn't actually see the show, but my sister in Japan and my grandmother in Trenton, N.J., both watched it, and they were shocked to see me get so much exposure. They called to tell me I was naked on TV.

I couldn't believe it.

On my way to work the next day, I heard people on the radio talking about me appearing naked on the show. They were saying how shocking it was to see me in my birthday suit on a family show.

When I got to the Broncos facility, I walked past one of my teammates who was sitting in his locker and he said, "Vance have you heard all the stuff they've been saying on the radio about you?"

"Yeah," I said. "I heard them talking about how surprised they were to see me naked on TV."

"No, I'm talking about the contests they were having," he said. "This morning women were calling in for the Guess Vance's Length Contest."

"No shit." I hadn't heard any of that. Although I had shown my dick to a lot of women individually over the years, I was very embarrassed to have people all over the city and possibly the country talking about my dick.

"You could sue them," my teammate said. "It's totally irresponsible for them to put you on TV naked, and now you have to deal with radio shows making up contests based on your dick. I think you could sue *Inside the NFL* very easily."

I walked away from his locker thinking that I just might sue. But after a few minutes, I pretty much forgot about it. My appearances in different courts had been such a negative experience over the years, that I didn't relish the idea of going to court again, even if I stood to gain some money. I just put the idea out of my head.

But then things kept getting worse and worse. I heard more radio talk about my dick. There were contests for people who wanted to guess Vance's shape. There were contests for people who wanted to compare Vance's member to a vegetable. There were contests for people who wanted to guess how hairy Vance was on a scale of 1 to 10 — with a newborn baby being a 1.

It got to the point that it was just humiliating. Everyone seemed to be talking about it.

Finally, I contacted my attorney and we put a suit together. The first thing we had to do was get a copy of the show. We called HBO, and they sent us the show, but it was the edited version. I did not appear on the tape.

So then we called NFL Films and they sent us the unedited version. At the end of the tape Broncos' Head Coach Dan Reeves was making a speech and handing out game balls. During all of that, I was standing in the background completely naked and facing the camera. My arms were crossed and the rest of me was just staring at the world.

Even filing the suit was embarrassing, because I had to sit and watch the tape with different people. The first time it was three attorneys from my lawyers' firm. There were two men, a woman and me sitting in a conference room while the tape rolled and we all watched my naked body.

When we met with HBO's attorney, we were sitting in a huge conference room with a big screen projection TV. There were seven people in the room including me. The audience included three male attorneys, two female attorneys and my wife. The tape started playing.

The image we saw was Dan Reeves giving his post-game speech and congratulating the team on the victory. I was standing in the background of the picture with no clothes on. The camera kept panning back and forth as Dan paced a bit during his approximately two-minute speech — I was naked in the background for the entire two minutes. Days after the show aired, one of my other teammates told me that I was on the screen naked for so long that his wife had time to see me, go to the kitchen to get him and return to the living room to watch me flash my stuff on television.

During his speech, Dan announced that he was giving me a game ball for a touchdown that I had scored in the final minutes. He and I moved closer together as the ball exchanged hands.

The camera focused on me. All of me.

While watching the tape with the lawyers, someone hit the pause button at that moment so my image would stay on screen while everyone got a close-up look to verify that it was me.

I was totally embarrassed.

After that meeting, my attorney and I filed suit in federal court. We were asking for $1 million in damages.

When we met with the judge he told us that it might be in our mutual best interest to try to settle this out of court. The judge warned HBO that Colorado juries generally side with the individual in suits against big companies. And the judge warned me that in my case, a lot of people knew my colorful past and a jury might not be very sympathetic for me. He told HBO to think about it, and he told me to think about it, and he even gave us a ball-park figure of what we should settle for.

Unfortunately, I am not allowed to reveal the financial details of our settlement because of a contractual agreement with HBO, but I can tell you basically what happened.

My attorneys and I went to meet with the woman who was HBO's attorney. She was the toughest lawyer I have ever seen. She was a total bad-ass. She sat there by herself and was hard as a rock. She wouldn't give us anything.

Just so you understand the situation, let's say the judge suggested that we settle for $1. Well this woman came in and offered us a nickel, and she wouldn't budge. She kept telling me that I could take it to court if I wanted to, but if I won, HBO would simply appeal and they'd keep dragging it out. She said I may never get any money. If I did get money, I would owe so much in attorney fees that it would be like I never got any money.

I was really afraid of that happening. My attorney was going to get one-third of whatever the settlement was, but I had to pay for all of the associated costs of the suit. If we had to fly people in for a deposition, I had to pay for it. All court fees came out of my pocket. Any other miscellaneous charge was my expense. So if the suit got dragged out over several years, there was the very real possibility that I might actually lose money after paying all of the fees. My only hope would be that the jury would make HBO pay for all of my legal fees, but there's no guarantee that will happen.

So we kept negotiating with HBO and we finally agreed upon a settlement.

I was very happy about the result. It was one of the few times in my career, that I came out on top in a lawsuit or court appearance.

13

Recovery

About four months elapsed between the night that Holly and I said that we loved each other in club Jubilation and the day we got married.

During that period, I was still having problems.

One night during the middle of June in 1991, Holly and I met up at a club, and we were just hanging out. We left the club at about 2 a.m. and were heading to my house. Holly was driving a Geo Tracker, and I asked her to trade cars with me because I had never driven a Tracker.

She said, "Okay." and took off in my Nissan 300 ZX.

I took off after her, but I was hungry so I decided to stop in at a Taco Bell and get some food. It was a warm night, so I was driving with my shirt off. I thought I was really cool. I thought I was a "hunk" as I cruised bare-chested through the drive-through lane at Taco Bell.

After I got my food, I headed home again. All of a sudden I cruised right past Chri and a girlfriend of hers. Chri and I were separated, but not yet divorced. It wasn't that unusual for me to see her on Highway 285, because my house was very near her parents' house, and there were only two ways to get to that area. So I often saw Chri on the highway even after our divorce was final. But that night she pulled up even with me, and was yelling something at me. I told her to pull over, so she sped up in front of me and stopped on the side of the road.

I pulled up next to her so that my passenger-side window was adjacent to her driver's-side window. She recognized Holly's truck, and she wanted to know what I was doing driving Holly's truck in the middle of the night without a shirt on.

I tried to explain to her what was happening, but she was pissed and wouldn't listen. We were screaming at each other, and I was yelling, "Let me explain it to you." We were both sitting there at a dead-stop when she suddenly gunned her engine and tried to take off. I hit the gas, too, and tried to cut her off. I ended up running right into her car.

After that I was scared, so I took off. She and her friend went to the police and filed a complaint. When my phone rang at 3:30 or 4 a.m., I didn't answer it because I thought it was Chri.

The next morning, I was driving to work when I heard on the radio that there was a warrant out for my arrest. There were people driving by me on the road doing double-takes. I was used to that, because people always recognized me when I went out in public, but now they were doing double-takes and then pointing at me because they had just heard on the radio that I was wanted by the police. I was really embarrassed.

I decided to turn myself in.

The police took me into a room and told me about the charges that had been filed against me. They told me that Chri said I rammed her car with the intent of hurting her, and she thought her life was danger. Although that's not really how everything happened, her friend corroborated the story.

They charged me with intent to harm with a vehicle or something like that. I can't remember the name of the exact charge, but it was some sort of assault with a vehicle.

I was going to try to fight the charges, but I knew that Chri's story was fundamentally right. I knew that I had hit her car. I knew that I was wrong. Plus, I just wanted to get it over with. The season was quickly approaching, and I didn't want to be distracted from football. If we went to trial, it might take a year for our case to be heard, and I didn't think I could live for a year with the threat of going to jail hanging over my head. I said if they're going to stick me in there, then stick me in there now. So my lawyer worked out a plea bargain, and I pled guilty to criminal mischief. I was sentenced to seven days in the Arapahoe County Jail. I was also ordered to pay $1,000 to a battered women's shelter, and to enroll in a domestic violence program.

A couple of days before going to court, I suffered a partially torn knee ligament in the Broncos' pre-season game against the San Francisco Forty-Niners. I appeared in court wearing a knee-brace, so my sentence included a 3 1/2-hour furlough everyday so that I could go to the Broncos' facility for rehab on my knee.

The Arapahoe County Jail is located about 300 yards from the Broncos' training facility. I went to court on a Friday, Aug. 9, 1991, and the portion of Broncos' training camp held at the University of Northern Colorado ended that Sunday. By the time I reported to jail on Tuesday, the team had moved back down to the regular facility for the remaining two weeks of camp.

After I was sentenced, I was interviewed by a newspaper reporter about spending time in jail. "The bad news is I do have to go to jail. . ." I said. "The good news is, I'm in love again."

I was deeply in love with Holly. It really meant a lot to me to have Holly's confidence and support during that time in my life. I really needed a friend, and she was there for me.

Although I didn't want to spend time in jail, it was probably one of the best things that ever happened to me. It was sobering. It was tangible evidence that my life was out of control. If I didn't change, I would either end up in prison or end up dead.

During my jail time, I told reporters that I was going to leave "The Vance" behind bars. The character I had created had to go. Jail seemed like the right place for him to live, so I decided to leave him inside when I came out.

Some movies I've seen actually make prison look sort of attractive. It looks like a cool place, where cool dudes hang out and talk a lot of cool shit, but here's the reality: jail sucks.

It's a real dreary, cold place. It's dark with lots of walls and few windows. There's always lots of noise with inmates screaming and cells clanging in the background. I felt like a little kid going to a new school for the first day, except that there were no teachers — just a bunch of bad ass kids. The school was full of bullies.

They put me into a cell by myself. It was about 15 feet by 15 feet with a bed and a toilet. There was just one tiny window in the door that I could look out of. I'd never been in a situation where I had to sit in a waiting room or anything and not have even a magazine to read. So I was standing at the door with my face pressed against the little window saying, "Can somebody please give me a magazine to read in here?"

I was petrified. The jail officers were telling me to shut up and sit my ass down.

I was emotionally out of control. My only link to the real world was the telephone and the television. I called Holly every chance I got. My father came to town to be with me, too, which really meant a lot to me. Plus, I was permitted to leave for a few hours everyday to rehab my knee, and I was so grateful for that. But it sucked, because after my rehab each day, I never wanted to return to jail. But I knew that I had to go back in.

My blood pressure skyrocketed the minute I walked into the place. It was so high that the prison officials were really concerned about me. They thought I was going to have a stroke or a heart attack. My blood pressure was about 190 over 150. I'd had high blood pressure before, but nothing like that. Before then, the highest I'd ever experienced was about 160 over 110. But it was never high to the point that I could have had a heart attack or a vein could have ruptured.

But I was so emotionally keyed up during jail, that my blood pressure was out of control. The doctors at the prison ended up giving me some Valium to calm me down, but I still spent most of my time in the infirmary. In fact, nearly all of my time was spent in the medical ward. That was fine with me because I was scared as hell of going out into the general population. I thought there might be some guy who were

L.A. Raiders' fans and would kick my ass. That seemed like a very real possibility to me. After all those years of seeing people yelling and screaming at the stadium and seeing people get into brawls during games, I figured it wasn't unreasonable to think that some dedicated Raiders' fan might take it upon himself to knock the shit out of some hot shot Broncos' receiver.

When I wasn't in the infirmary, I stayed in my cell reading books the entire time. There I was, Vance Johnson, the stud receiver for the Denver Broncos serving time, just like thieves and rapists and other hoodlums. I kept asking myself, "What am I doing here?"

Vance Johnson isn't supposed to go to jail. Vance Johnson is supposed to get a break. Vance Johnson is supposed to get fined or get slapped on the wrist and told to "not do that again." I couldn't believe I was in jail.

I just had hours and hours of time to sit and think about all of the bad things that I had done in my life. Unless you've been to jail, you can't even imagine what it's like to sit in a tiny room by yourself for 24 hours and just think. You feel like you're going to lose your damned mind. You don't realize how much freedom you have until someone takes it away. Losing the right to run to the corner 7-11 or the right to go see a movie or the right to go out to dinner or the right to go visit a friend is a terrible feeling. Imagine locking yourself in your bedroom — or better yet your bathroom — and pretend that you are not allowed to leave that room for any reason. You can't go into the kitchen to get a drink of water. You can't go into the garage to look for a tape in the car. You can't go into the living room to watch television. You can't do shit, until someone comes and opens the door and tells you that you can go into the backyard for 30 minutes.

That loss of freedom is demoralizing.

I was released after four days, because I had served "good" time. I was so happy to be out of there. I had served only four days with a 3 1/2-hour furlough everyday, but it felt like I had been in a long, long time. I can't begin to imagine how people manage to serve years and years in prison. I don't think I would have survived for a month.

After I got out of jail, I had to spend a year in a domestic abuse program headed by a counselor named Michael Lindsey.

In the beginning, I hated Michael Lindsey. But his program saved my life.

Michael Lindsey is a very calm and collected person, who has a strong heart and a lot of fire and desire to continue to fight against domestic violence. He cares more than anyone I've ever known. And he's set in his ways about how to do things, and he pushes you to do things his way. Anyone who comes into contact with him realizes that he's there to help and he'll always be there to help you.

He became like a father to me, because he guided me in different ways and helped me get out of the emotional troubles that I was having. I could go to him and say, "Last night, I felt violent as hell." I knew that I could trust him.

And I knew that he had so much faith in me. After a while, I tried to live right just because I didn't want to let him down. I wanted to validate all of the faith that he had in me.

He told me stories about the time he served in Vietnam and how he watched his entire platoon get killed and how he had to be strong in that chaotic and violent setting. He used his experiences to show me that I could overcome the chaos in my life, too.

He is the most powerful man I've ever known in my life. There are a lot of rich, powerful men in the world, but as far as I'm concerned, there is no one who is more powerful than Michael Lindsey.

I wish that other Broncos' players who had trouble over the years had a chance to meet and work with Michael Lindsey the way I did. I know that things would have turned out differently in their lives.

• • • • •

After serving my time in jail, and then spending four weeks on injured reserve while my knee healed, I was really worried about what people in Denver thought about me. Even though I did a lot of crazy, stupid things during my heyday, I was still very well regarded in Denver. I think people looked at me as someone who was just living a fun life. I was spending a lot of money, driving fast cars, sporting wild hairdos and living the life of a womanizer. My lifestyle was out of control, but I think it was the type of lifestyle that people were willing to forgive.

I wasn't out doing or selling drugs. I wasn't molesting children. I wasn't robbing banks. I was just being very immature in my life, and I think people tended to forgive me for that.

I think they looked at me and said, "Oh, that Vance is a character." I gave everyone a bunch of crazy haircuts and wild cars and off-the-wall stories to to talk about, and I think that served as a form of entertainment for a lot of people. Everyone began to look forward to the sequels. "What's Vance going to do next?" they'd wonder. So when I went out and did the next crazy thing, they weren't pissed off at me, they were glad that I had given them something else to talk about.

So even when I was at my worst, I think people generally still liked me.

But I wasn't so sure about that when I got out of jail.

Somehow, after the "Men Who Beat Women" article, a lot of people refused to believe the charges. They were still on my side. They wrote letters to the *Rocky Mountain News* criticizing the paper for lying about me. And I was in denial about my abuse problem, so I criticized the newspaper, too.

But then I went to jail for four days for ramming my estranged wife's car. I had been ordered to spend a year in a domestic abuse program. Suddenly I had confirmed my abusive nature. People might forgive me for living a crazy lifestyle, but I didn't think they would be very sympathetic toward a wife beater.

After I served my time in the county jail, I spent four weeks on injured reserve rehabilitating my knee. When the Broncos put me back on the active roster, I was worried about the reception I would receive at the stadium.

I was not longer just a fun-loving guy whose shenanigans gave everyone a grin.

Incidentally, remember the woman who used to sit outside the Broncos facility and wait for me? Remember also the woman who came up to my dorm room late one night during training camp? Well, both of those one-night-stands resulted in pregnancy. At about this time, both of those women filed paternity suits against me.

So not only was I a confirmed abuser, I was also a confirmed philanderer.

All of a sudden, I was a guy whose offenses weren't so laughable anymore.

I was nervous about what people were going to think about me now. I didn't know if the fans at the stadium would boo or clap for me. I was going to be introduced in the starting lineup that game, and I decided that if the fans booed me when I ran out onto the field then I would just keep on running right out of the gate, onto Interstate 25 and all the way down to Arizona. If the fans hated me, I didn't think I would have the courage to perform.

I was very relieved to hear a lot of cheers for me when I ran onto the field. That was one of the things I always loved about the Denver fans. They were always very kind to me and always stood behind me, even when I was running around the city like an idiot.

• • • • •

Even though I wanted to change my life for myself, there is no way I could have done it without Holly. Years before we got together, I realized that I was living in chaos. I knew that I needed to change my life, but I couldn't get the motivation or the maturity to make the transition. I think I needed someone who was strong and who loved me and who was willing to stand by me through the tough times.

And Holly was that person for me. It's crazy, but I used to think that in order for a relationship to work, the woman I was with would basically have to be just like my mother. She had to be a church-going, God-loving, God-fearing woman. She had to be a wonderful cook, be honest, have an understanding of how to pay bills, know how to take care of me, know how to take care of the kids, and be somewhat successful in her field of work. I felt that I was never going to be happy because I would never find anyone like that.

I began to realize that I could not go into relationships with those types of lofty expectations. I knew that you need to love someone for who they are and what they are and not try to change them. In my case, I was "The Vance" to the world, but inside I was a completely different person. Holly helped to bring that other person out.

I love Holly with all my heart. She's the perfect woman for me, and she doesn't have half the qualities I used to think I needed in a spouse. I hope she doesn't get mad at me after she reads this, but she can't cook.

But, I really wanted to have a happy life. I wanted to be a good husband. I wanted to be a good father. I wanted to be a good person. But I didn't know how to do any of that. I had to learn it all from scratch.

Through Michael Lindsey's program, I was supposed to learn how to control myself, and how to be a good husband, a good father and a good person. I was really excited about this program because I wanted to be all of those things. But at the same time, I hated it because it was really hard for me to change my life. It seemed easier to keep living in the chaos than to do everything that was required to change.

Michael Lindsey's program is group therapy for men with domestic violence problems.

I was sitting with this group of men, and they all had domestic abuse problems. These men ranged from being carpenters to bank tellers to business owners. Some guys made $10,000 a year, and there were two or three guys who made more than $5 million a year. It was surprising to me that all of those guys had problems and they were all struggling to get through this process. It's not just a problem that poor people have or unemployed people have or over stressed people have. Even men with good jobs, nice houses, nice families, nice everything can have abuse problems.

One day Michael Lindsey told us that the percentage of guys who will actually be able to change their lives is really low. He said a lot of guys will try, but most of them won't make it. To make it, you have to be really dedicated to making the change. It's not going to just happen — It takes a lot of work.

I was looking around the group at all of the guys who were in there. Some guys were in the group because they slapped their wives once or twice. Some guys were there because they'd hit someone with a fucking hatchet. Some were there because they had screamed at their wives or had affairs on them. Some were in there because they had beaten their dads up.

Then there was me. I had beaten up women in my life. I was Vance Johnson, the guy who was getting away with all the shit he was doing. While one guy was nearly in tears because he had slapped his wife, I was sitting there thinking, "I slapped my wives all the time." While another guy was saying that he had screamed at his wife, I was thinking "I screamed at my wives all the time." While another guy was confessing that he'd had an affair, I was thinking "I've had hundreds and maybe thousands of affairs."

I was looking around that room thinking, "Take anything that any of these guys have done and you have to multiply it times 100 or 500 to make it as bad as the things that I have done." I knew that I had done a lot worse shit than anyone else who was sitting in that room. If the percentage of regular group members who change is really small, then what's the percentage for someone like me? What was the likelihood that I could change? I was thinking, if all the guys in the group were like me, then the percentage of guys who change would be zero.

I was really afraid back then. I wanted to be a better person, but I was really disheartened. I thought there was no chance for me to get better.

A lot of us were just starting in the program at the time, but there were a couple of guys who had been in therapy for a year or two. Every meeting they'd stand up and admit that they had a problem. They said admitting your problem is the only way that you can change.

Well, the rest of us were rookies in the program, and we'd sit there saying things like, "I never hit anybody, I'm not supposed to be here," or "I accidentally hit her one time," or "She hit me, so I hit her back. She started it," or "Yeah, I slap my wife every once in a while, but I don't have a problem with it. That's just the way things work."

Every time a guy got up and said something like that, I understood him. I agreed with them. Even though I wanted to change my life, I really didn't think I had a problem. I just figured I needed to tone it down a little bit, but I didn't have a real problem.

In the beginning, I really felt out of place in that room. I was a Denver Bronco. I was a high-profile person. I was well-known. Everyone knew about all of the terrible things that I was doing. That millionaire business owner on the other side of the room might control the lives of 200 or 300 people, but those people didn't know that he had a problem. They didn't know that he was beating his wife.

But me, Everybody knew. The papers had reported that I was abusive. The television stations had said that I had a problem. Everyone knew about my crazy temper. Everyone knew that the courts had ordered me into this domestic abuse program. It was hard for me to be in that room. This was a process I felt I needed to go through by myself. I didn't need or want to have the world looking over my shoulder to see how I was doing. But I didn't have a choice. The Vance had led a very public life, so The Vance had to heal in public, too.

I didn't say much in the group. I just sat and listened to other guys talk. One guy would get up and say, "You know, I'm really fucking close to just knocking the fucking shit out of my wife." I was sitting there listening to him thinking, "So am I."

I could identify with him. I could understand him. I began to realize that I wasn't the only one who had those crazy thoughts. I wasn't the only one who was abusive. But I still wasn't ready to admit it. Once I admitted it, I would have to tell them about all of the crazy shit that I did. I had done too much bad shit during the past seven years. Even though everyone in the group was very supportive, I didn't think they would like me if I told them everything that I had done.

Meanwhile, a lot of the other guys had crossed the line. They had stood up in front of the group and said, "I am an abusive person." They were waiting for me to admit it, too, but I wouldn't do it. I would tell them stories about things that happened in my life, but I wouldn't admit my problem.

I remember one day they asked me to tell them what had happened on the night I rammed Chri's car. I told the story, but at the end I said, "She started driving, and I started driving, and she ran into my car, but I'm the one who got blamed for it. I'm the one who had to go to jail for it."

The guys gave me hell. "That's not what really happened, Vance," they said. "Why don't you tell us the truth?"

Later, I would say that "She started driving, and I started driving and our cars accidentally collided."

"That's not what really happened, Vance," they said again. "Why don't you tell us the truth?"

I was really getting pissed off at them. How in the hell would they know what really happened? They weren't there. I was. I was the one who knew what happened. But eventually, they forced me to be honest with myself and with them. Finally, I stood up one day and said, "She started to drive away, and I tried to cut her off, and I rammed right into her. I hit her car. I'm glad I hit her car. I wanted to hit her car. Are you happy now? Are you happy?" I was really mad that they had forced me to say it, but I was relieved, too. I had admitted the truth, and instead of hating me, everyone in the group loved me. I felt closer to them because I was honest.

That was a big turning point for me. I finally admitted that I had a problem. For years, I had known that I had a problem, and I needed to change my life. But I never made it a priority. I never committed myself to a course of action, because it was easier to continue to live a crazy life than to submit to the discipline of trying to change.

When I first got into the group, I think some of the guys looked at me in awe and said to themselves, "Holy Shit! That's Vance Johnson." But after I broke down crying saying that I was an abusive person and that I wanted to change, I think they saw me as a regular person. They saw me as a hard-headed, young black kid with a lot of money and a lot of problems. When I got inside that room with them, I was no longer the stud football player. I was just Vance. They never once treated me like "The Vance."

In fact — I now know I did this to myself — but when I first joined the group, I felt totally inadequate. I was the only black person in the room, and I felt bad about that. I had less education that most of the other guys. I wasn't nearly as successful as most of them. The only time I felt successful was when I was on the football field. I wasn't very literate — at least not compared to those intelligent men.

I was just really ashamed of myself as a human being whenever I wasn't on the field. I think they sensed these feelings I was having. Sometimes I'd be sitting there not saying anything and not participating. They'd stop everything and say, "You know Vance, whenever you want to be a part of this, then you can be but you have to feel like you're a part of it." Sometimes they treated me like a kid, because I acted like a kid.

And that was one of the things that Michael Lindsey asked us right from the beginning. He said, "How old do you feel right now?" I said, "13 years old." No one in the group was surprised because I acted like I was 13 years old. After months and years went by he'd ask again, "How old do you feel right now?" I'd say, "Now I'm 19."

If I asked myself that question today, I'd say that I'm 20 or 21 years old. Today, I'm actually 31 years old, but emotionally I feel like someone who is college age. So I still have a long way to go to become a total man.

But when I first started meeting with the group, I felt like a 13 year old, so it was really hard for me to be in a group of 15 other men and tell them all of the terrible, horrible things I had done in my life. It was hard to say, "I slapped my wife" or "I hit my wife" or "I pushed my wife" or "I restrained my wife."

I can say it now because I know that I was wrong, and that I was a different person back then. I would never hit my wife now. I could never hit another woman or anyone else again. Now if I go to a group meeting and I hear someone say, "You know, I'm really fucking close to just knocking the fucking shit out of my wife," I'm shocked.

I sit there thinking, "How can you say you want to hit your wife? How can you even be thinking that? Don't you know how wrong that is?" Then I think, "Damn Vance, not too long ago, you were thinking the same kinds of things. But now you know there is no way you are every going to hit your wife." I could feel myself changing. Michael had said that only a handful of men will be able to change, and I'm determined to be one of them.

I really began to depend on the group. They were the people who understood me. They were the people who could help me. I really wanted to change, and I realized how much I needed the group in my life but, there was a catch. After you get through the initial meetings and admit your problem, you have to continually earn the right to be in the group. If you are abusive you can be kicked out of the group. Since I was dependent on the group, I had to work hard at not being an abusive person, because I didn't want to be kicked out.

And that in itself was a chore, because I was still really stubborn and hard-headed and Michael Lindsey would always challenge me. He would single me out and tell me that if I wanted to quit I could just leave. He told me that no one was going to make me stay in the group. I had to want to stay there. He'd stand up in front of everyone and say, "I see that you want to change, but if you're not willing to change, you don't have to. But you can't stay here if you're not going to change."

There were many times when I would just get up and walk out because I was so pissed off at the guys in the group for holding me accountable for all of the things that I had done. I sat in that room with them and knew that I had not been very smart or intelligent, and I hadn't handled things the way that I was supposed to.

But Michael Lindsey always said it's not going to come easily and it's not going to come fast. That's why it makes me laugh when I hear people say, "I went to counseling for a couple of months and now I'm all better." You might get a quick fix in a couple of months, but it takes years to deal with the underlying problems that are the roots of your behavior.

While I was going through this process, I had the additional obstacle of having to go into a chaotic environment everyday. In the locker room, guys were always talking about girls they had slept with or cars they had bought or clubs they had gone to. It was hard to hear them talk about it because it was like a string tugging at me trying to pull me back into the chaos.

During the 1993 season, I even took on the role of an advisor for some of the younger players. I could see that some of them were on the same road to destruction that I had been on a few years earlier, and I tried to warn them about the pitfalls. I tried to give them some advice so that they might be able to turn back before they hit bottom like I did. But they didn't listen to me. Of course, I can understand that because when I was in my heyday, I wasn't willing to listen to anyone either.

I remember during the 1993 training camp, a bunch of us were sitting in the locker room up at the University of Northern Colorado talking. I was just sitting in the corner listening to the guys talk about different girls they had gotten pregnant. Even some of the married guys were bragging about how many women they had slept with and how many children they were supporting without their wives' knowledge.

I spoke up for the first time during that conversation and said, "How would you feel if your wives were doing the same thing to you? What would you do if you found out your wife was having an affair on you?"

"I'd kick her fucking ass," said one player and everyone else laughed and agreed that that was the right answer.

"I'd beat the shit out of that bitch," another player said.

It was hard for me, because I'd had a whole bunch of affairs on my first two wives, and I had been abusive to my first two wives. A couple of years earlier, I probably would have laughed right along with those guys. Actually, I shouldn't even use the word, "probably." I know I would have laughed right along with them. But after working with Michael Lindsey and the rest of the men in the group, I was beginning to learn what was right and what was wrong.

After that, the other players started talking specifically about different times they had hit their wives or other girlfriends. One player talked about how he was driving with his wife or girlfriend and he saw her looking at a man in the car next to theirs. He started yelling at her and pushing her. Then he pulled over to the side of the road and punched her. He said he looked around to see if anyone was watching him, and then he punched her a few more times and started slapping her and trying to shove her out of the car. He said he would have kicked her, but he couldn't get his feet over the console.

The whole time he was telling the story, guys were laughing their asses off and screaming out, "Yeah, I had to do the same thing to my girl."

It just wasn't funny to me anymore. Every week I was exposed to two completely opposite groups of men. In one group — the football players — a lot of guys who were fabulously wealthy, young, mostly immature and mostly irresponsible. They were egotistical, abusive and arrogant and didn't care about their families or their wives or about anyone. They were basically carbon copies of the person that I used to be.

Members of the other group of men — Michael Lindsey's group — were generally older, more responsible, more mature, more caring, more sincere. They were strong men who stood up week after week and took responsibility for their actions.

Being in the locker room everyday did make things tougher on me in the beginning, but later, as I began to really change, I think the other players actually made changing easier for me. The difference between the guys in the group and the guys in the locker room was so dramatic that I could clearly see the person that I used to be. I'd walk into the locker room with the new attitudes that I'd learned in group, and I would come face to face with the type of person I used to be. One of the other players might say something I used to say or talk about doing something I used to do. It would embarrass me to think that I used to do those things.

I think the Broncos' new head coach, Wade Phillips, really wanted to change the type of players who were on his team. One of the first things he did when he took over during the 1993 off-season, was get rid of a lot of the troublemakers. He traded some guys, cut some others and basically cleaned house. That was a weird time for me because I really wasn't nervous at all. You'd think that I would have been nervous as hell because of all the crazy shit that I had done in the past but there had been such a significant change in my behavior during 1991 and 1992, that I didn't feel that I could be fired on the basis of my lifestyle. I didn't feel like the team's sore thumb anymore. I didn't feel like the guy that the team worried about and said, "Oh Lord, what is he going to do next." I had changed a lot and I felt that Wade knew that about me. So I wasn't really worried about getting fired when the ax was falling on so many other guys.

Wade did another thing that I thought was really interesting. Midway through the 1993 season, he called a team meeting and told us that a couple of women from the Broncos' new cheerleading squad were coming to talk to us. A bunch of the guys in the room started grinning and high-fiving each other talking about how they were going to "get them one" of those cheerleaders. The women were supposed to give a presentation to us the next day.

The following day, we were all sitting in the team meeting room when three women walked in. One of them was a black lady who looked to be in her 50s. Another was an Hispanic lady who was about 40 and the third was a really pretty black girl who was about 21 or 22. She had a really pretty face and a nice body, and as soon as she came in a bunch of guys started whispering to each other. It was obvious that she was one of the new cheerleaders. Players were talking back and forth about how sexy she was and how they were going to try to get her phone number after the meeting ended.

One guy just flat-out guaranteed that he would fuck her by the end of the week.

Wade introduced them to us and told us that they were here to talk to us about something very important.

First the older black lady got up and said she was from center for AIDS prevention in Atlanta. She was a pretty hip chick. She asked us all to stand up.

"If you've ever had sex without using a condom, please sit down."

Everyone in the room sat down, except for one of our coaches who was standing in the back of the room. We all looked at him and one of the players yelled, "Man, you got four kids sit your ass down!" We all cracked up laughing.

"Yeah, but I've only had sex with my wife," he said.

"But you've had unprotected sex with you wife, have you not?" the woman said.

"Yes," he said.

"Then please take your seat."

He finally sat down, and everyone started ragging on him.

"The reason I made you all stand up and then sit back down was to show you that every single one of you has put yourself at risk for the HIV virus.," the woman said. "And one of the things I want to encourage all of you to do is to use a condom when you have sex as a means of protecting yourselves from the HIV virus."

Someone in the back of the room yelled out, "A condom don't fit me," and everyone started laughing. The woman laughed too, and then she asked if there was anyone else in the room who was too well-endowed to fit into a condom.

Everyone started laughing again and a bunch of guys were holding their hands up in the air with their palms about a foot apart indicating how long their dicks were. A couple of guys yelled out that even with the condom rolled out all the way it still only covered half of their length. Guys were high-fiving each other, laughing and having a good time.

The lady was still laughing, too. Then she pulled a huge cucumber out of a bag and said, "Does anyone in here have a penis bigger than this?" One guy yelled out, "Yeah, I do," which sparked some more laughter. But as she held it up in the air, it was obvious that no one outside of the circus could have a dick bigger than that.

Then she took a small packet out of her bag and said, "this is a regular sized lubricated condom." She ripped it open and then unrolled it onto the cucumber until the entire vegetable was covered. She held it up for all of us to see.

"Now what was that line again?" she said. "'But baby, I just don't fit into a condom.' Yeah, in your dreams you don't."

We all fell out laughing.

She went on to talk a lot more about AIDS. Then the Hispanic lady got up and talked to us a little bit about the HIV virus and how to avoid it.

Finally, the really good looking 25-year-old chick got up and started talking, and you could have heard a pin drop when she said, "I'm HIV positive."

She had gotten raped by a guy when she was 13 or 14 years old, and had later had sex with her first real boyfriend when she was 16. About a year or so later she found out she was HIV positive when she tried to join the military. We were all sitting there stunned. She was a really pretty girl. She looked as healthy as anyone we knew. If she hadn't told us that she was HIV positive, a bunch of guys would have been trying to get her phone number so they could try to have sex with her. And if it was up to him, one player would have had sex with her before the end of the week.

She'd been carrying the virus for a lot of years, but fortunately she hadn't developed full-blown AIDS yet. She said there was a chance that she could live a completely normal life and never contract AIDS. But there was a chance that she could be diagnosed with the disease the next day and begin the quick decline into death.

It was a really powerful presentation. It made all of us realize that even the most attractive, clean looking woman could be carrying the AIDS virus. I was really nervous when I was sitting there because I had slept with so many women over the years. I was constantly having sex without protection and it's is just plain luck that I never caught AIDS.

That presentation was sobering. Everyone had been laughing a few minutes earlier, talking about how they couldn't wear condoms, but after that young girl got up there, no one had a word to say. You could almost hear the thoughts running through guys' heads trying to catalogue when they had slept with lately, and whether or not they might have the virus.

It really made us think about how dangerous unprotected sex was and how easy it was to catch the HIV virus. I know I learned a lot from the presentation, and I hope some of my teammates did, too.

Unfortunately, in the locker room the very next day, guys were again talking about different girls they had slept with the previous night. It was like all that talk of AIDS didn't faze them.

It scared me. I was glad that I wasn't living that type of life anymore.

• • • • •

During most of the "changing" process, I just didn't hang out with anyone else on the team. I couldn't. I was like an alcoholic. An alcoholic is supposed to stay away from bars, and not hang around people who are going to be drinking. I was the same way. I couldn't go to bars with the guys. I couldn't just run around the streets popping into clubs and expect to stay in control of myself. I knew that I had a problem, and I needed to get myself out of that environment, until I had gone through enough of a change to be able to resist the temptations. I knew that if I went out with the guys I would probably have a good time, and I might decide to fall back into that lifestyle.

During the 1993 season, a lot of the younger players would invite me to go out with them. I think a lot of them knew about my past reputation, and they figured I would be a fun guy go party with. But I always made up some excuse for not going. I would often jokingly say, "Man, all the crazy shit I've done, you know my wife won't let me go out."

Or I would say that I had other plans or I would say anything just to avoid the situation.

But every year we have rookies' night out. Once a year, the rookies at every position have to take their teammates at that position to dinner. The rookie receivers had to take the veteran receivers out. The rookie running backs treat the veteran running backs, etc. All of the receivers were making plans for our night out, and I was trying to get out of it. I kept saying, "I probably won't make it," and they kept saying, "What? You've gotta come V.J., it's rookies' night out. Everybody's got to come."

I didn't want to go.

But finally I agreed to go with them just so that they would get off my back. Part of the rookies' responsibility is to provide a limousine to drive around and pick up all the players. And the young guys had to pick up the tab at whatever bars or restaurants we went to that night.

Since I didn't want to get stuck hanging out at a strip bar or a nightclub with all of the guys, I told the rookies not to worry about picking me up in the limo. I would just drive myself and meet them at the restaurant.

We had 7 p.m. reservations at Morton's of Chicago steakhouse, and I arrived just a couple minutes after that. The limo had not yet arrived. I immediately changed our reservation to 8 p.m., and the people at Morton's were really nice about it. I was sitting in the bar waiting for the guys to show up, and feeling really stressed about the whole situation. The restaurant was really filling up. People were sitting in the lounge area waiting for tables, and I could see our reserved table sitting there empty all the way in the back. I was really uncomfortable because I could see people looking at that table and asking the hostess if they could be seated there.

Back in my chaotic days, if I was waiting for Mark Jackson or some of the other fellas to show up and we kept a table in a restaurant out of commission, I didn't think anything of it. I figured we were the Broncos, and the restaurant managers were so lucky to have us in their store that they shouldn't mind putting up with the wait. I always thought that people who were waiting to be seated would see me there and figure out that the table was for me, and then they wouldn't mind. It would give them something to brag about later. "Yeah, we had to wait 30 minutes to be seated. There was one table open, but they were saving it for a bunch of Broncos. I saw Vance Johnson sitting in the bar having a drink waiting."

That was the attitude I used to have, and it was an attitude I shared with a lot of my teammates.

But sitting in Morton's that night, I realized my attitudes had changed a lot since those days. I felt really bad about what was happening. I didn't think the people who were waiting felt "lucky" to be waiting for a group of Broncos.

As 7:30 p.m. came and went I kept looking at the door waiting for the guys to arrive. At 8 p.m. they still hadn't shown up. At 8:15 p.m. I talked to the manager of the restaurant and thanked him for holding our table and assured him that the other guys should arrive shortly. At 9 p.m., there were 30 or 40 people waiting to be seated, and the guys still were not there. No one had called to say they were running late or anything. So I gave our reservations away, and three families were able to be seated. I apologized over and over to the people at Morton's. I really felt bad for what we had done.

That was another time when I was really able to see the person that I used to be. I used to be late everywhere I went. If I was supposed to do an autograph session, I'd be late. I always made people wait for me, and I thought it was no big deal. I figured they were so lucky to have me coming to meet them, that they wouldn't mind waiting 15 minutes or an hour or even several hours for me to show up. When I finally did show up, I would waltz into the room like it was no big deal.

But sitting in Morton's that night, I had an opportunity to see what happens on the other end of a player's late arrival. The restaurant was holding three tables for us, and by doing that they added 10 or 15 minutes to everyone else's wait. The restaurant was losing money because they couldn't seat anyone at those tables. They were losing money because the length of the wait probably turned some customers away. They were frustrating their customers who weren't being seated but could see that a block of tables was still open.

Yes, I think the people at Morton's were happy to have a bunch of Broncos' players coming in, but I know they didn't appreciate the delayed arrival. They didn't appreciate its effect on their business or its effect on all of their other customers.

That was the night that I really began to understand how completely inconsiderate I used to be. Seeing things like that really helped me along when I was trying to change my life, because it gave me a different perspective on some of my former actions. It gave me a chance to see how "un-cool" it is to be inconsiderate of other people.

Shortly after I canceled the reservation, I went home.

The next day the guys told me that they showed up about 15 minutes after I left, and the people at Morton's were really happy to have their business. The players weren't the least bit concerned about being 2 hours and 15 minutes late. They figured the people at the restaurant were lucky to have them, no matter how late they were.

It sounded really familiar.

• • • • •

Like I said earlier, Holly really helped me during this entire process. She is such an independent, hard-headed, strong person that she wouldn't put up with any of my shit. Holly said she would leave me in a second if she found out I was doing any of my old shit again. When we got into an argument, she'd stand her ground and argue right back at me. I have never hit Holly. We have never been in a physical fight, but we have had a whole lot of in-your-face screaming matches.

During my first marriage, Angela once said, "Vance, you need some fucking help. You're crazy." That was the first time in my life that anyone ever told me that I was crazy or suggested that I needed professional help. She would say similar things later in our relationship, but I never listened to her. I thought she was the one who had a problem.

When Chri and I were together, she said, "Vance, you really need to see someone. I think you really need to get some help, because you shouldn't be doing all these things." I pretty much blew that off, too. Once again, I figured she was the one who had the real problem.

When Holly told me I had a problem, it was different. I listened to her and I agreed with her. She said, "Vance, you are fucking out of your mind. You don't make any sense. I don't think you really know where you're coming from. You really need some help. You need some fucking help. You need to quit lying to your group, and tell them the truth. They can help you. You seriously need it."

Of course, part of the reason I listened to Holly was that I wanted to change my life. The time was right for me to hear that sort of message, so I was receptive to it. I knew that I had a problem, but I needed people like Holly and Michael Lindsey to push me and help me stay on track.

Every time we got into an argument, Holly would threaten to call Michael and tell on me. I didn't want her to do that because Michael would bring up the incident in group and everyone would get on my ass for being abusive. It used to piss me off when Holly did that.

We'd argue and argue, but if I got close to her and acted like I might hit her, she would grab the phone and say, "Go ahead! Go ahead! Do it! I've got the phone. I'm calling Michael! I'm calling Michael!" She had the number memorized, and she'd start dialing. "It's ringing," she'd say. "I'm going to tell him everything!"

I'd be yelling at her to "put down the damned phone!" It worked. Her doing that would stop me from being abusive. But it was terrible. I said, "I'm going to leave you for this, Holly. You can't be doing shit like that. You've got to be on my side. You've got to stand by me."

"That's your fucking problem right now," she said. "Every fucking woman you've ever been with has been standing by your side and lying for you all the damned time, but you were still mean and abusive to them. Well, I'm not going to stand for it. I'm going to call the cops on you if you fuck up."

I'd be sitting up some nights thinking, "Do I love this woman?" I wondered how I could love a woman who said she was going to get me in trouble with the police? How could I love a woman who was trying to get me kicked out of the group? How could I love a woman who was telling my family, her family and everyone we knew everything that was happening in our home? Very slowly, I began to realize that Holly loved me and she wanted me to change. That's why she threatened to get me in trouble. She made it easier for me to focus on not fucking up.

One of the things that I learned in group therapy that really helped me with my problem was that there are often physical cues in my body that can alert me when I am about to get really angry. Men in the group said, "You need to find out what your body does just before you lose control."

When I first got into that group I was sitting there thinking, "What the fuck are you guys talking about, something happens before you 'go off' on someone? Nothing happens to me. I just go off."

But months later, I was getting into an argument with Holly. I was getting really angry, and all of a sudden my underarms started dripping like a water faucet. I just busted up laughing, I said, "I got it. I fucking got it! I start sweating before I go off."

I was so surprised that I stopped being angry, and I told Holly. Then I started thinking back to all of the other times that I had gone off, and I realized that I had always sweated a lot under my arms right before I lost control. I started to understand that I only sweat a lot on three occasions: 1) When I'm working out hard and exerting myself 2) When I'm really nervous about something and 3) When I am really really angry and I'm about to lose control.

I know the idea of me sweating under my arms when I'm about to lose control might sound crazy to some people, but it's really pretty normal. I've learned that the human body experiences a physical change whenever a person's attitude changes. When you feel sad, your body produces tears. When you feel nervous, your body puts sweat on your palms or butterflies in your stomach. When you feel stressed out, your body raises the blood pressure. When you feel angry, your body might make blood vessels bulge out of your forehead. Your mental state of health can cause a lot of changes in your body, and I learned that if I pay attention to what my body is telling me, then I can stay more in control of my emotions.

I learned to control my sweat by anticipating its arrival. If Holly and I were arguing and I felt myself start to get wet under the arms I would say, "I've got to leave, because I'm starting to sweat." I would go for a drive in the car or for a walk or for a run. I would just go do something else until I calmed down. When I got back, we'd continue our conversation. Eventually, I got to the point that when I was in an argument and I was getting angry, I would say to myself, "I'm going to start sweating soon." Then I would feel the sweat getting ready to come. Then I'd feel the sweat come. When it came, I would do something else for a little while.

I got progressively better at paying attention to my underarms. I reached the point where I didn't have to start sweating before I made myself stop. I'd say, "Honey, we need to stop because I'm going to start sweating and you know what's going to happen when I start sweating." I was like the Incredible Hulk: "Don't make me angry. You won't like me when I'm angry."

Now, I'm to the point that I never sweat unless I'm working out or I'm really nervous. Now when I get angry, it's a very cool anger. It's more like just being disappointed in something. I rarely get really pissed off anymore.

•••••

While all of that was happening, Holly was still being strong for me. We both wanted our marriage to work, so we were really working hard to make things right. The night in the club when Holly and I said that we loved each other and that we wanted to be together, was really the night that I took the first big steps toward changing my life. Before then, I had been seeing a counselor because I wanted to change, but I still had a long way to go.

Holly kept telling me that I shouldn't hang out with Mark Jackson because he's a really bad influence on me.

See, at that point, Mark and I were still good friends. When I was mad at Holly, I would sometimes take off and go hang out with Mark. He was my buddy. I was really distrustful of all women, because I had been sued by so many over the years. But I knew I could trust Mark. I said, "Shit, Holly's just my wife. She's wife number three. The first two didn't love me, and neither does she. But Mark is my buddy. He's been with me through all of this shit."

So I would hang with him.

"Can't you see that he's a bad role model for you, Vance?" Holly would say. "You need to hang out with good people. You need to hang out with people who are living the type of life that you want to lead. You can't hang out with Mark because he's part of your old life. He's part of the life you're trying to let go."

The guys in the group were telling me the same thing. They said if I was hanging out with Mark, then I was just putting myself into position to walk right back into the chaos.

I really was committed to changing my life, so I tried to cut back on the amount of time that I spent with Mark. But it wasn't easy because he really was my best friend. He was the first true best friend that I ever had in my life. He was someone whose friendship I had come to depend on. Although I distrusted most people, I really trusted Mark.

But I was committed to changing my life, and I knew that I couldn't continue to hang out with Mark if I wanted to lead a different lifestyle.

And, honestly, I don't think Mark wanted to hang out with me as much either, because I wasn't as much fun as I used to be. I was trying to move in a different direction, and I didn't have the enthusiasm that I used to have for the chaotic lifestyle.

I would make up excuses sometimes when he wanted me to go hang out with him. I would sometimes say that I didn't feel well. I would sometimes blame Holly. I would make up any excuse that seemed reasonable. I tried to completely avoid going to nightclubs with him. I knew going to a club would be the end of my recovery.

Despite all my efforts to avoid Mark, we were still roommates whenever the Broncos had an away game, and that was hard. I guess it wouldn't have been too tough for me to go to the Broncos' front office and tell them that I wanted them to change my roommate for the road games. They would have done it. But I didn't want to do that. I wanted to get away from bad behavior, but I really didn't want to get away from Mark. He was my good, good friend, and that would be lost if I went to the Broncos and said, "I want a new roommate." I would lose my only real friend on the team.

Since 1986, Mark and I had been meeting girls on road trips and having sex with them in our hotel rooms. Every road game we would meet a couple of new girls.

Usually after a little while, I'd be tired of having sex, and would fall asleep, but Mark was a sex fiend. He could have sex with girls all night long and still get up the next day and play well on the field. I never understood how he could do it. I would have been dragging on the field, but it never seemed to bother Mark.

By 1990, we had travelled enough to have a short list of girls we could call to meet us in whatever city we played in.

As I mentioned in a previous chapter, Mark and I were constantly meeting girls — even in the middle of football games. During one game at Mile High Stadium in Denver, during 1990 I believe, the Broncos were winning pretty handily. It was the fourth quarter, and people were beginning to file out of the stadium. A bunch of players were standing together talking near the Gatorade table when we saw a really beautiful girl walking down the aisle on the other side of the fence that separates the stands from the field.

We were all checking her out, and a couple of guys gave her wolf whistles. She was very pretty.

I wanted to impress all of the guys, and further inflate my ego, so despite the fact that my wife Chri was in the stands with two of my children, I was figuring out a way to talk to this woman.

I grabbed one of the ball boys and asked him to go talk to the girl for me. I said, "Tell her that Vance Johnson wants her phone number."

He walked over to her, conveyed my message, and I nodded and smiled to her when she looked in my direction.

All of the guys were clapping me on the back and calling me a stud when she got out a pen and wrote down her phone number. The ball boy delivered the paper to me, and I felt like a cool guy.

Of course, I didn't feel so cool when I walked out of the stadium with my wife and my two kids and saw this woman standing right next to my car. She was obviously waiting for me, and I was scared to death. I didn't know what I was going to do. What lie could I make up to tell Chri when this woman says "Hi" to me?

The four of us kept walking toward the car, and I tried to avoid eye contact with the woman. Fortunately for me, I think she knew I was with my wife, so she didn't say anything to us. She just watched us walk by and get into our car.

I was very relieved.

I called her later that week and had an affair with her. I even flew her to Seattle when we played the Seahawks because I wanted her to be with me in the hotel. Her parents lived in Seattle, so it seemed good for me to take her to that city.

Mark and I were constantly doing things like that. We were always picking up women, and we were always trying to figure out whom we could fuck next.

But that was all before I got into counseling and started trying to live a different way. During the 1992 season, I was trying to change, but Mark was still doing the same things we had been doing for years. He was still bringing girls up to the room, and I would be lying in my bed listening to them have sex. It was hard.

Mark didn't really understand why I wanted to change. The life we were living was a lot of fun. At times, it did seem foolish of me to be letting go of all those good times. But it had become too chaotic for me. I couldn't deal with it anymore. I knew it was time for me to settle down. But Mark was still really deep into that lifestyle, so it was hard for him to see what I was talking about.

Before the 1992 season started, Mark was always calling to see if I would go out with him. Sometimes I would go. Sometimes I wouldn't. We went to the dog tracks together, and often I'd go hang out at his restaurant, Scribbles, which wasn't far from my house.

But our relationship was deteriorating. With each passing day we got further and further apart as friends. Eventually, we were still friendly to each other at work, but we almost never went out together after work.

During the 1993 off-season, Mark signed as a free agent with the New York Giants. That transaction added geographical distance to the emotional distance that was already present in our relationship.

• • • • •

Holly made me accountable for everything. She made me take responsibility for my life and for my actions. I had to learn to be a responsible person. She made me learn how to pay bills. Before then I honestly didn't know how. During high school and college, I'd never had any friends in far away places, so I never wrote letters to anyone. I never had bills that I had to pay, so I never learned how to do that. I know this sounds crazy, but when I got into the NFL, I really didn't even know how to mail a letter.

And the importance of paying bills was lost on me. I tried to do it at first, but it just wasn't a priority in my life. I'd get bills at my house and they would stay stacked on my kitchen table for months. I would never sit down and write out checks and lick stamps and seal envelopes and mail the letters. It just didn't seem important to me. I finally turned everything over to my agent. I'd send him my bills, and he would pay them for me. But my bills were always late, by the time I got around to mailing them to my agent. Even if he was sending in payments immediately, they would still arrive late.

But I didn't care. During my second or third year in the league, someone said something to me about bad credit. I called my agent to ask him what that meant. He gave me a basic explanation of how credit worked. I said, "Do I have bad credit?"

He said, "Vance, don't worry about it. Money buys credit."

So I didn't worry about it anymore. In my mind I had a lot of money, so I had a lot of credit.

But Holly taught me a lot about taking care of bills, and being responsible and having good credit. When the Broncos went on road trips, she'd only give me $20 to take with me.

On every road game, about a dozen players participate in poker and dice games. The stakes are usually $100 to $200 per roll in dice or $20 a hand in poker. It's not unusual for a guy to lose $2,000 or $3,000 during the flight to or from an away game. I was one of those guys. I was always gambling. But Holly put a stop to it.

I'd sit in my seat and watch sometimes or I'd look out the window or I'd read a magazine. But I only had $20 in my pocket, and I knew I couldn't lose it on dice or cards. The guys started wondering why I wasn't gambling with them on the plane. I told them I didn't feel like it. The truth was that Holly wouldn't let me.

She helped me that way. She was strong enough to make demands of me that forced me to live the right way. Of course, she could only do that if I was willing to submit to those changes. But that's why we're together. We complement each other well. A lot of times, Holly made change easier for me because I could pin the blame for certain things on her. I was the one who was saying, "Okay, I'll only take $20 on the trip with me." It might have been Holly's idea, but I had to go along with it. But then if one of my teammates asked me if I wanted to gamble, I could jokingly say, "Man, you know my wife won't let me carry any money." I'd make it sound like a joke and like the truth at the same time. The other guy might laugh, and say, "Yeah, my wife was trying to tell me not to spend so much money, too."

Being able to pin the blame for certain things on Holly really helped take the pressure off me. I could pretend that it was my wife who was changing things — not me.

Even though she's strong, Holly still had a lot of fears. I'd had so many affairs over the years, and I'd done so many bad things, that we could not just sweep all that under a rug and forget about it. It would be like throwing a blanket on top of an elephant. It doesn't hide the problem, it just looks like an elephant wearing a blanket.

I've always been a really early riser, and a lot of times, I'd go into the Broncos' facility hours before any other players got there. I'd work out in the weight room or talk to the trainers or do anything to kill time. But after Holly and I got together, that became a problem. Holly had fears about me having affairs on her, so when I said I was leaving in the morning at 7 a.m., and she knew I didn't have to be at work until 9 a.m., she wondered what was going on. Sometimes, I'd stay after work and lift weights or do some extra running or watch some film. By the time I got home, Holly would be a basket case. She'd be trembling with fears that I was out somewhere having an affair.

Her fears were justified, because in my past relationships, I had hundreds of affairs. In my past relationships, I'd leave the house and go have an affair on my way to work. Or I'd have an affair on my way home from work. So when Holly didn't know where I was, she assumed I was having an affair. At first we didn't know how to deal with this problem, but finally Michael Lindsey said that in order for Holly to learn to trust me and have faith in me, she needs to know that when I say I'm going somewhere, I'm actually going there.

He suggested that I let Holly drop me off places instead of driving myself. Then all of the other guys in the group jumped in and told me that's what I should do. Well, I was still really hard-headed, and I told them that they were crazy if they thought I was going to get my wife to drive me everywhere. I wasn't going to give someone that kind of power over me to know what my every move is every day of the week. They couldn't make me do it, and I wasn't going to to do it.

Less than a week later, a couple of the guys saw Holly drive off after she dropped me off at the group meeting.

During the meeting, they told me that it was good that I had finally seen the light and that I was going to allow Holly to drop me off. I said, "This is a one time deal. There were certain circumstances that came up. That's why she dropped me off. It had nothing to do with you guys it's not going to happen again."

The next day Holly dropped me off at work.

It turned out that I was arguing against the guys with my mouth, but my mind was moving in the direction of what I knew was right. I was too stubborn to just come out and say, "Yeah, you guys are right. I should let Holly drop me off." Instead, I vowed that I would never let it happen, and then I proceeded to do the right thing.

So Holly started to drop me off everywhere I went. If I was going to work, she'd drop me off in the morning and pick me up in the afternoon. She'd deliver me to the group meetings. She'd come with me to the grocery store. If I went to the corner to get gas, Holly came with me. She'd drop me off for golfing and pick me up. Drop me off at the airport and pick me up.

Even when the Broncos went on road trips, I'd check in with Holly. Before the team left, I'd give Holly the itinerary, and she would have to call me in my room at certain times. She'd know what time the team dinner was, and she'd call five minutes after the meal had ended to see if I'd come back to the room. She'd know what time our meetings were, what time curfew was and what time we were leaving for the stadium.

At the team's request, the hotels on the road discontinue incoming-call service to players' rooms when curfew begins. Players can still call out, but no one can call in. So I'd call Holly after curfew to let her know that I was in my room.

All of this was driving me crazy, because I had to give up so much of my freedom just so she could learn to trust me. It was really tough, and sometimes I wanted to quit because I didn't want to give someone that kind of power over me. I was afraid that by giving her the luxury of checking up on my all the time, she would eventually get used to it, and she would control my life.

But I was willing to take that risk because I love Holly with all my heart, and I desperately wanted us to have a good marriage. Plus, Holly and Michael Lindsey were the only two people on the planet who had confidence in me. They believed in me. They stood by me. When everyone else thought I was just a spoiled jerk who should be taken out into a field and shot, Holly and Michael were telling me that I was important. They cared about me. They were going to help me in whatever way they could. Without their support there's no way I could ever have made it this far in the process of changing my life. And even when I was still on the fringe of the chaos, I knew that Holly loved me, so I was willing to take the chance of giving her some control in my life. I was willing to do whatever was necessary to help Holly learn to trust me.

It was a slow process, but Holly had to learn that when I say "X" I mean "X," and I'm not trying to fool her. I had such a history of being dishonest and deceitful, that Holly had to learn that if I said I was going to the Broncos' facility, she could rest assured that that was where I was going.

Eventually, she started to trust me more, and I began to drive myself to different places. But I was still checking in. If I left for work early, then I'd call Holly when I got there, and I would yell something to Steve Antonopulos, the Broncos' trainer and make him say something. He would never know why I was talking to him when I had my wife on the phone, but it was a way to let her know that I was where I said I was. If I stayed at work late, I'd do the same thing.

I was willing to give up a lot of freedom, because I desperately wanted to be trusted. I needed to be trusted. I needed to reach the point where my wife could look me in the eye, and she and I would both know that I was telling the truth. I had been dishonest to so many people for so long that I had forgotten what honesty was. I had even been lying to myself.

One of the things I learned in the men's group was that change will not come without sacrifice. I came from an abusive background, and I had a lot of affairs, but I wanted my marriage to work. So instead of just being The Vance, and running around the city doing whatever I wanted, whenever I wanted, I had to be accountable. I had to act more like an adult than a 2-year-old. I had to learn that I can't have everything that I want. I had to learn that in order to have one thing, I had to sacrifice another thing. In order to have a good relationship with Holly, I had to give up some of my freedom for a while.

I was learning to be honest with the guys in the group. I was learning to make my mind accessible to the lessons I could learn from other men in the group. I wanted to be normal. I wanted to have a good life. I wanted to have my children living with me and looking up to me. I wanted to have a wonderful wife and to be in love with her and to have her trust me. I learned that there is nothing better than being in a relationship with someone who has faith in you and who depends on you to be strong and responsible. When that person trusts you with her heart and her life, it's the ultimate trust. There is nothing in this world that can compare to it.

• • • • •

Holly's comments are indicated by italics.

After the night we finally got together, our relationship developed very quickly and very naturally. We'd been getting to know each other for six years, so when we finally started a relationship, we had a lot of history together.

But despite our history, I was very naive about everything. I really had no idea of just how chaotic Vance was. I thought I knew, but I later learned that I had no clue.

I knew that he was just one of those guys who had a lot of money and who liked to flaunt his money around town. I had known other guys who were like that, and I figured Vance was in the same category as them. On a scale of one to 10, I knew he was probably a seven or an eight, which was pretty high on the scale. But as our relationship started to develop and Vance started to open up to me, I began to realize that he was far worse than anyone I had never known. On a scale of one to 10 he was a 50.

But during the six years that we had been on-again, off-again friends, I never realized the extent to which he was having affairs and buying cars and basically living a chaotic life. I knew that he had cheated on his first wife, but I figured he had had one affair maybe two. That seemed within the realm of reality to me. I knew that he had cheated on his second wife, but again I figured one or two affairs. All of the other women I saw him with were people he was dating while he and Chri were separated, and I guess I didn't count all of those because his marriage was already on the outs.

I knew that he talked to a lot of girls, but I didn't think he wined and dined them and slept with them or kept calling them. It wasn't until much later that I learned that he'd had hundreds of affairs on his wives. He hid the truth well.

By the time I started to realize how bad Vance had been, I was already deeply in love with him. I had committed my heart to him.

I thought about leaving him at times, but I stayed with him, because I could see that he was sincere about wanting to change his life. We were talking one day, and he broke down and started crying and started telling me how bad he was and how many affairs he had and all of the terrible things he had done. That was a hard day for both of us. It was tough for Vance to tell me all of that, and it was tough for me to hear it. But it reassured me in a way, because I knew that he wanted to change. I knew that he wouldn't have confessed to all of the chaos in his life unless he wanted to get rid of it. And if he was willing to make that commitment, then I was willing to stand beside him and help him.

At the beginning of our relationship, he was going through divorce proceedings with Chri. During that process, Vance really seemed to get his head on straight. It was like the divorce was what he wanted, and he wanted to handle it appropriately. He wanted Chri to be comfortable because he felt like he had really hurt her. And I think in a lot of ways he did really hurt her.

He was sorry about all the things that had happened between him and Chri. But, strangely, I didn't really feel threatened by those feelings of remorse because I knew it was over between them. I had inadvertently walked right into the middle of their failing relationship, and I had been involved in a lot of their problems. There was a time when I wanted them to work things out. They were married, and I thought that people should work out their problems rather than get divorced.

But it didn't work for them, and I knew that it never would. So I didn't feel threatened by Vance's feelings, and in some ways, the pain he was feeling was attractive to me. It was a side of Vance that no one ever saw, but he shared that with me. I could see that he really did want to change his life. I could see that he really was hurting inside because of a lot of the things that he had done. I could see how sorry he felt about hurting Chri, and I knew that Vance was trying to change.

He was really honest with his feelings, and I trusted and believed in him. I knew that he could change. I was very optimistic.

He's proven me right.

• • • • •

One night shortly after we started our relationship, we met at a club and hung out and danced together for a little while. When we left, we were planning to go to Vance's house, but we were in separate cars. I was driving a Geo Tracker, and Vance was driving a Nissan 300ZX. As we got ready to leave, we decided to switch cars, which was fine with me because I thought I'd be able to keep up with Vance if I was in his car. Vance loved to drive fast, and often when I followed him somewhere, he would leave me in the dust. He didn't do it on purpose. He just had a heavy foot, and he'd dart ahead of me and have to slow down and wait for me to catch up. So when he suggested that we trade cars, I was all for it. He still drove fast in my car, but it was just easier for me to keep up with him when I was driving his sports car.

On our way home we were both hungry so we went through the drive-through at a Taco Bell — the sit-down portion of the restaurant was closed — and then we parked and sat together in the same car in the parking lot eating our food.

Afterward we got back on the road, and Vance was following me. We started racing each other, trying to beat each other home. Then I looked in my rear-view mirror and saw a white Eagle Talon pull up beside Vance. I could tell that someone in that car was talking to him. They were just driving side-by-side like there was something going on. Then they both suddenly pulled off the highway. In my mirror, I could see the Talon stop in the dirt just off the road at the bottom of the exit. Vance pulled up next to the car, and he was halfway on the shoulder and halfway on the road. That was the last I saw of them, because I continued on my way home.

I was curious about what was going on, but the next exit was still several miles ahead, and that was the exit I needed to take to get to Vance's house. I knew something was going on, and I knew that Chri drove a white Eagle Talon, but beyond that, I didn't know what had happened.

I got home and waited for Vance to return, and this is the story that he told me. He said Chri pulled up next to him on the highway and stared yelling at him and calling him a "fucking asshole" because he was driving my car. She darted off the highway at the next exit, and Vance followed her. She pulled over onto the dirt just off the highway, and Vance pulled up next to her. They rolled down their windows and argued. She started to take off, but he decided that he was going to go first. They were both peeling out at the same time. She was sort of turning to the left, to get back onto the road, and Vance was moving straight ahead. The front right bumper of my car (with Vance driving) collided with the left rear fender of her car.

She sped off, going home, and he sped off taking the back way to our house.

In the meantime, I was sitting in the house. The telephone rang. It was Chri.

She said, "I just want you to know that Vance has been stalking me all night. He followed me from the club, followed me home and ran into me with your car."

I said, "I know that's a lie because we went to the club together and we were following each other home. I saw you in the rear-view mirror, I thought it was you, and I guess it was."

She hung up. See, Chri knew what my car looked like, so she knew that Vance was driving my car. But Vance changed cars so often, that she didn't realize that the 300ZX in front of her was Vance's car, with me driving it. She figured that since she called the house and I was there, then I must have been there all night.

The whole situation with Chri was one of the reasons that I usually believed Vance's story before I believed something I heard from someone else. She was always making up stories to try to drive a wedge between Vance and me. Some of Vance's former girlfriends would say things about him in the media or to people that we knew, and Vance would say, "They're just saying that because they're mad at me for breaking up with them." At first, I didn't believe Vance when he said that because I couldn't imagine myself making up stories about him if we ever broke up. But after going through everything with Chri, and knowing how often she lied about Vance, it was easy to believe that a lot of women were simply angry at Vance. I thought, "Maybe girls do get their hearts broken and make up crazy stories." It became easier to believe that Vance was telling me the truth. It's kind of strange, but all of those lies actually helped make our relationship stronger.

Anyway, after Chri called me that night, my heart was pounding. Vance had been in an accident, and he wasn't home yet. I didn't know if he was hurt or if the car had broken down or if he was on his way home. I didn't know anything. I was just waiting, and I was worried.

A few minutes later, Vance came home and he told me everything that had happened. He was completely candid with me, and I believed him because I had seen the situation developing in my rear-view mirror.

The next morning, Vance and I were driving to the Broncos' facility. I was going to drop him off at work, and we heard on the radio that Vance Johnson rammed his estranged wife's car. It was such a weird thing, because we were sitting in the car listening to the radio and suddenly it felt like people in other cars were looking at us. We felt like everyone was listening to the same radio station, recognized Vance and knew that the police were looking for him.

Vance turned himself in that day, and several months later he settled the case and agreed to spend seven days in jail.

I thought it was ridiculous to send him to jail, because it was a pretty minor incident. I think there are a lot of people who do a lot worse who don't have to go to jail. I'm not saying that they shouldn't go to jail. I'm just saying that they don't go to jail.

What Vance did was wrong, but I don't think the courts were fair to him because they placed 100 percent of the blame on him, when part of it belonged to Chri. But I think they made an example out of Vance because he was a celebrity. The average citizen probably would not have gone to jail.

But Vance's stay in jail turned out for the better in the end, because it brought him together with Michael Lindsey.

• • • • •

Michael Lindsey is an amazing man. He is very professional and he knows his job really well. In my opinion, his best attribute is that he understands women and he knows how they differ from men.

If Vance and I are discussing one of our arguments, Michael can listen to the things that I say, and tell Vance what I was saying in terms that Vance can understand. And I would be sitting there saying, "Yes," that's what I was trying to say.

One very simple example of that came up when Vance and I were talking about an argument we'd had. During that fight, I told Vance to "Get out!" and he left.

But during the counseling session, Michael explained to Vance that when a woman says, "get out," she doesn't always mean "get out." What she sometimes means is, "Come here and hold me and tell me that I'm worth something to you." Michael's ability to understand what women were really saying was just amazing, and through him, I learned a lot about how to communicate with Vance, and Vance learned how to understand me.

Michael is a very demanding man who is unwilling to accept anything less than 100 percent effort to make your relationship work. He might like you as an individual, but he keeps everything on a professional level. And he certainly doesn't beat around the bush about anything. He can be brutally honest with the truth, especially if he doesn't think you're working hard enough to improve your relationship.

Another great thing that Michael does is confront you when you try to put the blame on someone else. He doesn't give you an outlet, and he pushes you until you realize that you have the problem. And you have to work on yourself to get rid of the problem.

One time Vance and I got into a big argument at home, and then when we went to our counseling session, I told Michael about it. I knew that Vance was wrong because he had started the argument. He had blown up at me over something, and I wanted Michael to tell Vance that he was wrong.

Instead, Michael asked me why I had argued with Vance. I didn't understand why he was questioning me. It was obvious that Vance was the one who started the argument., I was just defending myself.

But Michael kept challenging me until I understood that if Vance starts an argument with me and I keep it going, then I'm at fault as much as he is. I began to understand that most of the time in a relationship, both people are to blame for whatever problems arise. And if Vance and I could understand that, then we could spend less time pointing fingers at each other, and more time working together to resolve our problems.

Through Michael, I started to realize that I just needed to worry about myself, and to work on the way I was thinking. I'd have to let Vance take care of himself at his own pace.

After the first few joint sessions, Michael put me in touch with my own counselor in order to make sure that I stayed in touch with my own feelings. I had to make sure that I was taking care of myself emotionally during the process of change that Vance was going through.

At that stage, it would have been easy for me to get so wrapped up in trying to help Vance solve his problems that I forgot about my own needs and my own problems. Michael wanted to make sure that didn't happen.

I had problems of my own that were contributing to our arguments. For one, I began to realize that I had problems trusting men. Since my parents had divorced at a young age, and then my father died, I had this fear of abandonment that made it hard for me to get close to men. I had to overcome that in order to learn to trust Vance.

I had to learn that the only person I could control was myself. I can't control Vance. I can't tell him what to do. I can't make him do anything. All I can do is trust him and whether he follows through on his end or not, is his responsibility. That was a hard lesson to learn, and I'm still learning it, although it amazes me how far we have progressed during the past three years.

I think the toughest days were in the very beginning when Vance and I were seeing Michael together. I would hear Vance and Michael talking about this "need" for the chaos. Sometimes he would get into a fight with one of his other wives, or some woman would hurt his feelings, and he would feel a "need" to have an affair or a "need" to buy expensive cars or a "need" to get drunk.

I didn't buy it. I thought it was just a big excuse Vance used in order explain why he was going out and doing all of those crazy things.

I looked at Vance against the backdrop of myself, and every other person that I knew, and I never knew anyone who was as crazy as Vance. I had friends who would get into a fight with their significant others and who would flee to another friend's house or to a bar to hang out for a while. But I had never known anyone who had to sleep with a lot of other people or buy six different cars in order to hide pain.

I never knew anyone like that until Vance.

But slowly through the counseling, I began to understand him more. I started to notice the way Vance acted whenever he felt pain. Whenever we got into arguments he would always want to leave. He'd be rushing out the door when I wanted him to stay and talk, so that we could try to resolve our problems. Through counseling, we learned that I'm the type of person who wants to sit down on the couch and talk through problems until they don't exist any more. Vance is the type of person who likes to go off by himself and work through problems on his own.

Part of our compromise has been that instead of having to leave the house when we argue, Vance will just go into another room or into the basement until he's ready to talk. I agree not to bother him while he's spending this time by himself, and he agrees to talk through the problem after he's cooled down, but that's been hard for me. I want to talk right away, and it's tough to sit in one room and wonder what he's thinking in another room.

Even when he felt physical pain, he withdrew into himself. Every time he got injured on the field, I would watch him pull back and become distant. He wouldn't want to talk, and he'd want to spend a lot of time by himself. I could see that he was in pain, and I'd want to help him, but he would be silently pushing me away.

Slowly I began to understand that when he withdraws himself, he is shielding his emotions from further pain. I began to understand that when he feels that way, he craves attention without fear of being rejected. So he would go out in one of his expensive sports cars, pick up a girl and have sex with her, so that he could feel better about himself without exposing himself to further pain by being intimate with anyone. (It took me a long time to understand this, but to Vance, having sex and being intimate were two completely different things. He and I struggled with that for a long time, because I didn't want him to just have sex with me. I wanted him to be intimate with me. It's been a slow process, but we're both learning how to be intimate together.)

I think a lot of people — male and female — experience the types of feelings that Vance had, but in him everything was much more pronounced because of who he was. He was always someone who craved the limelight, and who wanted to be envied by other people. But he was also a very insecure man, and he measured his self-worth by how many receptions he had on the football field, or how many women he slept with or how much he spent on his car or how many parties he went to in a week. So whenever he got his feelings hurt, he would rush out and try to mend himself though all of those shallow measurements.

After I started to understand Vance better, I was more able to help him as he worked to change his life. I learned how to react to him. I learned how to respond when he felt hurt. I learned how to relate my feelings to him when something really bothered me.

Today I'm still learning to follow through and to stick to the lessons I learned in counseling.

• • • • •

I never wanted to have children because I thought it would be so hard to care for a child. I always thought about my mother and how hard she had struggled to raise me and the twins, and I just didn't think I had it in me to do that.

But after Vance and I got engaged, we started talking about having kids. And for the first time in my life, I could imagine it. At every other point in my life when I imagined having a child, I saw me and a kid. But when I was talking about it with Vance, I realized that it was me, Vance and a kid. That realization kind of shocked me because before then I was never consciously aware that I didn't see my children having a father in the home.

I didn't have a father in my house when I was young and then I lost my real dad when I was young, so it never really occurred to me to think that there is a father involved with parenting.

Once I understood that Vance and I would be having children together, it really got excited about having a child.

But I was afraid that I wouldn't be able to get pregnant.

Mother had a tough time getting pregnant. Before she got pregnant with me, she spent two years trying to conceive a child. She visited doctors all the time, followed a bunch of different medical recommendations and basically tried every old wives' trick in the book, but nothing worked. She could not get pregnant. Finally, her doctor told her to take a vacation and go to sea level. He said, just go sit on the beach and relax and don't think about it. She went to California for a week's vacation, and she got pregnant.

You can draw your own conclusions from that. It was probably just coincidence that she got pregnant while she was in California, but it was amazing that after two years of trying to get pregnant, she was able to do it at sea level.

With that in mind, I didn't think I could get pregnant. Before Vance, I had obviously had other relationships, and I was usually always careful, but there have been a handful of occasions when I wasn't careful. Fortunately, I never got pregnant.

I moved into his house in May 1991, and we got engaged two weeks later.

After we got engaged, we started talking about children and how many children we wanted and when we wanted to have them and all of that. We were just trying to make sure that we were on the same page, so that we didn't end up married and then find out that I wanted five children and he couldn't do that because he already had children.

During this talk I said, "Vance would it upset you if I can't get pregnant?"

"Of course not," he said.

"But if I can get pregnant, would you like to have a child?" I said.

He said, "I would definitely love to have a child with you."

So we decided that we would have one child, maybe two, but we'd make the decision about a second one after the first one was born — if I could get pregnant.

It took my mom two years, so I figured I'd have to work at least that long. We planned our wedding for February of 1992. We were planning to have a big wedding with a beautiful dress and bridesmaids and groomsmen and everything else, so we needed time to plan.

Then we talked about when we should start trying to have a child.

"Should we start now?" I said. "That way if I have to go see the doctors, I can start that now, and then after we get married we won't have to wait as long to have a child. Or should we just wait until after we get married."

Vance said, "Let's try now," because he really wanted us to have a baby together. "But will you be okay with it, and will it be okay with your family if you end up pregnant before we get married?"

I agreed that if we ended up pregnant before the wedding that would be wonderful. But in the back of my mind, I thought there was only a remote chance that I could get pregnant period, let alone before the wedding.

I had been on the pill for many years, and after that discussion, I had three or four days of pills left before my cycle. So I finished that pack of pills just so I'd be on schedule. Then, after my cycle, Vance and I had a lot of fun trying to get pregnant. We worked at it every day, and it was especially fun because we were newly engaged.

I never saw my period again.

It was instant pregnancy. We were both really happy because we didn't think we'd be able to get pregnant. So, our daughter, Paris was planned, even though it probably didn't look like it to a lot of people, but she really was.

We moved the wedding up to October 11, 1991, so that my pregnancy wouldn't yet be showing.

The pregnancy was another factor that contributed to my willingness to stay with Vance as he tried to rid himself of his chaotic lifestyle. When I got pregnant, I was just beginning to understand how crazy Vance was. Every day, I was learning something new. By the time I figured out the entire picture, and realized that Vance was a wild man, I was already in love with him. I was living in his house. I was engaged to him. And I was pregnant with his child. So when all of the negative truth came out about Vance, I had a lot of compelling reasons to dig in my heels and help him in his tug-of-war against the chaos.

During all of this, I was very optimistic about our future together, because I could see how hard Vance was trying. I knew that he had initiated counseling on his own a couple of years earlier by going to see Dr. Rakowski regularly. Then, after the car-bashing incident, Vance was forced to attend Michael Lindsey's group therapy. So I was sitting there thinking, "Okay, the man I love has a lot of problems from the past. But I know he wants to change, and he's getting help for his problem." That reality made it easier for me to stay with Vance. If I had found out all of those bad things about him and I could see that he was not trying to change, I would have left him. I would have had to do that for myself because I could not have survived with someone who was going to lead a life that was as chaotic as Vance's.

Anyway, in 1992, our daughter Paris was born on March 12. That is the day before Vance's birthday, and I tried so hard to hold out for one more day, but I couldn't do it. Vance was wonderful when we had the baby. He came in with my best friend Natalie, and he sat there on the bed with me all night when I was in labor. The next morning after Paris was born, he went out and got two big stuffed animals, one for me and one for her. Then he stayed in the hospital with me again that night. He was really wonderful.

Paris was my first child, and she was Vance's seventh.

When we first got engaged, it was hard for me to get used to suddenly being a step-mother to all of those children. There was that feeling of "instant family" that was kind of scary. It took a little bit of time for me to adjust to that, but as I met some of the children, it really came easily for me because they're all great kids.

Unfortunately, Vance and I rarely see Nicole and Vance, Jr., his first two children. They both live in other states, and Vance, Jr.'s mom really doesn't want Vance to see his child. And Vance has two children from two one-night stands, but he rarely sees them. I've had a chance to spend a lot of time with Vaughn and Vincent — Angela's children — and they are really special.

I don't know how often Vance saw his kids before he and I got together, but I got the impression that he didn't get to spend a whole lot of time with them. But I always wanted him to bring them around. When I got pregnant with Paris, I wanted the other kids to visit and see my stomach, and know that they had another stepsister coming. I wanted all of the kids to be close. I'm sure some people probably wonder how I can care for children who are from my husband's previous relationships, but it's easy for me.

I was very comfortable with the patchwork family that we were creating, because that's exactly the type of home that I grew up in, and I loved all of my stepbrothers and sisters. I also had a really good relationship with my stepfather, Gordon. So all of this came really naturally for me. Actually, it seemed more normal to me than a traditional family.

But I never told any of Vance's first six children that I was their stepmother. They all had their own mothers, and I didn't want them to ever think that I was trying to replace their mothers. But one of the most rewarding days for me came about a year ago, when Vaughn, Vance's third child, came over and said to me, "You're my stepmom, huh?"

Apparently one of his friends at school was talking about his stepmother and through him, Vaughn learned what that meant.

I said, "Yes."

That conversation really warmed my heart and made me feel that he and I were working toward a loving relationship. I thought that maybe he was beginning to accept me as his daddy's partner.

• • • • •

At the very beginning of our relationship, I rarely felt threatened by other women or worried that Vance would have affairs on me. If we were out somewhere and a pretty girl flirted with him, I wouldn't get mad. Instead, I would be flattered because Vance was with me, and I felt that she wished he was with her.

As our relationship developed, Vance opened up to me more and more, and he told me the straight truth about his past. That's when I started to get scared. I would say to myself, "I hope he doesn't want to go back to that type of lifestyle. I hope he doesn't want to have affairs anymore."

Accepting his past was difficult. I was trying to deal with it and accept it and keep my mind focused on the changes that he was making and on the understanding that he was not going to be the same person that he was. But sometimes, I would just get scared.

And other times, it was just hard because I'd get blind-sided by some story from Vance's past. As part of Vance's therapy, he was learning to be more honest about the things that he had done in his life. So sometimes if I was curious about some relationship he'd had, I would ask him a question, and he would just flat-out tell me the truth.

It would be like getting hit in the head with a brick. I had to sit there and learn to handle it. I eventually reached the point where I quit asking questions. I didn't want or need to know any more. Later, our relationship would develop to the point where we could talk about anything and everything, and I could accept and deal with his past. But during that first year, I was just overwhelmed. I couldn't listen to any more.

Trying to juggle him being honest and telling myself that this is okay and having this fear inside of "Oh, I hope he doesn't still want to do stuff like that."

I knew that Vance loved me and he was committed to me, but after hearing all of his stories from the past, I worried that it would be hard for him to be monogamous. I had a lot of fear about that.

If Vance was supposed to be home at 5 p.m. and he didn't get home until 6 p.m. my first thought would be that he was having an affair. It didn't hit me that way every time, but most of the time during those first few months, I had that type of fear any time he was even a little bit late.

Once day, he went out golfing, then he came home and said he was going golfing again.

I said, "Okay." I never wanted to stop him from doing anything, but I was still really afraid. I didn't understand why he would want to go golfing twice in the same day. It sounded suspicious to me, but I didn't know what to say. I really loved Vance, and I trusted his heart. But I was sometimes afraid that he wouldn't be able to control his impulses. But I was trying to show him that I trusted him and that I believed in him, so I wasn't going to say anything about him going golfing again.

But I think he could tell by the look on my face that I was scared. He said, "Why don't you drive me over to the golf course and then pick me up after I'm done?"

I said, "Okay." I was very relieved. Then I knew that he was telling me the truth, and I was right for wanting to trust him. After that, my driving him places became part of our regular routine. It was something Vance offered to me that made that whole transition period easier for both of us.

During all of this, we've both had to have a lot of faith and hope and trust in each other. It has been a really tough couple of years for us, but Vance has changed so much and is still changing and that makes everything easier. By the way, I no longer drive him around everywhere.

It's been kind of like being with a little kid. Vance had to break himself down to when he was 7 years old — or some age around then — and then start over so that he could see life in a different way as well as react in a different way.

Dealing with all of the changes that Vance was making, was a constant struggle for both of us. And you'd probably think that the abuse was one of the biggest issues, but Vance has never hit me, and I've never been overly scared that he would hit me. Part of the reason for my lack of fear was an incident that happened back when were just friends, long before we really started to date seriously. I was mad at Vance about something — I can't remember what — and I started crying. We were standing beside his car, and I said, "whatever," and turned away from him. Vance grabbed me by the shoulders and turned me back toward him, and said, "Will you settle down?"

He just stood there inches from my face staring at me, and I guess I had a scared look on my face.

He jerked his hands off of me, held them up and said, "I would never lay a hand on you. I would never hurt you."

I was surprised to hear him say that, because him hitting me was the last thing on my mind at that point. I don't know if I looked scared or not, but I wasn't scared at all, I was just angry. But his reaction made me realize that he was sensitive. He was very conscious about what people were saying about him, and what I might be thinking about him.

So as we tried to work through our problems and build a happy marriage, Vance and I had our arguments but he never hit me. I think he knew that if he ever struck me, I would leave him immediately. I had been in an abusive relationship in the past, and I wasn't going to allow myself to get into that situation again.

Vance was really honest with me about his past abusiveness, and I knew that he was committed to curing that problem. I told him that he was either going to stick to what he said and continue to get help or he was going to lose me. Abuse was probably the one thing that I absolutely would not tolerate. I figured we could work through any other type of problem, but if Vance started hitting me, that would be too much for me to overcome.

So there were times when we argued and Vance and I were in each other's faces yelling and screaming, and there were times when I threatened to call Michael Lindsey or the police. When I said things like that, they weren't idle threats meant to scare Vance. *I fully intended to make the call. I was determined to be strong for Vance, and I was going to make him own up if he stepped in the wrong direction. I was always honest with Michael Lindsey, because I wanted to spend the rest of my life with Vance. And the only way for that to happen, was for Vance to get better.*

Part of the reason I was able to deal with everything that was going on and continue to be strong was that I really loved Vance, and I loved myself. I was going to win whether it was with him or without him. If the best thing was for me to not be with him, then I wasn't going to be with him. Knowing that just helped me to keep my head on straight through the whole thing. And loving him so much made it easier for me to try to be a support. I just always had to try to see clear and see what was going on. I had to be honest with myself. I was strong because I knew where I didn't want to be in the relationship. It made it easier to be strong to see him and know him the way that I do and know that he was sincere about wanting to change. If any part of me could help to keep him on track, then I was determined to follow through and be strong for him.

And today I am so happy that we hung in and fought together, because Vance is a much different person now that when we got engaged. He is much more intimate, responsible, considerate and controlled.

He's more financially secure. He's not a rambunctious spender like he used to be. A lot of the stimulations, such as sex, women, fast cars and partying have disappeared. The gambling, the car buying and everything else have been scaled back. He's more relaxed. Even my family has noticed a difference from when they first met him to now. He used to be kind of antsy all the time, like he couldn't get comfortable or like he couldn't stay long. Now he seems to feel very relaxed around my family.

The biggest factor in all of these changes is that Vance feels good about himself. He knows he's a good person now. He knows how to make himself happy with his family and friends, rather than with short-term stimulations that don't last. Different things are important to him. The other day, he dressed our daughter, Paris, and the two of them went to the circus together. You would never have seen him do something like that in the past. If he did, he'd be jittery and get it over with. In the past when he had visitation with Vaughn and Vincent, he'd take them out somewhere and then take them right back to Angela. He didn't really "spend" time with them, he just "put in" time with them. It wasn't that he didn't love them, he just was living such a fast and crazy life that he was uptight all the time. He couldn't relax. He couldn't just spend time with his boys because he had too many other things on his mind.

Now he's settled down a lot and when he picks up the boys, he'll take them to the movies, go get dinner and then ask them if they want to spend the night. Now that his lifestyle has settled down, he's a much better father to all of his kids. He seriously enjoys it now. He appreciates the smaller things a lot more. He used to take a lot of things for granted.

Vance is just more happy with himself. He likes himself. I think he disliked himself before. In the past, he was always trying to convince himself of what a great person he was and how great it was to have all that money. He bought fancy new cars because he thought it would make him feel happy. He pursued a bunch of women because he thought the conquests would make him feel happy. He spent a lot of money because he thought that would make him feel happy. He tried to impress people because he thought that would make him feel happy.

I remember him trying to impress me when we first started dating. I mentioned earlier, that the night that we first made love, he let me drive his Porsche. At the time, I didn't think he was trying to impress me. Back then, I thought he was just being nice. I figured he knew I was from a middle-class family, and I had probably never even been in a Porsche before. So he was just letting me drive it to be nice. But I later realized, that he was showing off his car. It was his way of trying to impress me.

Another time he and I went to a seafood restaurant and Vance really clicked with our waiter, who was a young teenager. At the end of the meal Vance tipped him $100. I think Vance thought that I would be impressed that he liked this kid so much that he was giving him $100, but where I came from, that was ridiculous. I thought it was stupid. I didn't get it at all. To me $100 is a lot of money, so I couldn't relate.

But as time passed, I think Vance began to realize that impressing me or anyone else with material things was not very satisfying for him.

He learned that whatever need he was trying to fill couldn't be filled from the outside. It had to be filled inside of Vance's mind and there wasn't enough money in the world to supply that need. Vance had to learn that happiness came from within, and its survival didn't depend on any external factors.

• • • • •

From the very beginning of our relationship, our difference in our perspectives of money was a huge hurdle for us to overcome.

Vance was trying to change his life in every way, and spending money was one of the habits that he wanted to curtail. He was constantly see-sawing back and forth. One day he would be talking about how desperately he needed to go out and buy the new Porsche that just came out, and the next week he'd be talking about how we needed to save money, invest for the future, buy a Mazda 626 and pay if off in cash, have a truck for the snow and nothing more. But then a month later, he'd be talking about buying a Corvette ZR-1 and saying, "We won't worry about getting a truck. We'll get one next winter when it snows."

It was tough to deal with the swings. I'm really good with money and being responsible. I can't sleep at night if I think one of our bills is going to be even a day late, so I tried to instill that in Vance. At first I tried to fight Vance whenever he wanted to go spend a lot of money. I would yell and scream at him. I'd say, "This is ridiculous! We've got to pay this bill, and this other money needs to stay in the bank!" But that approach didn't work very well. And then I thought, "Here's a man trying to change, and I'm giving him a really bad reaction."

So then I just started trying to reason with Vance. If he wanted to buy a new car, I would make a list and show him all of the bills and say, "This is all we have left." I'd show him the benefits that we could gain by choosing one route over the other. I'd say, "If we don't buy the Porsche, we can have this much money in the bank on X date, instead of only having this much if we do buy the Porsche." That approach worked a lot better. Vance would usually choose the wiser path, but a short time later, he would want to buy the car again. In the end, I always just had to let him do whatever he wanted, because he was a grown man. It was his money that he had earned on the football field, and the ultimate decision was his. But I kept preaching the importance of taking care of money, and eventually it began to sink in.

I think another thing that helped was that I wasn't going out and spending a lot of money, so Vance didn't think I was trying to stop him from spending because I wanted to get something. Vance always felt that women tried to control him or take advantage of him. He didn't trust women at all, because he thought they all had ulterior motives. So I think it helped a lot that I didn't have my own agenda in terms of trying to spend money.

He told me that Angela used to get pissed at him when he lost money gambling, bought a new car or gave money to his mother because she wanted to use the money to buy jewelry or clothes. They had a lot of arguments about spending. But after Vance saw that I wasn't going out and buying things, he began to realize that I was trying to make things better for our family and not just for myself. I think that made a big difference to him.

It was a really tough situation because there were so many negative situations in Vance's past. So I always had to think ahead about what I said and did because Vance would take things in differently than I meant them. I didn't want Vance to associate me with things in the past, so I'd always have to come at a different angle than straight on, because it would affect him differently.

Vance vacillated back and forth with his gambling, too. He'd go through a period in which he wanted to gamble all the time. Then he'd swear off gambling and say he's never going to do it again. Then he'd want to go gamble again.

I like to play cards, but I don't really like to spend a lot of money gambling. Part of the problem that Vance and I had was that when I went gambling, I considered the money spent already. If I took $1,000 to go gambling, I wrote off that $1,000 as lost money from the start, in the same way I would have if I bought clothes.

On the other hand, when Vance went gambling, he really thought he was going to win money. He'd go to Las Vegas with $5,000 thinking that he was going to turn it into $60,000 to buy a Porsche. Then when he lost the $5,000, he'd start chasing it with more money thinking that he could win it back.

It was frustrating for me, but I had to let Vance be Vance. I couldn't try to control him and tell him that he wasn't allowed to go gambling because it was his money. But even back then, Vance knew that he was wrong for doing it. And I knew that he knew and that made a big difference for me.

So instead of me being the nagging wife always pulling on his ear, I would talk to Michael Lindsey, so that he could bring it up in a casual way. Or I would call a good friend of ours who is a banker, and he would talk to Vance. Sometimes just hearing it from someone other than me would make a big difference.

I always tried to keep myself on Vance's side. I always wanted Vance to see me as an ally, so I had to be careful how I approached a lot of things. I wanted to help him change, but I didn't want to sour our relationship by becoming a source of resentment for him.

Now, Vance has really changed a lot. Now he just wants to save money. He's very conscious of how much things cost. Sometimes, it seems as if he has made a 180-degree turn from where he used to be. He will occasionally go through periods where everything costs too much. When he feels like that, he won't spend $20.

But that's a rare thing. Vance is still very generous, and that's just part of who he is. He's always buying nice, special things for the people he loves, and I don't think that part of him will ever change.

• • • • •

Vance is a much different person now than the one he was as recently as three years ago. He's still working hard to change, and he still goes to counseling regularly. But the work isn't as intense as it used to be. Once Vance was able to overhaul his general way of thinking, all of the other changes involved in being a good husband and father began to happen naturally.

Basically, Vance has just changed the way he looks at himself and at the world, and it amazes me to see how powerful a change in perspective can be. I've begun to realize that perspective is everything. For example, if a person was standing at the bottom of the Grand Canyon, he would have a different perspective and outlook than someone standing at the top of the Grand Canyon. In a way that's how Vance was living. He was at the bottom of the Grand Canyon surrounded by high walls of chaos. He could look up and see the tops of the cliffs, but it looked like an impossible climb. It seemed easier to just continue to camp on the bottom than to make the effort required to climb out.

But then he met a guide, named Michael Lindsey, who knew of a trail that led all the way to the top. The trail was very narrow and very long and it was treacherous climb. But if Vance was careful and if he always kept his attention focused on the next step, then he could get out of the canyon.

And that's what Vance did. He climbed out of the "Grand Canyon," and now he stands on top and his perspective has changed. Now the bottom doesn't look so appealing to him anymore. From the top, the bottom just looks like a long fall. From where he stands now, a tumble off the cliff would mean certain death. From where he stands now, the sunrise and sunset are beautiful, and his car is parked behind him, and the highways to the rest of the world are open to him. From where he stands now,

Vance can see that life has a lot more to offer him than the confining, chaotic walls of the canyon.

• • • • •

 I'm really proud of Vance for signing with the San Diego Chargers this year. At first it was a little scary because Vance would be leaving his counselor and all of his friends who have supported him during his change. But I knew he was ready for the change. Vance had regained control of his life, and he would be the same person regardless, whether he was living in Denver, San Diego or Timbuktu.

 And it's been a really good change for him. It's been a fresh start. Vance isn't as concerned as he used to be about what people think of him, but he still cares about what his fans think of him, and he wants them to know that he's changed. San Diego has been a new beginning for Vance, and it feels good to him for people to know that he is who he says he is.

 I just think he's blessed to have an opportunity for a new beginning.

Epilogue

I hope someone will benefit from my writing this book. I was a little scared to tell everyone all of these bad stories about myself, but I felt it was something I needed to do. I know that other men suffer from the same problems that I had, and I know that some of them need professional help.

Just a few years ago, I was one of those men.

And my recovery has been a long, hard journey.

By the time I finally sought professional help, I had already dug such a deep hole for myself that there didn't appear to be any way I could climb out. It took people like Holly and Michael Lindsey and the other men in the group to help pull me out of that hole.

The hard part is that other people can't just attach a rope to you and pull you out of a pit of chaos. All they can do is drop a rope down to you and wait for you to grab onto it. Then you have to do all the climbing yourself and all the other people can do is make sure that rope is securely anchored around a sturdy tree or a big rock. If they keep encouraging you and if you keep climbing, you can eventually get out of the hole, but it's a hard journey.

I'm not out of the hole yet, but I can see the top. I know that I can get there if I just keep climbing.

Appendix

Vance Johnson's Toys

Listed below are some of the toys I've owned during my career. I'm positive that I've left four or five cars off this list. I bought so many cars during my career, that I simply can't recall all of them.

Automobiles (40)
1985 Porsche 944
1986 Corvette
1986 Porsche 911 Targa
1986 Mercury Tracer
1962 Corvette convertible
1987 red Corvette
1967 red Corvette convertible
1966 big block blue Corvette
1988 Porsche 911 turbo convertible
1987 Ferarri 328 GTS
1993 Mercedes 300 E
1993 Lexus Coupe
1992 Chevy truck
1988 Porsche 911 Carerra
1991 Mercedes 190 E
1962 Mercedes 190SL
1958 Mercedes 190SL
1989 Corvette
1991 Corvette convertible.
1989 Porsche 911 Turbo
1966 vintage Limosine Cadillac
1988 Porsche 911 slant-nose
1991 Isuzu Trooper
1993 Mazda 626
1992 VW Rabbit convertible
1989 Porsche 944

1987 Jeep Cherokee
1989 Jeep Laredo
1990 Cadillac Elante
1991 Nissan 300ZX
1990 Porsche 911 Turbo
1992 Porsche 911 Turbo slant-nose
1988 Mazda RX7
1989 Mazda RX7
1993 Jaguar XJS
1989 Jaguar XJS convertible
1985 Ford Bronco
1986 Chevy Blazer
1991 Eagle Talon
1993 Toyota Land Cruiser

Motorcycles (6)
Kawasaki 900
Ninja 1000
Ninja 900
Ninja 600
Kawasaki 600
1993 Harley Davidson Fat Boy.

Boats (3)
19-foot bayliner outboard
25-foot bayliner outboard
21-foot bayliner outboard

VANCE JOHNSON'S NFL STATISTICS

Year	Club	Games	Starts	RECEIVING No.	RECEIVING Yds.	RECEIVING Avg.	RECEIVING TD	RUSHING Att.	RUSHING Yds	RUSHING Avg.	RUSHING TD
1985	-Denver	16	7	51	721	14.1	3	10	36	3.6	0
1986	-Denver	12	7	31	363	11.7	2	5	15	3	0
1987	-Denver	11	9	42	684	16.3	7	1	-8	-8	0
1988	-Denver	16	13	68	896	13.2	5	1	1	1	0
1989	-Denver	16	16	76	1095	14.4	7	0	0	0	0
1990	-Denver	16	13	54	747	13.8	3	0	0	0	0
1991	-Denver	10	0	21	208	9.9	3	0	0	.0	0
1992	-Denver	11	6	24	294	12.3	2	0	0	0	0
1993	-Denver	10	8	36	517	14.4	5	0	0	0	0
	TOTAL	118	79	403	5525	13.7	37	17	44	2.6	0

Year	Club	PUNT RETURNS No.	PUNT RETURNS Yds.	PUNT RETURNS Avg.	PUNT RETURNS TD	KICKOFF RETURNS No.	KICKOFF RETURNS Yds	KICKOFF RETURNS Avg.	KICKOFF RETURNS TD
1985	-Denver	30	260	8.7	0	30	740	24.7	0
1986	-Denver	3	36	12	0	2	21	10.5	0
1987	-Denver	1	9	9	0	7	140	20	0
1988	-Denver	0	0	0	0	0	0	0	0
1989	-Denver	12	118	9.8	0	0	0	0	0
1990	-Denver	11	92	8.4	0	6	126	21	0
1991	-Denver	24	174	7.3	0	0	0	0	0
1992	-Denver	0	0	0	0	0	0	0	0
1993	-Denver	0	0	0	0	0	0	0	0
	TOTAL	81	689	8.5	0	45	1027	22.8	0

About The Co-Author

Reggie Rivers, 26, is a fourth-year running back for the Denver Broncos and a weekly sports columnist for the *Rocky Mountain News*. He graduated from Southwest Texas State University with a bachelor's degree in journalism in May of 1991. During his college tenure, he served internships with the *San Antonio Light,* the *Austin American-Statesman* and *Newsday* newspapers.

The Vance: The Beginning and The End is his first attempt as an author.